After Legal Equality

Groups seeking legal equality often take a victory as the end of the line. Once judgment is granted or a law is passed, coalitions disband and life goes on in a new state of equality. Policy makers too may assume that a troublesome file is now closed. This collection arises from the urgent sense that law reforms driven by equality call for fresh lines of inquiry. In unintended ways, reforms may harm their intended beneficiaries. They may also worsen the disadvantage of other groups. Committed to tackling these important issues beyond the boundaries that often confine legal scholarship, this book pursues an interdisciplinary consideration of efforts to advance equality, as it explores the developments, challenges, and consequences that arise from law reforms aiming to deliver equality in the areas of sexuality, kinship, and family relations. With an international array of contributors, *After Legal Equality: Family, Sex, Kinship* will be an invaluable resource for those with interests in this area.

Robert Leckey is Associate Professor and William Dawson Scholar in the Faculty of Law, McGill University, where he conducts research in comparative family and constitutional law. He is author of *Contextual Subjects: Family, State, and Relational Theory* and co-editor of *Queer Theory: Law, Culture, Empire*.

Social Justice

Series editors: Sarah Lamble, *Birkbeck College, University of London, UK*, Davina Cooper, *University of Kent, UK*, and Sarah Keenan, *SOAS, UK*

Social Justice is a new, theoretically engaged, interdisciplinary series exploring the changing values, politics and institutional forms through which claims for equality, democracy and liberation are expressed, manifested and fought over in the contemporary world. The series addresses a range of contexts, from transnational political fora, to nation-state and regional controversies, to small-scale social experiments. At its heart is a concern, and inter-disciplinary engagement, with the present and future politics of power, as constituted through territory, gender, sexuality, ethnicity, economics, ecology and culture.

Foregrounding struggle, imagined alternatives and the embedding of new norms, *Social Justice* critically explores how change is wrought through law and governance, everyday social and bodily practices, dissident knowledges, and movements for citizenship, belonging and reinvented community.

Titles in this series:

Intersectionality and Beyond
Law, Power and the Politics of Location
Emily Grabham, Davina Cooper, Jane Krishnadas and Didi Herman (eds), 2009

Regulating Sexuality
Legal Consciousness in Lesbian and Gay Lives
Rosie Harding, 2010

Rights of Passage
Sidewalks and the Regulation of Public Flow
Nicholas Blomley, 2010

Anarchism and Sexuality
Jamie Heckert and Richard Cleminson (eds), 2011

Queer Necropolitics
Jin Haritaworn, Adi Kuntsman and Silvia Posocco (eds), 2014

After Legal Equality
Family, Sex, Kinship
Robert Leckey (ed.), 2014

Forthcoming:

Power, Politics and the Emotions
Impossible Governance?
Shona Hunter

Law, Environmental Illness and Medical Uncertainty
Tarryn Phillips

Global Justice and Desire
Queering Economy
Nikita Dhawan, Antke Engel, Christoph H. E. Holzhey and Volker Woltersdorff (eds)

Chronotopes of Law
Jurisdiction, Scale and Governance
Mariana Valverde

Protest, Property and the Commons
Lucy Finchett-Maddock

Regulating Sex After Aids
Queer Risks and Contagion Politics
Neil Cobb

Subversive Property
Law and the Production of Spaces of Belonging
Sarah Keenan

After Legal Equality

Family, sex, kinship

Edited by
Robert Leckey

Routledge
Taylor & Francis Group

LONDON AND NEW YORK

First published 2015
by Routledge
2 Park Square, Milton Park, Abingdon, Oxfordshire OX14 4RN

and by Routledge
711 Third Avenue, New York, NY 10017

a GlassHouse Book

Routledge is an imprint of the Taylor and Francis Group, an informa business

First issued in paperback 2015

British Library Cataloguing in Publication Data
A catalogue record for this book is available from the British Library

Library of Congress Cataloging-in-Publication Data
  After legal equality: family, sex, kinship/edited by Robert Leckey.
  pages cm—(Social justice)
  Includes bibliographical references and index.
  1. Same-sex marriage—Law and legislation. 2. Gay couples—Legal
  status, laws, etc. 3. Equality before the law. 4. Homosexuality—Law
  and legislation. 5. Gay rights. 6. Queer theory. I. Leckey, Robert,
  editor of compilation.
  K699.A84 2014
  346.01'68—dc23
  2014001223

ISBN 978-0-415-72161-5 (hbk)
ISBN 978-1-138-64476-2 (pbk)
ISBN 978-1-315-86303-0 (ebk)

Typeset in Garamond by
Florence Production Ltd, Stoodleigh, Devon

Contents

Notes on contributors

Susan B. Boyd is Professor of Law and holds the research Chair in Feminist Legal Studies in the Faculty of Law at Allard Hall, University of British Columbia.

Kim Brooks is Dean of the Schulich School of Law, Dalhousie University, and Senior Research Fellow in the Taxation Law and Policy Research Institute at Monash University.

Richard Collier is Professor of Law and Social Theory at Newcastle Law School, Newcastle University.

Catherine Donovan is Professor of Social Relations at the University of Sunderland.

Roderick A. Ferguson is Professor in the Department of African American Studies and the Department of Gender and Women's Studies at the University of Illinois, Chicago.

Rosie Harding is Senior Lecturer in the Birmingham Law School, University of Birmingham.

Jonathan Herring is Professor of Law, University of Oxford.

Janet R. Jakobsen is Professor of Women's Studies and Director of the Barnard Center for Research on Women at Barnard College, Columbia University.

Robert Leckey is Associate Professor and William Dawson Scholar in the Faculty of Law and Director of the Paul-André Crépeau Centre for Private and Comparative Law, McGill University.

Daniel Monk is Reader in Law at Birkbeck, University of London.

Helen Reece is Reader in Law at the London School of Economics.

Claire F.L. Young is Professor in the Faculty of Law at Allard Hall, University of British Columbia.

Acknowledgements

This collection emerged from a workshop called 'After equality: Family, sex, kinship', hosted at McGill University on 11–13 April 2013. Other papers will appear, in 2015, in the *Canadian Journal of Women and the Law* (27(1)). Thanks are owed to the Connection Program of the Social Sciences and Humanities Research Council of Canada (file no. 611–2012–0004), to the Paul-André Crépeau Centre for Private and Comparative Law and the Institute for Gender, Sexuality, and Feminist Studies, both of McGill University. Thanks also to Régine Tremblay, Manon Berthiaume, Bethany Hastie, Iris Graham, Catherine Le Guerrier, Allison Render and Marc Roy, as well as to Colin Perrin and Rebekah Jenkins at Routledge. I gratefully acknowledge the permission granted by photographer Valerie Simmons to reproduce her image of the dancer and choreographer José Navas.

Robert Leckey
Montreal, January 2014

Table of cases

Chapter 1

Introduction

After legal equality

Robert Leckey

Groups seeking equality sometimes take a legal victory as the end of the line. Once judgment is granted, or a law is passed, coalitions disband, and life goes on in a new state of equality. For their part, policymakers may assume that a troublesome file is now closed. This collection, and the larger project of which it is part, arises from the sense that law reforms made under the banner of equality invite fresh lines of enquiry. For example, such reforms may worsen the disadvantage of other groups, as where recognizing same-sex couples can indirectly intensify distinctions by race or class. Redrawing the lines of legal 'family' might also further marginalize non-normative caring and kinship networks. Moreover, legal reforms in equality's name may, in unintended ways, harm even their intended beneficiaries. Efforts to protect religious women from patriarchal practices, for example, may undermine their religious freedom and deny their agency. These matters are complex and cut across different social fields. Addressing them can be uncomfortable. However, scholars, civil-society organizations and policymakers need to know about them.

To be sure, compared with situations in which there is nothing akin to equality (see, e.g., Kondakov 2013), the state of affairs 'after legal equality' may appear to be less urgent. At least at first blush, it is not a matter of life and death, although some argue that gay-rights projects collaborate in the uneven distribution of life chances (Spade 2011; Haritaworn *et al.* 2014). Considering the questions raised in this collection is nevertheless important, in order to ensure that change in the name of legal equality does not perpetuate disadvantage or stall social change.

Although some scholarly projects arise from a grand idea, my inspiration for this collection and the preceding workshop emerged by induction from small, concrete cases. In 2007, the Court of Appeal in my home jurisdiction of Quebec ordered two former lesbian partners to share the custody of girls of whom only one was the legal mother, by adoption. Had it been possible at the time, the women would have adopted the girls together. Although, under the province's civil law, the children had only one 'mother' – the other woman being a legal stranger towards them – the judges used the everyday language of family, referring to the children's 'two mothers'.[1] I wrote favourably about that approach and result, characterizing it as 'a judicial willingness to make space for manifold existing forms of family', an attempt to bridge the gap between social and legislative discourse (Leckey 2009: 565–6 (footnote omitted)).

Several years later, the same tribunal again ordered former lesbian partners to share custody of a child of whom only one was the legal mother. This time, the mother had given birth to the child. The child was younger than the girls in the previous case, and the duration of the couple's family life with the child was shorter. This time, law reforms had offered an avenue by which the birth mother might have established parental status for her partner, but she had declined to do so. The judges, nevertheless, spoke once more of the child having 'two mothers', whatever the law said.[2] I assessed this second case more cautiously. I posed the question whether, 'now that two women may become legal spouses and that a child may have two mothers, might judges too readily interpret facts from the diverse ecology of queer kinship through the script of two equal mothers?' (Leckey 2013b: 13). While grappling with such instances in my scholarly life, my activist life has involved reorienting a national lesbian, gay, bisexual and trans human-rights organization for which no subsequent priority has matched the broad-based support rallied by a successful campaign for equal marriage.

In conversation with colleagues and friends, these examples quickly joined with others. They helped in formulating a research agenda – the title of this volume – that is distinct from scholarship laying out the advantages or disadvantages of a legal reform or prescribing doctrinal paths for achieving it. As with any research agenda, its contours are contestable: it might have included more or less. On the side of more, the terms might have extended to regulation of the workplace and of political processes. The agenda might also have encompassed reforms justified on bases other than equality, such as liberty, privacy, health, children's welfare, individual responsibility (think of welfare reform) or security. Equality, though, is especially rich, given the ontological conceptualizing that it induces about the majority, the claimant group, and the relation between them, as well as its 'fit' with liberal and neo-liberal discourses. On the side of less, it would have been possible to focus on equality from a single vantage, such as gender or sexual orientation, or on a single issue within family regulation, such as measures to foster 'equal parenting' by fathers and mothers. The hope is that the terms framing the agenda – including the subtitle, *Family, sex, kinship* – capture a middle ground, providing sufficient focus while stimulating productive connections across sites.

Researching 'after legal equality'

This collection presents new research, gathering under its rubric authors from England and Wales, the United States and Canada. Under an overarching theme of kinship and care, the chapters are organized into three parts: Care and justice under neo-liberalism, States' reach, and Sex and love. The recognition of same-sex relationships – primarily conjugal ones – emerges as the prevalent site of investigation, but chapters also address care more broadly, gender relations in parenting, cohabitation and organizing for racial equality. This gathering embodies an effort to transcend the barriers that often confine legal scholarship within law and, via specialized journals, within fields. For example, the collection sets scholars of family law in conversation with tax specialists. Disciplinarily, it juxtaposes socio-legal scholarship with the work of specialists in sociology, American studies and women's studies.

Before elaborating on the collection's register and methods and setting out its themes, it may be helpful to distinguish various understandings of the object of research 'after legal equality'. Although their boundaries are porous, such research might focus on at least five phenomena.

First, the dismantlement of achievements won in the name of legal equality. One might study instances in which conservative or other forces disassemble institutions or structures set up with a view to bringing about equality for one group or another. A recent example is the US Supreme Court's invalidation of the Voting Rights Act (see Jakobsen and Ferguson, both in this volume).[3] Arguably, such dismantlement should be assessed in a larger context. Thus Ferguson (159), discussing the same court's decision a day later to strike down the Defense of Marriage Act,[4] reads the judgments as together suggesting, 'that the mainstreaming of homosexuality within the US took place via the marginalization of anti-racist protections'. The destruction or reengineering of the welfare state offers other examples.

Second, the backlash following a historically marginalized or disadvantaged group's legal and social advances. Feminist gains in family law or criminal law may trigger a backlash (see, e.g., Boyd *et al.* 2007), as may achievements in rights for gay men and lesbians. Advocates for one group may borrow or co-opt the discourse of equality used by another, opposing group. Thus, fathers' rights groups have asserted fathers' right to parent equally and children's right to have two equal parents, in response to claims for substantive equality grounded in mothers' disproportionate caring work (see, e.g., Crowley 2006).

Third, the intuition (or evidence) that lobbying or litigation relying on legal equality has reached its limit. Equality as a political or legal argument has proven more effective at addressing some kinds of issue than others. In a number of contexts, equality has helped to obtain formally identical treatment, but failed to achieve significant redistribution or substantive equality (Hunter 2008).

Fourth, the impact for those left behind or further disadvantaged. Efforts to study such impact might pursue a number of enquiries. Which inequalities have reforms driven by equality exacerbated? How does enacting formal equality play against abiding substantive inequalities? Specifically, have reforms justified by equality in terms of gender or sexual orientation intensified inequality on other bases, such as class, race and ability? Crucially, class does not generate an 'equality' claim articulable in law, something that may intensify the effects of other markers of social position, such as race. 'Success' at changing law might further stigmatize non-normative sex (Warner 2000) or non-normative families (Barker 2012), although that may be an empirical rather than a conceptual question. It might also intensify the legal and social favours accorded to privileged, coupled forms of family (Brake 2012), although the character of such favours and the social meaning of marriage vary by jurisdiction and by era. For example, marriage's significance in the US is not necessarily universal. By advantaging those who are privileged except for their sexual orientation, equality efforts risk further legitimating legal and social structures soldered to discrimination based on race, gender, class and nationality (see, e.g., Young and Boyd 2006; Kandaswarmy 2008; Lenon 2011; Joshi 2014).

Have the reforms benefitted some members of a disadvantaged group and not others? As feminist and queer critics have noted in connection with the push for same-sex marriage, the rising tide of successful equality claims does not lift all boats. The 'options' that legal reforms make available – for gay men and lesbians, marriage and legally acknowledged parenthood – do not benefit or appeal to all groups or subgroups equally. New inclusions may produce new exclusions. Moreover, 'equality' campaigns, as for same-sex marriage, may visit unwelcome effects on those who would not decide to take up the new legal possibilities. In this respect, it is significant that expanded 'recognition' of spousal status may not be optional. For purposes of social programmes, it sometimes applies mandatorily, deeming cohabiting couples to be 'spouses', aggregating their incomes and reducing their benefits, irrespective of their wishes (see Young, in this volume).

Fifth, the effects for legal reform's intended beneficiaries. This understanding of 'after legal equality' presses against the assumption that legal 'success' represents an endpoint for legal reform and political organizing. Research might scrutinize the courts' or legislatures' selected means and anticipate and observe unintended consequences. How are reforms playing out? Are people taking advantage of the mechanisms made available, such as forms of family recognition or remedies? Where legislative drafters have copied existing legislative regimes for new contexts, how effective is that approach? Assumptions of sameness call for scrutiny, in particular concerning the regulation of same-sex couples (see Monk, in this volume; Leckey 2013a) and their status as parents (see, e.g., Diduck 2007). A newly accessible regime of family law may interact problematically with the legal arrangements made by same-sex couples – pre-equality, as it were – using the devices of the ordinary private law, such as wills (Monk 2011).

It may be possible, then, to identify the benefits of legislation recognizing families created and sustained by gay men and lesbians, as well as gaps in such regimes. Where reforms are already in place, such research may identify unintended consequences and point to additional, corrective reforms. Meanwhile, policymakers and governments in jurisdictions where reforms have not occurred can profit from the experience elsewhere. They may also find themselves judged against the yardstick of measures adopted in comparator states.

Other enquiries ripple outwards from legal regimes, reaching further into social practice and generating additional research questions. How have reforms altered conduct in their field of operation and beyond, such as the way people organize politically or where they congregate and live? Have legal rules that are ostensibly more equal reshaped kin configurations and practices or ways of talking about them? To what extent has a chosen legislative model 'channelled' social practice into it (Wallbank 2010), and how, methodologically, might we answer those questions? Looking back at the tools of law reform, how distortive is the image constructed for argumentative use before judges or elected lawmakers that the claimant group is the same as another group or sufficiently similar to it? (On campaigns for marriage, see Zylan 2011.) What subtleties and distinctive traits are stripped away when legal processes turn their gaze on a group heretofore 'outside' legal regulation? (Might the image on this volume's cover, by Montreal photographer Valerie Simmons, be read as an allegory of the strangely deadening effects of aiming to make one thing the same as another?) The diversity of social practices ensures that a process of legal recognition, through which one or more models will be picked out and given the state's imprimatur, will exclude some forms of practice and misrepresent others (Leckey 2011).

One finding from research 'after legal equality' may be that efforts to bring about formal equality – identical treatment of different individuals or groups – have not necessarily resulted in substantive equality. That observation has been made repeatedly, and this collection does not develop it. Instead, without pretence to exhaustiveness, this collection bears primarily on the fourth and fifth understandings of researching 'after legal equality'. I hope that it provides methodological, conceptual and theoretical resources for gathering and reframing existing research from different jurisdictions, and that it will inspire further work in other sites and concerning other groups. It may be worth identifying a few instances that exemplify the larger research agenda. On the gender and sexuality front, trans individuals' circumstances come to mind. A fine example of relevant research is Sharpe's (2012) painstaking analysis of the UK's Gender Recognition Act 2004 and its discriminatory premises and effects. Further, on family matters, the legal approach to surrogacy may register a concern for some intending parents' equality relative to others and a contingent conception of women's equality or capacity to choose (e.g., Campbell 2013: Ch. 3 Tremblay forthcoming). Turning to public policy, attention to areas such as welfare (see, e.g., Smith 2007) would align with this volume's chapters by specialists in taxation (Brooks and Young). Finally, religion warrants further analysis, whether in relation to legal efforts to advance women's equality by protecting them from religion (e.g., Korteweg and Selby 2012), perceived conflicts between freedom of religion and equality relating to sexual orientation (e.g., Cooper and Herman 2013) or other matters.

It is now appropriate to develop further the present collection's approach. In agreement with Hines and Taylor (2012: 2), that attending to advances around sexuality – and analogous matters – is 'both a methodological question and a theoretical challenge', this Introduction addresses the collection's register and methods, as well as its theoretical and thematic foundations.

Register and methods

Research 'after legal equality' may operate in a different register from work seeking to bring about law reform. It might bracket the binary logic of being for or against a given goal, such as access to marriage, and the doctrinal imperative of shoehorning social practice into existing categories. Such a juncture might make it more possible to 'complicate progressive narratives' and challenge the basis of claims for identical treatment (Monk 2011: 247). More than work prepared with an eye to judicial or parliamentary decision-making in the short or medium term, research 'after legal equality' may develop a critique that previously was politically unpalatable or simply not perceived (Harding 2011: 182; on the luxury of critique, see Brown and Halley 2002). Such research may be meditative, reflective or speculative. In this way, Monk aims 'to create a space for a "quiet empiricism", raising questions more than offering answers' (in this volume: 201 (reference omitted)). Of course, any opposition between advocacy or activism and research is contentious, and all research advances some perspective. Still, work 'after legal equality' may seek to deepen understanding, without issuing an immediately applicable policy recommendation. By contrast, moments of law reform, such as parliamentary hearings, pitting one group against another, offer less room for such enquiry.

Nonetheless, it would be wrong to imply that this collection of studies 'after legal equality' eschews policy prescription or offers no normative implications. Young favours an approach to taxation that focuses on the individual, not the conjugal couple. Although that is a view that she advocated two decades ago (Young 1994), it is now enriched by the experience of what 'equality' has brought and the heteronormative patterns it has failed to disturb. Other studies in this volume will inspire differing normative reflections in their readers. Reece's conclusion (129) that 'cohabitants' recalcitrance' – their failure to take responsibility for themselves by negotiating and concluding cohabitation agreements – 'may be something to celebrate' stands as a challenge to a prescriptive strand of legal policy literature. For some readers, though, her chapter's interdisciplinary discussion of the costs of concluding contracts on an individual basis, including the foreseeable hit to couples' optimism bias, will evoke the law-and-economics literature on default rules and strengthen the case for presumptively subjecting cohabitants to more robust protections. It is similarly possible to read Brooks's chapter on two levels. It is foremost a sociological endeavour, with the goal of better seeing conjugality at the margins. It may, however, lead some readers to worry about the intrusion that 'recognizing' family on an informal or functional basis occasions, and the apparently regressive way in which individuals with fewer resources appear least well placed to control their relationships' legal characterization. (The degree to which class privilege and social conventions inform metrics of intrusiveness would rightly temper such a reading.)

Beyond the question of its normative intensity, research 'after legal equality' raises methodological questions. The research agenda prefigured by this collection may call for different methods from debates for and against reforms. As the impact of legal reform on formerly excluded groups is a key question, empirical research is in order. The reforms in question are recent enough that fuller-scale empirical work must await the future; indeed, the complexity of legislation's impact necessitates a long-term view (Maclean and Kurczewski 2011: 106–10). Nevertheless, mid-term assessments may be fruitful. Researchers have already begun to trace how the availability of access to formal recognition of same-sex relationships may affect attitudes and ways of living (e.g., Balsam *et al.* 2008). Scholars have also examined the impact of legislated norms of equal or shared parenting (Fehlberg *et al.* 2011).

A shift in the scale and location of legal action post-equality may dictate a corresponding methodological shift. Where 'big' matters have been addressed in terms of equality, activism and pressures may be redirected towards more technical and interstitial legal matters. The implications of civil partnership and same-sex marriage in private international law or conflict of laws present an example (Cossman 2008). Regulations ostensibly based on health or risk concerns – in access to assisted reproduction or blood donation – that disproportionately affect a group are another.

To expand on this shift in scale, once equality has been 'achieved' via a human-rights judgment of general application or by legislation, the level and scale of relevant decision-making may change too. Equality's on-the-ground meaning will arise, for example, from discrete applications of law, as in individualized decisions respecting custody, residence orders or contact, made in a child's 'best interests' (Richman 2009). From an equality standpoint, the historical record of the latter concept's application is uneven, at best. Regimes that have been ostensibly purged of discrimination on their face may nevertheless prove problematic in their administration. A plain example is the adoption or fostering process (see Monk, in this volume). As an indication that it may be necessary to slice regimes finely, social workers' approval of same-sex couples as adopters may not be matched, downstream, by the placement of children with them (Sullivan and Harrington 2009). The lesser degree of transparency as the action shifts to policy, soft law and administrative decision-making – by contrast with publicly available judgments – mounts a thorny methodological challenge.

Concretely, then, with adjudication before apex courts and primary legislation in the national, state or provincial parliament behind it, scholarly attention 'after legal equality' may reconnect to research devoted to other sets of sources, such as soft law, and to less instrumental modes of reading. Indeed, research on regulation 'after legal equality' may have much in common with the pre-equality attention to soft law and policy, including at local levels, undertaken when groups such as gay men and lesbians were absent from higher-order laws (on 'sexing the city', see Cooper 1994; on 'post-equality', see Richardson and Monro 2012: Ch. 5). Same-sex marriage having been legislated in England and Wales, Harding (in this volume) brings critical discourse analysis to bear on the parliamentary debates that led to it. Research 'after legal equality' may privilege attention to the intimate, the archival and the micro. Think of work exploring queer parenting and kinship by examining stories, films and photographs (Hicks 2011; for a study of small-scale spaces, see Cooper 2013). Within this volume (100), Brooks reads legal tax cases for their portraits of individuals 'at the margins of conjugality', aiming to 'deriv[e] evidence about the texture' of their lives. Monk draws on interviews with solicitors who had experience of writing wills for gay men and lesbians, a revealing site of socio-legal enquiry, but not an obvious one. Nor are legal sources the only ones relevant. Consider Reece's assessment of Advicenow, a government-sponsored information website. The provision of information may merit analysis as a form of intervention and, indeed, of governance (see also, e.g., Reece 2003: Chaps 4, 5).

Critically, the micro character of suitable sources need not imply a small scope of relevance for the resulting findings. Even if focused on a minority group or formation in a circumscribed context, research 'after legal equality' stands to yield broader insights. For example, studying the friction between marriage law and gay and lesbian family life may provide insights applicable to other kinds of family, including the 'mainstream' different-sex couples for which such law was devised (Heaphy *et al.* 2013: 32; Leckey 2014).

Theory and themes

The complexities of post-reform politics may make it constructive to 'take a break' from prevailing theoretical constructs and commitments (Halley 2006). At minimum, it is worth studying their epistemic limits. Pre-equality, it sometimes appeared straightforward to characterize a minority group as oppressed or excluded by the majority. In contrast, a 'new era of legal recognition' around sexual orientation may create 'winners and losers within the lesbian and gay community', in the process 'test[ing] the very political notion of a community' (Monk 2010: 98). Queer theory has played an important role in this move, but Monk suggests that his chapter 'draws on, but at the same time troubles and complicates, queer critiques', troubling the 'new' binary of queer versus gay (211). As Donovan shows in her chapter, the problem of violence in same-sex relationships reveals the analytical limits of binary categories of gender. Collier calls for a 'move beyond considerations of gender differences', with a view to identifying 'the *common* problems that can face both parents, mothers and fathers' (in this volume: 69). At the same time, legal equality ignores some gender differences; grappling with them may draw on earlier feminist critiques of formal legal equality. This Introduction turns now to the overarching theme of kinship and care, afterwards addressing themes tied more directly to the collection's three parts.

Kinship and care

Referring to kinship, as opposed to family, may help to bring into view forms of affiliation that law has traditionally overlooked. Certainly, a rich sociological literature focuses on family as 'doing' or 'practices' (Morgan 1996, 2011). However, legal definitions of family remain confining (Wilkinson and Bell 2012). Concepts of kinship crystallize this collection's commitment to interdisciplinarity by showing how legal scholarship and theorizing may draw conceptual and empirical nourishment from fields such as sociology and anthropology. Recent years have witnessed a substantial, creative and often exciting outpouring of work on kinship (see, e.g., Carsten 2004), much of it assessing the impact of reproductive technologies (e.g., Franklin and McKinnon 2001; Strathern 2005; Franklin 2007, 2013). When traditional legal categories of sex, marriage, kinship and gender no longer suffice, anthropo-logical research may 'suggest alternatives for conceptualizing human affiliation outside reproductive ideologies and practices' (Borneman 2001: 31). Indeed, law's productive role, as opposed to its recognition role, connects intimately to lived and livable possibilities. Social practice and the demands made of contemporary law have disrupted assumptions that kinship must remain grounded on the 'presocial psychic place of the Mother and Father' (Butler 2000: 69). From within literary studies, Eng (2010: 136–7) draws attention to the 'prospects for a poststructuralist account of family and kinship', suggesting that reimagining family and kinship 'beyond the Oedipal . . . offers a host of political opportunities, economic responsibilities, and cultural commitments'.

Efforts to rethink the regulation of intimate relations may also draw on the abundant feminist work on an ethics of care (e.g., Noddings 1984; Gilligan 1993; Held 1995). Research has demonstrated the character of care work, how much is done, and by whom. Analysis 'after legal equality' unfolds against the backdrop of feminist work of decades past. Thus, Jakobsen and others in this volume question any purported dividing line between public and private spheres, alert to the underlying political and gendered politics of any such division (Boyd 1997; see also Halley and Rittich 2010).

Sociologists have made efforts to conceptualize family life, loosened from the strictures of heterosexual marriage and parentage. Some have expanded the categories of conjugality, highlighting the significant number of people who are 'living apart together' (e.g., Levin 2004). Smart (2007: 4) refers to 'personal life' as she seeks to explore 'those families and relationships which exist in our imaginings and memories'; Plummer (2003) proposes the concept of 'intimate citizenship'. A literature on friendship often, but not always, foregrounds sexual-orientation minorities (e.g., Nardi 1992, 1999).

However manifold the critiques of traditional notions and ideology around 'family', loosening their shackles – in law and in social practice – may prove difficult. Sociologists have remarked on the 'tenacity of the couple norm' (Roseneil *et al.* forthcoming; on 'the uncoupled', see Cobb 2012; see, also, Klinenberg 2012). Recent research involving same-sex couples indicates a strong focus on the monogamous romantic couple (Heaphy *et al.* 2013). Wilkinson (2012: 142) suggests that, if there is 'no longer compulsory heterosexuality, and no longer necessarily even compulsory monogamy', there may now be *'compulsory romantic love'*. That being said, such pressures may not operate in the same way for those disadvantaged by vectors such as race and class (or by their intersection), as they do for comparatively privileged groups.

If it is possible to read all the chapters in this collection as addressing big questions of kinship and care directly or obliquely, several gesture to related matters that, especially in the context of same-sex couples, offer promising avenues for research 'after legal equality'. Scholars outside law have extensively addressed the next two themes, sex and love, and then violence and power. In what is perhaps a reminder of the constraining influence of doctrines of legal equality and the strategic imperatives of advocacy, those themes are comparatively underrepresented in legal literature.

Sex and love

Aside from its role in procreation – assisted or otherwise – consensual sex is often largely absent from contemporary legal scholarship (but, see Brook 2014). Outside law, however, a substantial research addresses sex, attesting to the prevalence of non-monogamy within same-sex couples, especially among gay men (e.g., Barker and Langdridge 2010; Coelho 2011). A subset of this literature addresses implications for relationship therapists (Finn *et al.* 2012) and social workers who assist gay male couples (LaSala 2004). For anyone cognizant of this literature, it is a stretch to call the proliferation of varying conceptions of sexual and amorous fidelity, especially within male couples, even an open secret.

Yet, in places such as Canada, the US and the UK, advocacy for legal recognition of same-sex couples played the card of sameness, not only on economic interdependence but also on amatory commitment. As Stychin has observed, the discourse of equality rights has been accompanied by themes of 'social inclusion plus responsibility' and emphasis on recognition's 'civilising function' (2003: 40). For obvious strategic reasons, advocates did not draw judicial, legislative or public attention to the sexual practices in which formally recognized couples might foreseeably engage (on the UK Parliament's avoidance of sex entirely, see Herring, in this volume: 25; Barker 2006). Does this silence matter? The disconnect between the public discourse by which same-sex couples are just like normative different-sex couples may engender an alienation between gay men's public personae and their intimate queer selves (Joshi 2012). In addition, as Monk relates in this volume, it can have concrete effects when couples interact with administrative officials, as in connection with fostering and adoption. Two divides might be bridged productively. One lies between the extensive literatures on gay parenting and on gay sexual practices of non-monogamy. The other is between legal scholarship's focus on sameness and sociological and therapeutic literature's sensitivity to difference.

Relatedly, research 'after legal equality' might trace the discursive role that emotions have assumed in movements towards judicial or legislative reform. Love has emerged as a significant element in judicial and parliamentary discourse around same-sex marriage (Osterlund 2009; Grossi 2012). In this volume, Harding identifies love as a recurrent justification in debates regarding same-sex marriage for England and Wales. For her part, Donovan (in this volume) reports on the salience of love as a reason why individuals might stay in a violent same-sex relationship. Analysis of love's regulatory effects may evoke queer theorists' work in recent years on affect generally (see, e.g., Sedgwick 2003) and on particular emotions (e.g., Cvetkovich 2003). As if the view of love as governance instrument is not sombre enough, the question of love also raises matters of violence within intimate relationships.

Violence and power

The second issue where there is a gap between the social science and legal literatures is domestic or intimate violence in same-sex relationships. Understandably, discussion of this problem does not arise much in advocacy for legal equality, but, 'after legal equality', there might be space for considering it more fully. A burgeoning non-legal literature addresses violence in same-sex relationships (see, e.g., Ristock 2011), including the particular barriers to such individuals accessing support services (Simpson and Helfrich 2005). Some legal literature deals with same-sex domestic violence by underlining the policy imperative of assuring equal access to the criminal law or to civil remedies such as protective orders (Pfeifer 2005; Stapel 2008). Enquiry 'after legal equality' can ask whether new legal structures of recognition support relationships or, instead, isolate them, procuring for same-sex couples the marital privacy so persuasively challenged by feminist scholarship and activism. In this volume, Donovan draws on empirical findings to highlight the causes and character of same-sex couples' intimate violence. Coupled with Young's attention in this volume to how fiscal and economic regulation of couples induces and reproduces patterns of specialized labour and dependency, this research might lead some to worry whether family recognition has intensified the scope for abuse. These mentions of legal remedies for violence and the potential impact of public policies lead to the larger question of the state's role.

The state, recognition, and neo-liberalism

As should be already plain, this collection's focus on 'family, sex, kinship' and the broader research agenda it proposes are not limited to any private or intimate sphere. Its chapters are intensely bound up in 'public' questions of the state and, building on feminist scholarship, in troubling the public/private binary. Engaging with the role of the state is critical, because, despite reasons for disappointment – even for despair – regarding what the state can offer, many groups still 'desir[e] the state's desire' (Butler 2004: 105). As Ferguson argues, in this volume, contestable discursive and historiographical operations may have naturalized such desire. In this way, political and legal agendas concentrate on accessing the state's formal recognition, as by parental status or marriage for same-sex couples, or via informal, protective recognition on a functional basis. In other words, efforts to unmoor familial regulation from marriage or sex often end up urging the state to regulate more practices of intimacy (see Herring, in this volume; also 2013).

Arguably, however, it is necessary to sharpen the critical tools for assessing bids for state recognition, especially as the success of an equality claim appears to move the goalposts for further extension. Marshalling lines of enquiry for addressing the character of appropriate state action is delicate. Decades of feminist and other critical scholarship have made it impossible to speak incautiously or unselfconsciously of limits on the state's 'intervention', as 'non-intervention' is itself state action. Similarly, liberal discourses of autonomy and choice have been rightly criticized (although sometimes caricatured instead). Still, many will sense the need for a counterweight to the force of policies grounded in a claim to legal equality or justified on the basis of welfare or protection (for warning of 'post-liberalism's' 'uniquely interventionist' stance and 'coercive drive', see Reece 2003: 235, 237). Butler (2004: 117) rightly insists that 'legitimation is double-edged'. She emphasizes the importance of maintaining 'a critical and transformative relation to the norms that govern what will and will not count as an intelligible and recognizable alliance and kinship', including 'a critical relation to the desire for legitimation as such' and to 'the assumption that the state furnish these norms' (Butler, 2004: 117). Critical resources are also available outside the field of kinship, where scholars have scrutinized the 'demands for access to state violence' formulated by or on behalf of gay men, lesbians and trans people (Moran and Skeggs 2004: 19; see also Brown 1995).

Assessments on particular cases will vary, but identifying a relationship form for sociological purposes, or figuring it as kin, does not call straight-forwardly for subjecting it to legal recognition. Determining whether such a regulatory extension is appropriate would require assessing the foreseeable material or distributive consequences, including for those most financially vulnerable. But it also calls for reference, however tentative and qualified, to some idea of autonomy or agency (on the choice between the two, see Madhok *et al.* 2013: 5–7). It is notable that, when challenging the contours of family regulation in its major report on 'beyond conjugality', the Law Commission of Canada (2001: xii–xiii), rather than straightforwardly calling for their extension, emphasized autonomy as a key value and emphasized the question as to whether regulating via relationships is necessary in the first place. The case for regulating those who are living apart together is decidedly mixed (see, e.g., Duncan *et al.* 2012); that for regulating friendship is, perhaps, weaker still. It is far from plain that Jakobsen's 'network of alternative relation' (in this volume: 90) calls for assimilation with the more familiar objects of family law's grip.

Beyond adult relations, there are tensions between social, sexual and genetic bonds in relation to children and those who parent them. Inclinations to validate social parenting and to recognize genetic origins can pull strongly in opposing directions. Even as legislative drafters attempt to unmoor legal and social parentage from engenderment, making greater place for social parenting and intention (Boyd 2007), the normative persistence of the 'sexual family' merits attention (McCandless and Sheldon 2010; see also Harding and Boyd, both in this volume). Contrasting inclinations to enlarge the circle of family or kinship and to retract it are observable. 'After legal equality', there may be interest in recognizing more than two adults as a child's parents, for example, where assisted reproduction services are available without discrimination on the basis of sexual orientation or marital status. Simultaneously, efforts are made to protect the autonomy (in other contexts, a liberal concept repeatedly problematized by feminists) of individuals who set out to parent alone, notably single mothers by choice (Kelly 2012).

If one views these different configurations as equally valid, there may be little tension. From that angle, recognizing more simply increases the options and diversity within the ecology of family life. However, especially where children and their welfare or interests are involved – or, to ratchet up the rhetoric, even their 'right' to a genetic or social 'father' – social or legal practices may present some possibilities as 'better' or more 'responsible' than others (Leckey 2011: 341–2), thus reaffirming the sexual family. Here, again, surfaces the need for a counterweight to the welfare imperative, one that makes space for at least some conception of autonomy (on parenting post-separation, see Boyd 2010).

In any event, research taking stock of past legal reforms must also acknowledge the entwinement of alternative kinship practices with the material conditions of the neo-liberal state (Duggan 2003). It is not only that the retrenching welfare state makes the need for alternative kinship networks more urgent (Jakobsen, in this volume) or that it intensifies pressures on parents, before or after family breakdown (Collier, in this volume). Nor is it simply that work on gay and lesbian kinship regularly overlooks socio-economic status's abiding significance (Taylor 2009). It is, rather, that the recognition of alternative kinship forms parallels the rise of neo-liberalism in a non-coincidental way: neo-liberal politics 'explicitly recognize new models of family' (Woltersdorff 2011: 177). Shifts by which the state reprivatized the costs of social reproduction prepared the ground for expanding the contours of legally recognized family – that is, increasing the set of potential debtors of private support, such as same-sex spouses (Cossman 2002). Similarly, recognition of social parents within same-sex couples may have a poverty-law dimension, embedded in the post-welfare state's imperatives to seek out private support (Smith 2009).

The chapters of this collection

The collection is in three parts. Part I, 'Care and justice under neo-liberalism', addresses contemporary connections between family law and state policy concerning care and gender. Jonathan Herring's chapter emphasizes the importance of care and calls for family law to be reconceived around relations of care. He argues that the traditional focus on sex fails to capture family law's underlying aims, sets out indicia for caring relationships, and addresses objections to his proposal. In the next chapter, Susan B. Boyd uses laws on parenthood to study the contradiction between the trend towards formal equality and ongoing gendered patterns of care – including women's gendered inequality within heterosexual families – as well as the growing phenomenon of parenting by lesbians and by gay men and by single mothers by choice. She assesses the innovative potential of a new Family Law Act in British Columbia, Canada. In his chapter, Richard Collier suggests that our understanding of the political terrain around fathers' rights and shared parenting law can gain much from a richer and more nuanced engagement with the interconnections between fatherhood, law and gender. He contends that it is important to locate debates about fatherhood and law 'after legal equality' within a wider reconfiguration of gender and care under the political, economic and cultural conditions of neo-liberalism, one in which adequate support for post-separation parenting is in short order. Janet R. Jakobsen's chapter concludes this part, explicitly addressing contemporary conditions of neo-liberalism and the classification of care as a private matter. She argues that building possibilities for justice requires analysis of how private social relations such as those of gender and sexuality work with neo-liberal policy and the making of space for alternative relational understandings. By taking a queer approach to gender and sexuality, she calls us to shift, change and 'queer' the relation between public and private.

Part II, 'States' reach', pursues the enquiry about the appropriate role of the state, by interrogating what groups imagine and demand and showing how being recognized as family may play out. Kim Brooks reads the tax judgments applying Canadian law's recognition of conjugal couples as spouses, offering vignettes, at a micro-level, of life at 'the margins of conjugality'. The outcomes of the cases matter much less for her purposes than pausing to observe how state recognition of functional family plays out, including on whom the official gaze seems to rest most often. In her chapter, Helen Reece challenges the assumption of government and policy literature that responsible adults whose intimate relationships lie outside family law should take steps – inform themselves, negotiate and sign an agreement – in order to construct legal norms for themselves. She performs close readings of informational materials from Advicenow, a website sponsored by the British government. Drawing on psychological literature about optimism bias, among other things, Reece highlights the costs of making such agreements and invites us to take seriously the provision of information as a form of responsibilizing governance. Claire F.L. Young's chapter traces the impact, 'after legal equality', of gay men's and lesbians' recognition as spouses for purposes of income tax. Arguing for a governmental approach based on individuals, not the conjugal couple, she identifies the differential impact of inclusion as spouses across lines of gender and class. Some of the disadvantages flowing from spousal recognition relate to its impact on subsidies delivered through the tax system. The argument bears, then, on how the state should act, not on whether it should. This part's final chapter, by Roderick A. Ferguson, performs a genealogy of the contemporary claim for gay rights, identifying the historiographical operation by which past struggles for racial and sexual justice have been themselves refigured as claims for rights. He suggests that the current focus on obtaining equal rights from the state obscures a rich tradition of political thought and organizing that did not take the state's logics as their destination.

The collection's third part engages with 'Sex and love'. Drawing on empirical research concerning domestic violence within same-sex couples, Catherine Donovan points to the limits of the feminist understanding of domestic violence as a product of gender. She identifies features specific to the same-sex context and flags the recurrence of love as a factor in couples' staying together despite violence. Donovan argues for the need to attend to violence within the intimate sphere 'after legal equality', to ensure that new modes of legal recognition do not intensify abuses within those relationships.

In her chapter, Rosie Harding performs critical discourse analysis of key post-equality legal texts: parliamentary debates from England and Wales' Marriage (Same Sex Couples) Act 2013 and a family judgment concerning the relationships between men and the children born of their sperm donations to lesbians in civil partnerships. Harding delineates the robustness of heteronormative notions of marriage and love, on the part of parliamentarians, and the judge's susceptibility to the enduring lure of the sexual family. Finally, Daniel Monk's chapter challenges the prevalent separation in the literature between questions of gay sex and gay parenting, inviting us to consider the discursive and political salience of 'the child'. He studies two sites of queer kinship involving children: the difficulties encountered in the fostering process by a male couple who admitted that their relationship was non-monogamous and, based on interviews with solicitors, gay men's and lesbians' treatment of 'godchildren' in their wills. Monk subtly invites us to question the opposition between 'queer' and 'gay' and to reflect on the place of sex 'after legal equality'.

Acknowledgements

Funding was provided by the Social Sciences and Humanities Research Council of Canada and by McGill University's Fay Cotler Fund; I am grateful to Catherine Le Guerrier for her excellent research. For comments on earlier versions, I owe thanks to Susan B. Boyd, Kim Brooks, Davina Cooper, Iris Graham, Sarah Keenan, Sarah Lamble, Catherine Le Guerrier, Daniel Monk, Marc Roy and Régine Tremblay.

Notes

1   *Droit de la famille—072895* 2007 QCCA 1640, [2008] RJQ 49.
2   *Droit de la famille—102247* 2010 QCCA 1561, [2010] RJQ 1904.
3   *Shelby County v Holder* 133 SCt 2612 (2013).
4   *United States v Windsor* 133 SCt 2675 (2013).

References

Balsam, K.F., Beauchaine, T.P., Rothblum, E.D. and Solomon, S.E. (2008) 'Three-year follow-up of same-sex couples who had civil unions in Vermont, same-sex couples not in civil unions, and heterosexual married couples', *Developmental Psychology*, 44(1): 102–16.

Barker, M. and Langdridge, D. (2010) 'Whatever happened to non-monogamies? Critical reflections on recent research and theory', *Sexualities*, 13(6): 748–72.

Barker, N. (2006) 'Sex and the Civil Partnership Act: The future of (non) conjugality?', *Feminist Legal Studies*, 14(2): 241–59.

—— (2012) *Not the Marrying Kind: A Feminist Critique of Same-Sex Marriage*, Houndmills, UK: Palgrave Macmillan.

Borneman, J. (2001) 'Caring and being cared for: Displacing marriage, kinship, gender, and sexuality', in J.D. Faubion (ed.) *The Ethics of Kinship: Ethnographic Inquiries*, Lanham, MD: Rowman & Littlefield.

Boyd, S.B. (ed.) (1997) *Challenging the Public/Private Divide: Feminism, Law, and Public Policy*, Toronto: University of Toronto Press.

—— (2007) 'Gendering legal parenthood: Bio-genetic ties, internationality and responsibility', *Windsor Yearbook of Access to Justice*, 25(1): 63–94.

—— (2010) 'Autonomy for mothers? Relational theory and parenting apart', *Feminist Legal Studies*, 18(2): 137–58.

—— Chunn, D.E. and Lessard, H. (eds) (2007) *Reaction and Resistance: Feminism, Law, and Social Change*, Vancouver: UBC Press.

Brake, E. (2012) *Minimizing Marriage: Marriage, Morality, and the Law*, New York: Oxford University Press.

Brook, H. (2014) 'Zombie law: Conjugality, annulment, and the (married) living dead', *Feminist Legal Studies*, 22(1): 49–66.

Brown, W. (1995) *States of Injury: Power and Freedom in Late Modernity*, Princeton, NJ: Princeton University Press.

Brown, W. and Halley, J. (2002) 'Introduction', in W. Brown and J. Halley (eds) *Left Legalism/Left Critique*, Durham, NC: Duke University Press.

Butler, J. (2000) *Antigone's Claim: Kinship between Life and Death*, New York: Columbia University Press.

—— (2004) *Undoing Gender*, New York: Routledge.

Campbell, A. (2013) *Sister Wives, Surrogates and Sex Workers: Outlaws by Choice?*, Aldershot, UK: Ashgate.

Carsten, J. (2004) *After Kinship*, Cambridge, UK: Cambridge University Press.

Cobb, M. (2012) *Single: Arguments for the Uncoupled*, New York: NYU Press.

Coelho, T. (2011) 'Hearts, groins and the intricacies of gay male open relationships: Sexual desire and liberation revisited', *Sexualities*, 14(6): 653–68.

Cooper, D. (1994) *Sexing the City: Lesbian and Gay Politics within the Activist State*, London: Rivers Oram Press.

—— (2013) *Everyday Utopias: The Conceptual Life of Promising Spaces*, Durham, NC: Duke University Press.

—— and Herman, D. (2013) 'Up against the property logic of equality law: Conservative Christian accommodation and gay rights', *Feminist Legal Studies*, 21(1): 61–80.

Cossman, B. (2002) 'Family feuds: Neo-liberal and neo-conservative visions of the reprivatization project', in B. Cossman and J. Fudge (eds) *Privatization, Law, and the Challenge to Feminism*, Toronto: University of Toronto Press.

—— (2008) 'Betwixt and between recognition: Migrating same-sex marriages and the turn toward the private', *Law and Contemporary Problems*, 71(3): 153–68.

Crowley, J.E. (2006) 'Adopting "equality tools" from the toolboxes of their predecessors: The fathers' rights movement in the United States', in R. Collier and S. Sheldon (eds) *Fathers' Rights Activism and Law Reform in Comparative Perspective*, Oxford: Hart.

Cvetkovich, A. (2003) *An Archive of Feelings: Trauma, Sexuality, and Lesbian Public Cultures*, Durham, NC: Duke University Press.

Diduck, A. (2007) '"If only we can find the appropriate terms to use the issue will be solved": Law, identity and parenthood', *Child and Family Law Quarterly*, 19(4): 458–80.

Duggan, L. (2003) *The Twilight of Equality? Neoliberalism, Cultural Politics, and the Attack on Democracy*, Boston: Beacon Press.

Duncan, S., Carter, J., Phillips, M., Roseneil, S. and Stoilova, M. (2012) 'Legal rights for people who "live apart together"?', *Journal of Social Welfare and Family Law*, 34(4): 443–58.

Eng, D.L. (2010) *The Feeling of Kinship: Queer Liberalism and the Racialization of Intimacy*, Durham, NC: Duke University Press.

Fehlberg, B., Smyth, B., Maclean, M. and Roberts, C. (2011) 'Legislating for shared time parenting after separation: A research review', *International Journal of Law, Policy, and the Family*, 25(3): 318–37.

Finn, M.D., Tunariu, A.D. and Lee, K.C. (2012) 'A critical analysis of affirmative therapeutic engagements with consensual non-monogamy', *Sexual and Relationship Therapy*, 27(3): 205–16.

Franklin, S. (2007) *Dolly Mixtures: The Remaking of Genealogy*, Durham, NC: Duke University Press.

—— (2013) Biological Relatives: *IVF, Stem Cells, and the Future of Kinship*, Durham, NC: Duke University Press.

—— and McKinnon, S. (eds) (2001) *Relative Values: Reconfiguring Kinship Studies*, Durham, NC: Duke University Press.

Gilligan, C. (1993) *In a Different Voice: Psychological Theory and Women's Development*, Cambridge, MA: Harvard University Press.

Grossi, R. (2012) 'The meaning of love in the debate for legal recognition of same-sex marriage in Australia', *International Journal of Law in Context*, 8(4): 487–505.

Halley, J. (2006) *Split Decisions: How and Why to Take a Break from Feminism*, Princeton, NJ: Princeton University Press.

Halley, J. and Rittich, K. (2010) 'Critical directions in comparative family law: Genealogies and contemporary studies of family law exceptionalism', *American Journal of Comparative Law*, 58(4): 753–76.

Harding, R. (2011) *Regulating Sexuality: Legal Consciousness in Lesbian and Gay Lives*, New York: Routledge.

Haritaworn, J., Kuntsman, A. and Posocco, S. (eds) (2014) *Queer Necropolitics*, Abingdon, UK: Routledge.

Heaphy, B., Smart, C. and Einarsdottir, A. (2013) *Same Sex Marriages: New Generations, New Relationships*, Basingstoke, UK: Palgrave Macmillan.

Held, V. (ed.) (1995) *Justice and Care: Essential Readings in Feminist Ethics*, Boulder, CO: Westview Press.

Herring, J. (2013) *Caring and the Law*, Oxford: Hart.

Hicks, S. (2011) *Lesbian, Gay and Queer Parenting: Families, Intimacies, Genealogies*, Basingstoke, UK: Palgrave Macmillan.

Hines, S. and Taylor, Y. (2012) 'Introduction', in S. Hines and Y. Taylor (eds) *Sexualities: Past Reflections, Future Directions*, Basingstoke, UK: Palgrave Macmillan.

Hunter, R.C. (ed.) (2008) *Rethinking Equality Projects in Law: Feminist Challenges*, Oxford: Hart.

Joshi, Y. (2012) 'Respectable queerness', *Columbia Human Rights Law Review*, 43(2): 415–67.

—— (2014) 'The trouble with inclusion', *Virginia Journal of Social Policy and the Law*, 21(2): 207–65.

Kandaswarmy, P. (2008) 'State austerity and the racial politics of same-sex marriage in the US', *Sexualities*, 11(6): 706–25.

Kelly, F. (2012) 'Autonomous from the start: Single mothers by choice in the Canadian legal system', *Child and Family Law Quarterly*, 24(3): 257–83.

Klinenberg, E. (2012) *Going Solo: The Extraordinary Rise and Surprising Appeal of Living Alone*, New York: Penguin Press.

Kondakov, A. (2013) 'Resisting the silence: The use of tolerance and equality arguments by gay and lesbian activist groups in Russia', *Canadian Journal of Law and Society*, 28(3), 403–24.

Korteweg, A. and Selby, J.A. (eds) (2012) *Debating Sharia: Islam, Gender Politics, and Family Law Arbitration*, Toronto: University of Toronto Press.

Lasala, M.C. (2004) 'Extradyadic sex and gay male couples: Comparing monogamous and nonmonogamous relationships', *Families in Society*, 85(3): 405–12.

Law Commission of Canada (2001) *Beyond Conjugality: Recognizing and Supporting Close Personal Adult Relationships*, Ottawa: Minister of Public Works and Government Services.

Leckey, R. (2009) 'Family outside the book on the family', *Canadian Bar Review*, 88(3): 545–78.

—— (2011) 'Law reform, lesbian parenting, and the reflective claim', *Social and Legal Studies*, 20(3): 331–48.

—— (2013a) 'Marriage and the data on same-sex couples', *Journal of Social Welfare and Family Law*, 35(2), 171–91.

—— (2013b) 'Two mothers in law and fact', *Feminist Legal Studies*, 21(1): 1–19.

—— (2014) 'Must equal mean identical? Same-sex couples and marriage', *International Journal of Law in Context*, 10(1), 5–25.

Lenon, S. (2011) '"Why is our love an issue?": Same-sex marriage and the racial politics of the ordinary', *Social Identities*, 17(3): 351–72.

Levin, I. (2004) 'Living apart together: A new family form', *Current Sociology*, 52(2): 223–40.

Maclean, M. and Kurczewski, J. (2011) *Making Family Law: A Socio Legal Account of Legislative Process in England and Wales, 1985 to 2010*, Oxford: Hart.

McCandless, J. and Sheldon, S. (2010) 'The Human Fertilisation and Embryology Act (2008) and the tenacity of the sexual family form', *Modern Law Review*, 73(2): 175–207.

Madhok, S., Phillips, A. and Wilson, K. (2013) 'Introduction', in S. Madhok, A. Phillips and K. Wilson (eds) *Gender, Agency, and Coercion*, Basingstoke, UK: Palgrave Macmillan.

Monk, D. (2010) 'Commentary on Re G (Children) (Residence: Same-Sex Partner)', in R.C. Hunter, C. McGlynn and E. Rackley (eds) *Feminist Judgments: From Theory to Practice*, Oxford: Hart.

—— (2011) 'Sexuality and succession law: Beyond formal equality', *Feminist Legal Studies*, 19(3): 231–50.

Moran, L. and Skeggs, B. (2004) *Sexuality and the Politics of Violence and Safety*, London: Routledge.

Morgan, D.H.J. (1996) *Family Connections: An Introduction to Family Studies*, Cambridge, MA: Polity Press.

—— (2011) *Rethinking Family Practices*, Basingstoke, UK: Palgrave Macmillan.

Nardi, P.M. (ed.) (1992) *Men's Friendships*, Newbury Park, CA: Sage Publications.

—— (1999) *Gay Men's Friendships: Invincible Communities*, Chicago: University of Chicago Press.

Noddings, N. (1984) *Caring, a Feminine Approach to Ethics and Moral Education*, Berkeley: University of California Press.

Osterlund, K. (2009) 'Love, freedom and governance: Same-sex marriage in Canada', *Social and Legal Studies*, 18(1): 93–109.

Pfeifer, T.R. (2005) 'Out of the shadows: The positive impact of *Lawrence v. Texas* on victims of same-sex domestic violence', *Penn State Law Review*, 109(4): 1251–77.

Plummer, K. (2003) *Intimate Citizenship: Private Decisions and Public Dialogues*, Seattle: University of Washington Press.

Reece, H. (2003) *Divorcing Responsibly*, Oxford: Hart.

Richardson, D. and Monro, S. (2012) *Sexuality, Equality and Diversity*, New York: Palgrave Macmillan.

Richman, K.D. (2009) *Courting Change: Queer Parents, Judges, and the Transformation of American Family Law*, New York: New York University Press.

Ristock, J.L. (ed.) (2011) *Intimate Partner Violence in LGBTQ Lives*, New York: Routledge.

Roseneil, S., Crowhurst, I., Hellesund, T., Santos, A.C. and Stoilova, M. (forthcoming) *The Tenacity of the Couple Norm*, Basingstoke, UK: Palgrave Macmillan.

Sedgwick, E.K. (2003) *Touching Feeling: Affect, Pedagogy, Performativity*, Durham, NC: Duke University Press.

Sharpe, A. (2012) 'Transgender marriage and the legal obligation to disclose gender history', *Modern Law Review*, 75(1): 33–53.

Simpson, E.K. and Helfrich, C.A. (2005) 'Lesbian survivors of intimate partner violence: Provider perspectives on barriers to accessing services', *Journal of Gay and Lesbian Social Services*, 18(2): 39–59.

Smart, C. (2007) *Personal Life: New Directions in Sociological Thinking*, Cambridge, UK: Polity.

Smith, A.M. (2007) *Welfare Reform and Sexual Regulation*, New York: Cambridge University Press.

—— (2009) 'Reproductive technology, family law, and the postwelfare state: The California same-sex parents' rights "victories" of 2005', *Signs: Journal of Women in Culture and Society*, 34(4): 827–50.

Spade, D. (2011) *Normal Life: Administrative Violence, Critical Trans Politics, and the Limits of Law*, Brooklyn, NY: South End Press.

Stapel, S. (2008) 'Falling to pieces: New York State civil legal remedies available to lesbian, gay, bisexual, and transgender survivors of domestic violence', *New York Law School Law Review*, 52(2): 247–77.

Strathern, M. (2005) *Kinship, Law and the Unexpected: Relatives Are Always a Surprise*, New York: Cambridge University Press.

Stychin, C.F. (2003) *Governing Sexuality: The Changing Politics of Citizenship and Law Reform*, Oxford: Hart.

Sullivan, R. and Harrington, M. (2009) 'The politics and ethics of same-sex adoption', *Journal of GLBT Family Studies*, 5(3): 235–46.

Taylor, Y. (2009) *Lesbian and Gay Parenting: Securing Social and Educational Capital*, Basingstoke, UK: Palgrave Macmillan.

Tremblay, R. (forthcoming) 'Surrogates in Quebec: The good, the bad and the foreigner', *Canadian Journal of Women and the Law*, 27(1).

Wallbank, J. (2010) 'Channelling the messiness of diverse family lives: Resisting the calls to order and de-centring the hetero-normative family', *Journal of Social Welfare and Family Law*, 32(4): 353–68.

Warner, M. (2000) *The Trouble with Normal: Sex, Politics, and the Ethics of Queer Life*, Cambridge, MA: Harvard University Press.

Wilkinson, E. (2012) 'The romantic imaginary: Compulsory coupledom and single existence', in S. Hines and Y. Taylor (eds) *Sexualities: Past Reflections, Future Directions*, Basingstoke, UK: Palgrave Macmillan.

—— and Bell, D. (2012) 'Ties that blind: On not seeing (or looking) beyond "the family"', *Families, Relationships and Societies*, 1(3): 423–9.

Woltersdorff, V. (2011) 'Paradoxes of precarious sexualities', *Cultural Studies*, 25(2): 164–82.

Young, C.F.L. (1994) 'Taxing times for lesbians and gay men: Equality at what cost?', *Dalhousie Law Journal*, 17(2): 534–59.

—— and Boyd, S.B. (2006) 'Losing the feminist voice? Debates on the legal recognition of same sex partnerships in Canada', *Feminist Legal Studies*, 14(2): 213–40.

Zylan, Y. (2011) *States of Passion: Law, Identity, and the Social Construction of Desire*, Oxford: Oxford University Press.

Part I

Care and justice under neo-liberalism

Chapter 2

Making family law less sexy
... and more careful

Jonathan Herring

For a long time, sexual relationships have been the central focus of family law. Sex is seen as the defining feature of the kinds of relationship that constitute families and so are subject to family law. The concept of the nuclear family, with the two parents of opposite sex and their children, still has a powerful hold over family law as the ideal into which all other would-be families must fit.

There is no better example of this than the fierce campaigns in many countries to allow same-sex marriage (see Harding, in this volume). England's Civil Partnership Act 2004 created the status of civil partnership, which was said to be equivalent in legal terms to marriage, but excluded the parts of marriage law that related to sex, such as consummation and adultery. In England, the Marriage (Same Sex Couples) Act 2013 is striking in its attempts to fit same-sex couples into the heterosexual paradigm of marriage, and it struggles to do so. Workable definitions of adultery, consummation and presumptions of parenthood for same-sex couples could not be found, and so, despite the claims of 'equal marriage', students will still need to learn how same-sex and opposite-sex couples' marriages are different in law. The significance of these sexual elements and the way they are seen as central to marriage emphasize its sexual and heterosexual character.

Any move to equality raises the question: equal to what? The simplistic, and all too common, answer is: the prevailing norm. As feminist analysis has long demonstrated, formal equality of this manner does not necessarily lead to substantive equality (see, for example, Young, in this volume; Cooper 2004). However, one of the beneficial consequences of the debates surrounding same-sex marriage (on which see Harding, in this volume) has been a renewed analysis of what marriage and family law more generally are, and should be, about. This chapter explores how the debates on equalizing marriage have opened up new possibilities for structuring family law.

This chapter, echoing the calls of others, will argue in favour of focusing the interventions of family law on caring relationships, rather than sexual ones. In making this argument, I will not be undertaking a critical analysis of family law (see, e.g., Fineman 2004), but will deliberately adopt a mainstream legal approach by asking what the major goals are for family law. I will argue that each goal is far better served by emphasizing caring relationships rather than sexual ones. I hope to demonstrate that even using an orthodox method of legal analysis makes the case for moving to a care-centred family law.

I am specifically not arguing in favour of throwing open the door of family law widely to any relationship. I think the current coverage of family law is both too narrow and too wide. Nor am I in favour of leaving the regulation of care to private contracts. This chapter will emphasize the importance of care work and argue for a family law that is less sexy and more careful. Before developing these ideas, I need to set out my definition of care.

The four markers of care

There is a vast literature on the meaning and nature of care. I seek to summarize one suggestion as to the meaning of care (for an alternative approach, see Tronto 1983: 127–34). It is based on four key markers of care. These may be exhibited in different degrees. Although not providing a definition as such, they provide an indication of the extent to which an activity is or is not care (see Herring 2013: Ch. 2, for further discussion). Where all four markers are clearly present, there is undoubtedly care. When these markers are shown to a lesser extent, the behaviour moves away from the central understanding of care.

The four markers are as follows:

- meeting needs;
- respect;
- responsibility;
- relationality.

These terms need further explanation.

Meeting needs

We all have needs (Fineman 2011). Without the care and support of others, we would not survive for long. Being cared for and caring for others in meeting these needs is a universal experience (Held 2006). Dependency and care are inevitable parts of being human (Fineman 2004: Ch. 1). We are all profoundly dependent on others for our physical and psychological well-being. Although, in a person's lifespan, the extent of caring may vary during different ages, there is probably no point in our lives at which we neither are cared for by, nor are caring for, another, and often both at the same time (Feder Kittay 1999).

The meeting of the needs of its members is a central responsibility of society (Fineman 2004: xvii). Society has good reason to enable and support caring relationships to meet the needs of others. I argue that care should be understood broadly to include the meeting of a full range of a person's needs. These include, not only basic biological needs, such as food and shelter, but also broader social needs for emotion, relationships and play.

Respect

Respect is the second marker of care. This involves being alert to the needs of others and responding to those needs appropriately. It is about not treating the other as an object, but recognizing him or her as a fellow human being with whom one is in a relationship. This means that caring involves a degree of empathy and anticipation. It involves listening to the other and ensuring, where possible, that there is consent to what is being done. It involves accepting that what most people might want in a particular case is not necessarily what a particular individual wants.

Responsibility

The best caring involves assuming a responsibility to care for another. A person with needs must be able to rely on the giving of care to meet those needs. That cannot be guaranteed when caring is only done when it is convenient. The highest quality of caring relationship involves accepting a willingness to care, even where that was not one's preference. Of course, it may be that, in a particular situation, an individual is facing competing caring responsibilities and may not be able to meet all of them.

The classic liberal perspective is that one is 'born free' and that any responsibilities one takes on must be in some sense voluntarily assumed. However, for an ethic-of-care approach, with its starting point being that people are relational, the supposition is that there will be responsibilities for others. We are born into relationships that carry responsibilities with them. So, the response to a person in need is not an assessment of the extent to which you might owe them an obligation to assist, but rather an assessment of how one can meet that need, given other caring responsibilities (Sevenhuisen 2000).

Relationality

A central value in caring is that it should never be seen as unidirectional. Caring should be a relationship and, therefore, will require the person providing care to be open to receiving care (Dalmiya 2001). Caring relationships require both (or all) parties to be open to receiving the support and help of the other(s).

An ethic of care takes a particular view of the nature of the self, one that is constructed through, and finds its meanings in relation to, others (Crittenden 2001). Supporters of an ethic of care do not need entirely to reject the notion of an individual self, but simply to recognize that its identity and nature can only be appreciated through relation to others (Downie and Llewellyn 2011). It, therefore, is sceptical of approaches that seek to conceive of individual rights and interests understood in isolation from others.

The aims of family law

Much has been written on the functions of family law, and indeed whether it is wise to seek to identify its functions (e.g., Eekelaar 1984; Dewar 1998). The following are generally taken to be some of the goals of family law: the support and promotion of forms of intimate life; the protection of individuals from abuse within the course of family life; and the remedying of disadvantages and advantages caused by a relationship. I will not seek to justify here the wisdom of these purposes. My claim will be that, for each of these roles, the existence of a sexual relationship between the parties is irrelevant. Rather, a caring relationship should be key.

Promotion

Family law seeks to promote various kinds of relationship. It does this by providing social recognition through formal acknowledgement of certain kinds of relationship, and indeed through not providing formal acknowledgement of others. It also promotes the approved relationship with legal regulation and protection that constitute an attractive background against which to enter into intimate relationships.

Traditionally, family law has focused on sexual relationships, in particular marriage, as being the primary model of approved family life. Lynn Wardle (2011: 12) expresses the traditional view: 'Marriage is the primary expression of and preferred locus for the most meaningful and socially beneficial forms of intimate belonging.'

Even though, nowadays, marriage is offered to same-sex couples in some jurisdictions, and the rights of marriage have been extended to cohabitants to some extent, this is still done through the prism of marriage. For example, unmarried couples are 'treated as if they were married' for various purposes, and reference has already been made to the problems of fitting same-sex marriage into the heterosexual conception. Typically, textbooks on family law open with an explanation of the law of marriage, with an overly detailed analysis of the law on consummation. The authors explain that other relationships that are marriage-like (by which is meant, relatively stable sexual relationships) are protected in varying degrees. Moving on to parenthood, students are taught that parenthood is paradigmatically established through marriage or the biological link. Although textbooks on family law have extensive chapters on marriage, cohabitation and parenthood, little is written on broader family relationships, for example, the relationships between an adult child and her parent, a parent and an adult disabled child, a friend and someone with a disability. Nor is attention given to the position of older people in families. In the textbooks, sex and blood ties are presented as the meat and bones of family law.

This must be questioned. Are sexual relations between adults, or even particular kinds of sexual relationship, of such significance that they deserve promotion through the law? I would argue that what might make a relationship worthy of promotion by the state is care and mutual support, rather than sex. To be blunt, society does not really gain much from a couple's having sex, however pleasurable it may be for the participants! However, the state does benefit from care, particularly where that is of a person whose needs would otherwise fall on the state. It is such relationships that should receive the support of the state. Whether the relationship has a sexual side is a red herring.

It might be argued that, given the fluid nature of care, we can use sex as a proxy for care. However, that is a very weak argument. Nowadays, sex often takes place in the context of casual relationships. Any assumption that sex is a sign of commitment looks terribly old fashioned. Care can certainly take place outside a sexual relationship.

And, if sex is not a good marker of commitment or intimacy, why should it be of any legal significance? Traditionally, morality was seen as requiring that sex only take place within marriage, but few hold that view today. The only answer seems to be that society has an interest in ensuring that sex takes place in order to produce a sufficient number of children. However, the vast majority of sexual encounters do not produce children. Further, at least currently in most countries, it is the care of children that poses far greater challenges than their production.

If, therefore, marriage is not about the production of children, what is it about? It should be about the care of dependants. To quote Maxine Eichner (2010: 124):

> Because of its interest in the health, well-being, and dignity of its citizens, the liberal state has a vital interest in the success of relationships that foster caretaking, and should provide these relationships with the institutional support that will help them flourish.

Assuming it is unacceptable for individuals to be left in great need without any help, care must be performed. The question then arises: who is to meet the costs associated with that care? Currently, that largely falls on individuals within those relationships. However, if people stop caring, through choice or economic need, that burden falls on the state. As Jakobson notes (in this volume), the diminishing state help for those in need has made the private provision of care ever more significant. The state, therefore, has a strong interest in providing what support it can to ensure caring relationships continue (Carers UK 2011). There is much more to the state's interest than economics. The state has a core interest in ensuring that the needs of citizens are met, and that the distribution of care work is fair. In particular, the state has a role in ensuring that the division of care work does not exacerbate gender inequality (see Boyd, in this volume). This leaves open the complex question of how the state should promote caring relationships. This is a major issue, which is beyond the remit of this chapter, save that one important part of that can be through family law (for further discussion, see Herring 2013).

The protective function

One important role for family law is to prevent abuse within relationships. It will be argued that a sexual element is hardly a prerequisite for domestic abuse. The violence, structural inequality or coercive control that can mark domestic abuse can occur in non-sexual as well as sexual relationships. It is the intimacy of the relationship, not its sexual nature, that is key to the wrong in domestic abuse. Therefore, this function of family law is correctly focused, not on sexual relationships, but on intimate ones, typically marked by care. Restricting domestic violence to marriage or marriage-like relationships has meant that some forms of abuse have gone without an effective remedy, such as same-sex partner abuse (Donovan, in this volume), elder abuse (Herring 2010) and abuse by teenagers of their parents (Holt 2013).

In order to provide an effective response to abuse within intimate relationships, we need to identify the wrong that such abuse constitutes. I suggest that can be done by exploring three features of intimate abuse (building on Madden Dempsey 2006):

• harmful acts in an intimate relationship;
• acts perpetuating relational inequality;
• acts perpetuating societal disadvantage.

It is the intimacy of the relationship that is one element of the wrong of domestic abuse. This need not contain a sexual element, cohabitation or emotional warmth, but requires regular contact and a degree of dependency. It is in intimate relationships that the ability of the victim to escape from the violence is restricted.

Intimate abuse can be seen as a breach of trust. Intimate relationships involve becoming physically and emotionally vulnerable. The trust that is central to close relationships creates special obligations not to misuse that vulnerability (Eekelaar 2007: 4–47). The harm in abusive intimate relationships goes particularly deep. It is through our intimate relationships that we form our identity and sense of self. Intimate abuse strikes at the very conception of the self for the victim. Intimate relationship abuse, therefore, turns what should be a tool for self-affirmation and self-identification into a tool for alienation and self-betrayal. The victim almost becomes used as a tool against herself.

These arguments seem to point to the 'intimacy' requirement, better understood as not a point about the location of the incident so much as the nature of the relationship between the parties. Whether the parties are living together or whether they are related or having sex is much less relevant than whether their relationship is of the kind where there is deep trust and vulnerability. That will most typically arise in relationships involving care.

There is another reason why domestic abuse is best seen as occurring in intimate relationships that should be marked by care. The experiences of victims of domestic abuse show that it is best understood, not simply as a series of violent or abusive acts, but rather as a programme of 'coercive control' (to use Evan Stark's (2007) phrase) or 'patriarchal terrorism' or 'intimate terrorism' (to use Michael Johnson's (2005) phrase). The 'coercive control' model of intimate violence argues that understanding the impact of domestic abuse requires an appreciation of its controlling intent and impact. This can only be understood by looking at the relationship between the parties as a whole. The whole aim of the behaviour of the abuser is to dominate the victim and diminish her sense of self-worth. This is done by restricting the victim's access to work, isolating her from friends, manipulating the victim emotionally and using physical attacks. Again, the kinds of relationship where this can occur are not necessarily marked by sexual relationships, but are more likely marked by interdependence and care.

We have seen that intimate abuse is best seen as part of an inequality within the relationship. However, it also reflects broader inequalities within society (Madden Dempsey 2009: 112). Abuse within the relationship can be a tool used to maintain the dominance of one party in the relationship, usually the man. Abuse within intimate relationships reinforces and relies upon power exercised by men over women in society more generally. In such a view, intimate violence must be seen in its broader context as part of a set of power relationships that enable men to exercise control over women. The broader context is relevant for several reasons. It explains how domestic violence gets its power: the woman is disadvantaged, not only by the abuse in the home, but also by the lack of power outside the home. It may also explain why the law has been so reluctant and ineffective in responding to it.

A similar analysis can be made of the abuse of older people, children and vulnerable adults. Abuse of older people reflects wider societal attitudes towards older people. Elder abuse reflects and reinforces attitudes about older people in a way that interacts with the attitudes about them. Many of the victims are women, and then we see the interaction of both ageism and sexism in creating and reinforcing the structures that enable abuse to take place (Herring 2010: Ch. 3).

It is the devaluing and privatizing of care that leave what should be caring relationships open to abuse. The lack of social recognition for care work leads those in close caring relationships to face social exclusion and a lack of effective tools for self-protection. This leaves them open to abuse. Further, the devaluing of care, in relation to those both receiving and giving care, is reflected in abuse, which might stigmatize those in need as a 'drain on society', or carers reliant on welfare support as 'scroungers'.

When individuals enter what they believe to be a caring relationship, they are opening themselves up to the risk of intimate abuse. Family law, if it is to promote caring relationships and protect people from the wrongs of intimate abuse, must focus on caring relationships as being the ones where the protection is most required.

Remedial

Not only must family law seek to protect people from abuse, it must remedy the disadvantages that flow from relationships. This is particularly relevant in the context of financial orders on relationship breakdown. These are seen as designed to ensure a fair sharing of the economic advantages and disadvantages that flow from it. Here, I will summarize the primary arguments to justify such redistribution. These can be only sketched in outline, but the key point for this chapter is that the justifications apply particularly to caring relationships, rather than to marriage or sexual relationships per se.

Equal contribution to a partnership

According to this view, marriage should be regarded as analogous to a business partnership. The husband and wife co-operate together as a couple as part of a joint economic enterprise (Fehlberg 2005). It may be that one spouse is employed, and the other works at home, but they work together for their mutual gain just as in a business. Therefore, on divorce, each spouse should be entitled to his or her share of the profits of their enterprise, normally argued to be one-half each. For too long, the caring contribution to a marriage was not valued or recognized. One of the more appealing aspects of the approach is the weight that it attaches to carrying out caregiving obligations (Glennon 2010). It regards the matrimonial assets as the produce of the labour of them both and fit for division between them. There is no reason to restrict this reasoning to marriage. This argument applies whenever the members of the couple have entwined their lives. It will be in relationships of care that this intertwining will have occurred, and losses result.

Mutuality

It may be that the business model that sees marriage as involving equal contributions is not quite the right one. Shari Motro (2008: 1625) argues:

> Marriage is not fundamentally about equal contribution of labor. It is about two people joining the risks and rewards of their lives: merging their fates, committing to be 'in the same boat,' to sink or swim together, to contribute unequally at times if that's what it takes to keep the union afloat.

This way of putting the argument is interesting. On this model, marriage is not precisely an agreement to recognize as equal the contributions to the marriage, but rather an agreement to share the joys, slings and arrows of life. The model has considerable benefits. It views the family in the way we might assume that many couples do. The relationship may bring sickness, health, wealth or poverty, but the couple will share in that. Few families will seek to account for the contributions made. We are, as they say, all in this together.

These arguments apply to all caring relationships. An intertwining of lives normally leads to sharing of the joys of caring and the disadvantages of its burdens. In some cases, it may be that the relationship can be ended without a court order, because there is a fair share of these. Often, however, the sharing of the caring is not equal, and the disadvantages that result from the relationship will continue well beyond the marriage. It is the intermingling of lives in a caring relationship, especially as they carry indeterminable responsibilities and costs, that justifies the financial reordering on separation.

The state's interests

Most people who have written on the issue of justifications for redistribution of property on divorce have assumed that the issue is about achieving fairness between the parties themselves. However, it is arguable that financial orders on divorce can be justified by the interests of the state, regardless of what would be fair or just between the parties. So, what state interests are there here? These might include ensuring that, if possible, neither spouse becomes dependent on welfare payments, or promoting the stability of the family. Here, I will focus on the state's strongest interests in the promotion of caring relationships (Herring 2005a).

The response of society to the disadvantage flowing from care will have an impact on the way individuals respond to care needs. Obviously, a system that provided no kind of financial compensation or support to a person who lost out financially through childcare or other forms of care would discourage people from undertaking such care. By contrast, a society that did provide some kind of compensation would be making that a more attractive option. The availability of financial orders on divorce is one way a state could seek to encourage or discourage care. Lady Hale (2011: 4) has asked:

> Do we want to encourage responsible families, in which people are able to compromise their place in the world outside the home for the sake of

their partners, their children and their elderly or disabled relatives, and can be properly compensated for this if things go wrong? I continue to hope that we do.

How the law provides for financial orders on separation will directly impact on the decisions people may make over childcare and other obligations. It also contributes more widely to the societal response to caregiving and how it is regarded.

Not everyone will be convinced by these arguments. Lucinda Ferguson (2008) has argued that the state has overextended the appropriate interpersonal obligations owed between spouses and by parents to children in order to deal with poverty, which should instead be resolved by state support. There is much to be said in favour of Ferguson's argument. One of the difficulties with the current law is that the extent to which the claims of the spouse may be met or the goals of the state furthered depends on the wealth of the economically stronger spouse, still usually the husband. But, and it's an enormous but, the costs of doing this through state funds would be enormous. Especially in the current economic climate, it is hard to imagine it being taken on. Further, it would not capture the fact that the losses caused to the wife have resulted in the gains to the husband in terms of home and family life (Glennon 2010). Also, arranging financial orders flowing from caring relationships is not the only way the state should promote care. Other ways would be to provide funding for those who undertake care work or to restructure work around the norms of family care (Williams 1998).

Through financial orders on divorce, determined by the values of the law, our community is able to recognize the value and importance of care work. There is much more that our society needs to do to properly value that work, but this is a starting point.

That claim is central to the argument in this section. There may be some debate over elements of the distributions, such as the appropriateness of distinctions between those who have formalized their relationships in marriage or some equivalent status and those who have not, and the impact of the length of time the couple have lived together and the way they have structured their finances, but the sexual nature of the relationship seems particularly irrelevant (see Law Commission of Canada 2001). It is care that causes the kinds of relationship-based disadvantage that best justify the intervention of the law. We need financial orders on relationship breakdown that recognize the value of care, ensure the consequences of care are shared equally, and appreciate the intertwining of interests that takes place in intimate relationships. These should not be restricted to marriage but should apply to all relationships marked by care. Equality demands that we seek to promote a fair sharing of the burdens of care within relationships and across society. Inevitably, it is not always possible for an equal sharing of care; where unequal sharing takes place, the law should ensure that the disadvantages that flow from it are compensated.

Adjudicative

As to the adjudicative role, a primary function of family law is to ensure the making, at the end of a relationship, of a suitable distribution of the assets of the marriage and of suitable arrangements for any child who has been living with the parties. Again, both of these are required whether there is a sexual relationship between the parties or not.

Parents and care

Traditionally in family law relating to children, parents play a crucial role. Parents are given special rights that enable them to make decisions about children. Parents have particular responsibilities towards their children, which can be legally enforced. The state's ability to intervene in family life and remove a child from her parents is restricted to the severest of cases. In this legal regime, parenthood has traditionally been understood in biological terms. However, we have been seeing, in recent years, a move towards understanding parenthood in terms of the job of caring for the child, rather than the biological link (see Leckey, in this volume, discussing the notion of kinship). I will argue in this section that that is to be welcomed and should be developed.

The traditional approach has been that the biological link defines who is the father and who is the mother and who thereby acquires, or has the potential to acquire, the rights and responsibilities of parenthood. It would, however, be wrong to assume that it is biology that makes parenthood. Indeed, it will be argued that it is care of the child that is the central thread of parenthood. The argument that having a caring relationship with a child should be the source of parental rights is not to deny that children may have some kind of claim to be entitled to know of their genetic origins (although I would not accept the existence of such a right). Such a claim could, however, be met by granting children access to the information, without granting the status of parent.

Parental status should be earned by care and dedication to the child, something not shown simply by a biological link. It is the changing of the nappy, the wiping of the tear and the working out of maths together that make a parent, not the provision of an egg or sperm. Here are some of the reasons why parenthood should depend on care.

First, I argue that we should give parental status and parental rights in accordance with the principle of the promotion of the welfare of the child. Quite simply, we should give parental status and rights to those who are likely to make the best decisions for the child in question. That will be the person who knows the child best: the person who is caring for the child day to day.

Second, parental status should not be seen as a right one can assert, but as a responsibility granted in recognition of the work one has done in respect of the child (Boyd 2003; Wallbank 2010). As Barbara Bennett Woodhouse (1993: 1814) claims, there is a danger that the law is 'intent on securing children for adults who claim them', rather than 'seeking to provide adults for children who need them'. If we see parenthood in the nature of stewardship and parental status as a source not of power but of responsibilities, with the child's interests at heart, then they should be earned, not given as a right.

Third, there is much to be said in favour of the view that the law on the allocation of parenthood should match the perspective of the child. If the child regards an adult as a primary decision-maker, as a parent figure, then that is a strong indication the law should follow suit. Step-parents, same-sex partners, grandparents and others might be fully regarded by the child as a parent, and yet not be recognized as a parent by the law (Smart 2007). By contrast, a person with whom the child has little interaction, however strong the biological link, is unlikely to be seen by a child as a parent in a meaningful sense.

The current approach of the law is based on the heterosexual married model. The requirement that a child have one father and one mother reinforces that as a norm for parenthood. As we depart from the assumption that that model is the primary game in town, new vistas of what it means to be a parent are opened up (Kelly 2011). We can start to recognize the network of people that can play a role in a child's life. This includes recognition of the extent to which children care for other children and, indeed, for their parents.

Although welcome as liberalizations, the difficulty with both these approaches is that they retain a stark parent/non-parent divide. A better approach, it is submitted, is to recognize the range of adults who may be involved in a child's life, with particular focus on the nature of the relationship with the child. A teacher to whom a child is particularly close may thereby acquire a right to be involved in decision-making about education. One benefit of such an approach is that it avoids the norm of two opposite-sex parents, which still wields such a powerful influence in our law. The truth is that few families abide by such a straightforward model. As Laura Kessler (2007: 49) suggests, the current law demonizes 'difference, seeks to characterize as dysfunctional, disorganized, and deviant those families that do not conform with the nuclear, heterosexual, male-breadwinner, female-homemaker ideal'.

So, to conclude, parenthood should shift from focusing on blood ties to focusing on the caring relationship between child and other. Rights should flow from the relationship with the child, not the blood tie. If this is recognized, it has considerable significance. We move away from the idea that a child can have only two parents. In terms of legal rights, a range of adults might, depending on the context of their particular relationship, have a say in certain areas of the child's life, but the extent and nature of those rights will depend on the relationship.

Where there is a dispute concerning a child that a court must resolve, most jurisdictions require the court to focus on the welfare or best interests of the child. There is much to be said that is beneficial about the welfare principle: it ensures that the focus is on the child and enables an individual assessment of the needs of the child (Herring 2005b). However, we need an understanding of welfare based on an ethic of care to justify that approach. I have developed an approach I have called relationship-based welfare (Herring 1999).

Children, as we all do, live in the context of relationships. We cannot separate either the welfare or the rights of children from their parents. Their interests and rights are so intertwined and the parties so interdependent that to consider what order will promote the welfare of the child, as an isolated individual, and without consideration of the interests of the parents, as the courts suggest, is simply impossible.

A care-centred approach would require us to consider the child in the network of relationships within which he or she lives. Relationship-based welfare argues that children should be brought up in relationships that, overall, promote their welfare. Relationships are central to the lives of children and so should be at the centre of decisions about their lives. It is beneficial for a child to be brought up in a family that is based on relationships that are fair and just. A relationship based on unacceptable demands of a parent is not furthering a child's welfare. Indeed, it is impossible to construct an approach to looking at a child's welfare that ignores the web of relationships within which the child is brought up. Supporting the child means supporting the caregiver, and supporting the caregiver means supporting the child. So, a court can legitimately make an order that benefits a parent, but not a child, if that can be regarded as appropriate in the context of their past and ongoing relationship.

A central aspect of relationship-based welfare is that we need to take a long-term view when considering welfare. The danger with the welfare principle is that it can lead to taking a snapshot approach. The court looks at the pros and cons of a particular course of action at the time of the hearing and determines the correct result. The problem with this approach is that it focuses the court's attention simply on the current issues and fails to locate them as part of an ongoing relationship between the parties. What has happened to date in the relationship, and what will happen in the future between the parties, drops out of the picture.

Concerns with my approach

My argument in this chapter raises a number of concerns. First, how can we determine when the degree of care and commitment in a relationship is sufficient to justify state protection and legal recognition? I accept that the current family law legal system, with its focus on marriage and civil partners, has an ease of use that would be lost by a focus on care and commitment. Nevertheless, I believe that there are many relationships of care in which there is a need for family law's remedial, protective and supportive functions, but which fall outside its scope. The plight of those whose care goes unrecognized and unrewarded justifies any increased bureaucratic difficulties.

The temptation is to start to break down the category of caring relationships: parents, friends, partners. However, these categories tell us nothing about the disadvantages flowing from the caring. A friend may incur enormous sacrifices in a caring relationship with a friend, and spouses may incur none. Once we seek to separate out kinds of caring relationship, we are in danger of privileging the contexts of the caring relationship, rather than the work within it (Barker 2012: 204). It would be preferable to stick with the definition of caring relations used above, but give it more clarity by listing some indicators of when a relationship would fall within my definition, including an indication of the expected duration, the kinds of activity that would be considered caring, and factors that would suggest commitment to the relationship.

Second, and following on from this point, there is a danger that, if caring relationships are the focus of legal attention, then only those relationships that are analogous to a traditional form (parent–child, spouse) will be recognized (Brake 2012). This reflects the concern that equal marriage will work against same-sex relationships that do not fit the standard heterosexual marriage paradigm (Barker 2012). That is why the definition of care provided above is crucial. It should make plain that it is not the structure or form of the relationship that is important, but, rather, its caring content.

Third, there is a concern that the language of care, with its cosy terminology, ignores the power implicit in the concept of care, divides the carer from the cared for, sanitizes care involving abuse and manipulation, and disguises a range of cultural assumptions about the nature of care (Cooper 2007; see also Beasley and Bacchi 2007). These are genuine and important concerns, and it is certainly true that some of the writing on the ethic of care has been idealistic. This is why it is essential to be clear about what good care involves. For example, in the definition of caring above, I wrote about the importance of promoting caring relationships and the importance of respect. Further, as already argued, a care-based approach requires and enables an effective response to abuse.

Fourth, it may be that, if we are to centre care, we should abandon the terminology 'family law'. This claim is likely to be made by those who think that there is something 'fundamentally natural' (Santorum 2005: 28) about what a family is. It is difficult to respond to such an argument for those who see nothing 'natural' about a family. I can only note that family forms have varied enormously over the ages, and that the notion of what a family is, or what family life involves, changes between generations and societies. Even if there is such a thing as a natural family form, that does not tell us what the state should do about it. In any event, the label is of little importance: if we need to abandon the label of family law and replace it with relationship or caring law, we should do that.

There is, fifth, a deeper concern raised by John Eekelaar (2007), who notes that, if we attach legal obligations to selfless relationships, then there is a danger that these relationships will become polluted, with people using friendship for personal or material advantage. Further, one of the joys of intimate relationships is that they are 'law free' and outside public scrutiny. It is not the values of legal obligations that govern them, but love, trust and care. We should be wary of losing these virtues through regulation (see, further, Boyd and Young 2003). Indeed, the history of state intervention in intimate relationships demonstrates the dark side of state intrusion, which can reinforce inequalities and prejudicial attitudes about particular kinds of relationship. However, I would respond that the values of love, trust and care can only flourish if there is a legal protection from potential abuse caused by the vulnerabilities that arise, and if there are remedies for any injustice that results from the relationship. Although, therefore, as Eekelaar points out, there are dangers in legal intervention in relationships of care, there are graver dangers in not intervening. Given that the legal interventions that are proposed in this chapter primarily operate at the end of the relationship, adopting them is likely to protect those disadvantaged by relationships and is unlikely to pollute ongoing relationships.

Sixth, some who are very supportive of promoting care have recommended the use of contract law to govern care, rather than family law (e.g. Fineman 2004). One benefit of this is that it enables the parties to choose what counts as a caring relationship and achieve a market price for it. It can involve a recognition that traditionally family law has played a significant role in privatizing care and privileging certain kinds of relationship, both of which have contributed to the oppression of women (Boyd and Young 2003). However, I am not convinced by the contract model. It assumes that those on whom the costs of care currently fall most harshly are in a position to bargain to protect their rights. The current commercialization of care through the use of nannies, housekeepers and professional carers does not indicate that a contract offers a strong protection of their interests. Moreover, contracts work best where parties are able to predict their future abilities and obligations with a degree of certainty. However, the nature of caring is that its obligations are unpredictable and extensive (see, further, Reece, in this volume). Flexibility and being able to respond to care needs as they arise are essential to good care, and yet this being 'on call' is not readily reducible to a contract. A couple planning to set up home together and raise children cannot sensibly, at that point, construct a contract that can deal with all the vicissitudes that life might, or might not, throw at them. A fair sharing of the burdens and benefits can be determined after the event, but not before.

Conclusion

The debates over equal marriage pushed to the fore the questions about the nature of marriage and the role of family law. Traditionally, sexual relationships were seen as defining aspects of marriage and central to the kinds of relationship that deserved the ministrations of family law. Attempts to fit same-sex sexuality into the heterosexual model have proven problematic, opening up broader debates about the role of marriage and family. It has been argued here that doing so has laid bare the weakness of the case for centring sexual relationships as the heart of marriage or family law. The way ahead is to focus on care, rather than sex. Caring relationships are the ones that need promoting through family law, because they are the relationships that are key to the well-being of society. Caring relationships are the ones that can create vulnerability to abuse and should be the focus of protection. It is in caring relationships that the law is able to remedy the disadvantages that flow from relationships and so promote an equal sharing of the burdens of care. In short, family law needs to be less sexy and more careful.

References

Barker, N. (2012) *Not the Marrying Kind: A Feminist Critique of Same-Sex Marriage*, Basingstoke, UK: Palgrave.

Beasley, C. and Bacchi, C. (2007) 'Envisaging a new politics for an ethical future: Beyond trust, care and generosity – towards an ethic of "social flesh"', *Feminist Theory*, 8: 279–98.

Bennett Woodhouse, B. (1993) 'Hatching the egg: A child-centered perspective on parents' rights', *Cardozo Law Review*, 14: 1747–823.

Boyd, S. (2003) *Child Custody, Law and Women's Work*, Oxford: Oxford University Press.

Boyd, S.B. and Young, C.F.L. (2003) '"From same-sex to no sex"? Trends towards recognition of (same-sex) relationships in Canada', *Seattle Journal for Social Justice*, 1(3): 757–93.

Brake, E. (2012) *Minimizing Marriage: Marriage, Morality, and the Law*, New York: Oxford University Press.

Carers UK (2011) *Valuing Carers*, London: Carers UK.

Cooper, D. (2004) *Challenging Diversity: Rethinking Equality and the Value of Difference*, Cambridge: Cambridge University Press.

—— (2007) '"Well, you go there to get off": Visiting feminist care ethics through a women's bathhouse', *Feminist Theory*, 8(3): 243–62.

Crittenden, C. (2001) 'The principles of care', *Women & Politics*, 22: 81–112.

Dalmiya, V. (2002) 'Why should a knower care?', *Hypatia*, 17: 34–63.

Dewar, J. (1998) 'The normal chaos of family law', *Modern Law Review*, 61(4): 467–85.

Downie, J. and Llewellyn, J. (2011) *Being Relational*, Vancouver: UBC Press.

Eekelaar, J. (1984) *Family Law and Social Policy*, London: Weidenfeld & Nicholson.

—— (2007) *Family Law and Personal Life*, Oxford: Oxford University Press.

Eichner, M. (2010) *The Supportive State*, Oxford: Oxford University Press.

Feder Kittay, E. (1999) *Love's Labour: Essays on Women, Equality and Dependency*, Abingdon, UK: Routledge.

Fehlberg, B. (2005) ' "With all my worldly goods I thee endow"? The partnership theme in Australian matrimonial property law', *International Journal of Law, Policy, and the Family*, 19: 176–93.

Ferguson, L. (2008) 'Family, social inequalities and the persuasive force of interpersonal obligation', *International Journal of Law, Policy, and the Family*, 22: 61–84.

Fineman, M. (2004) *The Autonomy Myth*, New York: New Press.

—— (2011) 'Responsibility, family and the limits of equality: An American perspective', in C. Lind, H. Keating and J. Bridgeman (eds) *Taking Responsibility, Law and the Changing Family*, Abingdon, UK: Routledge.

Glennon, L. (2010) 'The limitations of equality discourses on the contours of intimate obligations', in J. Wallbank, S. Choudhry and J. Herring (eds) *Rights, Gender and Family Law*, Abingdon, UK: Routledge.

Hale, B. (2011) 'Equality and autonomy in family law', *Journal of Social Welfare and Family Law*, 33: 3–23.

Held, V. (2006) *The Ethics of Care*, New York: Oxford University Press.

Herring, J. (1999) 'The Human Rights Act and the welfare principle in family law – conflicting or complementary?', *Child and Family Law Quarterly*, 11: 223–41.

—— (2005a) 'Why financial orders on divorce should be unfair', *International Journal of Law, Policy, and the Family*, 19: 218–29.

—— (2005b) 'Farewell welfare', *Journal of Social Welfare and Family Law*, 27: 159–71.

—— (2010) *Older People in Law and Society*, Oxford: Oxford University Press.

—— (2013) *Caring and the Law*, Oxford: Hart.

Holt, A. (2013) *Adolescent-to-Parent Abuse*, Bristol, UK: Policy Press.

Johnson, M. (2005) 'Apples and oranges in child custody disputes: Intimate terrorism vs. situational couple violence', *Journal of Child Custody*, 2: 43–93.

Kelly, F. (2011) *Transforming Law's Family: The Legal Recognition of Planned Lesbian Families*, Vancouver: UBC Press.

Kessler, L. (2007) 'Community parenting', *Journal of Law and Policy*, 24: 47–102.

Law Commission of Canada (2001) *Beyond Conjugality*, Ottawa: Queen's Printer.

Madden Dempsey, M. (2006) 'What counts as domestic violence? A conceptual analysis', *William and Mary Journal of Women and the Law*, 12: 301–76.

—— (2009) *Prosecuting Domestic Violence*, Oxford: Oxford University Press.

Motro, S. (2008) 'Labor, luck, and love: Reconsidering the sanctity of separate property', *Northwestern University Law Review*, 102: 1623–721.

Santorum, R. (2005) *It Takes a Family*, Willmington, DE: Intercollegiate Studies Institute.

Sevenhuisen, S. (2000) 'Caring in the third way: The relation between obligation, responsibility and care in Third Way discourse', *Critical Social Policy*, 20: 20–46.

Smart, C. (2007) *Personal Life: New Directions in Sociological Thinking*, Cambridge: Polity.

Stark, E. (2007) *Coercive Control*, Oxford: Oxford University Press.

Tronto, J. (1983) *Moral Boundaries: A Political Argument for an Ethic of Care*, Abingdon, UK: Routledge.

Wallbank, J. (2010) '(En)Gendering the fusion of rights and responsibilities in the law of contact', in J. Wallbank, S. Choudhry and J. Herring (eds) *Rights, Gender and Family Law*, Abingdon, UK: Routledge.

Wardle, L. (2011) 'The boundaries of belonging: Allegiance, purpose and the definition of marriage', *BYU Journal of Public Law*, 25: 287–316.

Williams, J. (1998) 'Towards a reconstructive feminism: Reconstructing the relationship of market work and family work', *North Illinois University Law Review*, 19: 89–146.

Chapter 3

Equality

An uncomfortable fit in parenting law

Susan B. Boyd

Since the second wave of the women's movement and the emergence of the fathers' rights movement in the 1970s and 1980s, family law has moved towards formal legal equality and gender-neutral language. Early liberal feminists were optimistic about involving men as equal partners and parents and were keen to remove gender-based legal assumptions. Fathers' rights advocates lobbied for equal or joint custody norms and for mothers to have equal financial responsibilities, in order to redress what was, and still is, perceived as discrimination against men. In most modern family laws, male and female spouses now owe reciprocal duties of financial support, and disputes over children are determined by a child's best interests, rather than by assumptions based on gender. More recently, this gender-neutral language has accommodated the reality of same-sex partnerships and same-sex parenting.

These gender-neutral legal norms, however, sit uncomfortably next to familial realities that remain stubbornly gendered and unequal in certain respects, particularly because women still assume greater responsibility for domestic labour and childcare. Many feminists challenge calls for equal treatment of fathers and instead propose legal norms that recognize these unequal social relations. Even if the legal norms are gender-neutral on their face, they should include guidelines that direct attention to gendered patterns, or they should be interpreted so as to take account of gendered social realities still supported by social and economic structures. For instance, spousal support law should take account of the patterns of domestic labour in the family at issue. As for child custody, norms should direct attention to whether one parent has taken primary care responsibility for a child and whether domestic abuse is a factor (e.g., Boyd 2003; Shaffer and Bala 2003).

This chapter uses laws on parenthood to study the contradiction between the trend towards formal equality and ongoing gendered patterns of care, as well as the growing phenomenon of parenting by lesbians and gay men and by single mothers by choice, by which a woman plans to be a child's sole parent. Specifically, it assesses the innovative potential of the new Family Law Act (FLA)[1] in the Canadian province of British Columbia, which redefines legal parenthood and alters the regulation of post-separation parenting. The new definitions of legal parenthood respond to calls for the recognition of same-sex parenting and reproductive technologies. The new norms on post-separation parenting respond to calls for equal treatment of fathers, but they also take account of research on the troubling impact of shared parenting law reforms regulating post-separation disputes over children. As such, the FLA arguably eschews strict formal equality.

To assess whether it avoids the pitfalls of formal equality, the FLA is read against socio-legal literature on the normative dominance of the sexual family, by which significance is placed on the adult couple in a marriage or marriage-like relationship (Fineman 1995; McCandless and Sheldon 2010). Comparative reference to the legislation of other jurisdictions will be made, especially to recent legislation on parentage in the United Kingdom. The FLA's likely impact on women's autonomy is queried, given the gendered dynamics of care and the phenomenon of single mothers by choice. The chapter concludes by considering to what extent norms based on care (Herring, in this volume) can disrupt heteronormative assumptions about the sexual family and move beyond formal equality. A further question is whether law can take into account women's gendered inequality within heterosexual families, while simultaneously recognizing the dynamics of same-sex parenting.

The pitfalls of formal equality: a recap

The pitfalls of a formal equality approach in family law, which 'presumes the fundamental interchangeability of male and female parents as members of the liberal community' (Lessard 2004: 171), have been revealed on both theoretical and empirical levels. A formal equality approach posits that, based on their biogenetic ties, a child's birth mother and genetic father should both have parenting rights, thus asserting a 'sexual family' based on an implicit heteronormativity (Harding, in this volume). The distinction between parenthood based on biogenetic ties and social parenting has been key to the debate about defining legal parenthood, with feminist scholars and activists tending to emphasize the latter and responsibility for care, as well as, to some degree, intention (Boyd 2007). Fathers' rights advocates, in contrast, often argue that paternal rights, for instance the right to be named on birth registrations, should be based on biogenetic ties (Collier, in this volume; Lessard 2004). Legal interpretation too often adopts this approach. Even where legislation specifies that no man is to be treated as the father, if two women are the legal parents, as it does in the United Kingdom's Human Fertilisation and Embryology Act 2008, some judges have sought to find a father for the child (Harding, in this volume).

Feminist legal scholars emphasize the material underpinnings of women's relationship to family and care in an effort to counter arguments for equal and gender-blind treatment of mothers and fathers in parenting laws (e.g., Fineman 2001; Boyd 2003, 2012). They challenge the ways in which the hasty embrace of norms of equal parenting in the name of children's best interests ignores structurally embedded and deeply gendered patterns of care, as well as woman abuse. Paternal involvement has increased, and fathers are constructed as crucial to children's identity, but their care responsibilities have not reached equality with those of mothers (Duxbury and Higgins 2012), in part owing to structural impediments such as women's lower pay in the workforce and the lack of workplace accommodation of parental responsibilities and accessible daycare. These impediments are not likely to be removed under neo-liberal regimes (Jakobsen, in this volume). To give equal decision-making rights to both parents thus grants fathers equal rights without equal responsibilities and renders invisible women's care labour (Boyd 2003). At an ideological level, the equal parenting model reinforces the concept of the nuclear family with two opposite-sex parents and their children, a model that is premised on a (hetero)sexual paradigm (Fineman 1995; Herring, in this volume).

In addition, empirical research raises serious questions about the wisdom of equal or shared care. Shared parenting can work well for separated families who have the psychological and financial means to cooperate. However, in circumstances involving conflict, power dynamics or abuse, these norms can generate very difficult scenarios for mothers and children (Rhoades 2008; Fehlberg et al. 2009, 2011; Trinder 2010). Moreover, the research does not reveal a linear relationship between the amount of parenting time with each parent and children's having better outcomes (Shaffer 2007; Smyth 2009). Yet, when legislation gestures towards shared parenting, fathers may be led to believe that they are entitled to equally shared time. It appears that any legal presumption in favour of shared care can deflect attention away from violence or inhibit a parent from raising concerns about violence (Trinder 2010: 493). Given the extent of violence in the separating and divorcing population and the fact that it tends mainly to be directed against women (Brownridge 2006; Statistics Canada 2011), this latter finding is troubling, not only for mothers but for children who are affected by its impact. When children's rights to relationships with fathers are prioritized within the legal system, protection from harm seems to take a back seat. As such, formal equality can cause damage.

Looking at this research, it seems hard to deny that shared parenting laws reflect a focus on equal rights for fathers, rather than children's interests. Children in the UK who have lived in an 'equal shares' arrangement were unhappy, even miserable, when an equal shares approach was taken by their parents without listening to and consulting with them, recognizing them as separate beings and acknowledging their changing needs (Smart 2004). The move towards shared parenting rests on a political desire for fathers to be as engaged with children as mothers are (Collier and Sheldon 2008). Yet there is little evidence that law can achieve this goal, or that the amount or frequency of contact is either better or worse for children; instead, the evidence indicates that the quality of parent–child relationships has a greater impact on children's well-being (Trinder 2010: 488). In turn, the quality of parent–child relationships is largely dependent on parental well-being.

While these studies suggest that a nuanced approach to children's best interests would be preferable (Rhoades 2010), the fathers' rights movement has persuaded many in the media, the lay public and politics that fathers are discriminated against owing to a privileging of maternal claims, and that equal parenting norms would provide a key remedy (Collier, in this volume). Even in jurisdictions that stipulate that the best interests of the child should be the sole criteria for determining custody and access, a de facto presumption in favour of shared parenting has taken root (Kirouack 2007; Boyd 2010b; Kelly 2012b). Although the explanations for the dynamics of the fathers' rights movement are undoubtedly complex (Collier, in this volume), this discursive move ignores or underplays ongoing differences between maternal and paternal care patterns in relation to children and their material underpinnings. Women's advocacy that emphasizes women's social and economic realities and their relevance to parenting and norms to guide parenting disputes has often fallen on deaf ears, despite the care that advocates take to ground their arguments in a sophisticated equality analysis (Boyd 2008).

The next section asks whether the new law in British Columbia takes better account of these feminist voices, marking a departure from the formal equality of the sexual family and an effort to emphasize relations of care.

British Columbia's new Family Law Act: moving beyond formal equality?

The FLA replaces the Family Relations Act of 1978 (FRA).[2] The FRA had been updated over the years to take account of unmarried and same-sex partnerships, but not of the challenges that reproductive technologies pose for definitions of parenthood. Its provisions on guardianship and custody assumed a father and a mother: 'whether or not married to each other and for so long as they live together, the mother and father of a child are joint guardians' (FRA, s 27). If they separated, though, the person who usually had care and control of the child was sole guardian. If the parents had not been married to each other, were living separate and apart and did not share joint guardianship under the statute or an order, the mother was sole guardian (FRA, s 27(5)). These provisions represented a nod to the gendered nature of parenthood and care, increasingly rare in modern law, and protected the interests of single mothers wishing to parent alone. As for custody, the default position when the parents lived separate and apart was that the parent with whom the child usually resided could exercise custody, subject to orders or agreements. If conflicting claims were made, the person who usually had day-to-day personal care of the child had the right to exercise custody (FRA, ss 34(1)(b), 34(2)(d)). These latter provisions gestured in a gender-neutral fashion to fact situations involving asymmetrical responsibilities, notably primary care of a child by one parent. Judges could order that one or more persons exercise custody or access, and the best interests of the child were the paramount consideration (FRA, ss 24, 34, 35).

In July 2010, British Columbia's Ministry of the Attorney General released a White Paper proposing major changes to family law, including the (re)definition of parenthood and elimination of the language of 'custody' and 'access'. Unlike the UK's Human Fertilisation and Embryology Act 2008, which was an amending statute (McCandless and Sheldon 2010), the FLA was a brand-new statute that offered a fresh slate. It was the product of extensive background research and consultation with the community, including the legal profession, legal academics and NGOs such as fathers' rights advocates and those working with battered women. Feedback to discussion papers and proposals was given by feminist academics and women's groups concerned with legal parenthood and shared parenting norms. The final version of the FLA reflects some of this feedback.

Determining parentage

Part 3, on 'Parentage', is the most innovative part of the FLA and was unique internationally, at its inception, in allowing more than two legal parents. It defines parentage for all purposes of the law of British Columbia, changing the old law stating that a child is the 'child of his or her natural parents'.[3] Instead, 'a person is the child of his or her parents' and 'a child's parent is the person determined under this Part to be the child's parent' (FLA, s 23). In other words, parentage is a legally determined concept, and the 'naturalness' of biological definitions of parenthood is disrupted, arguably moving beyond dyadic heteronormativity. Nevertheless, outside the context of assisted reproduction,[4] on the birth of a child, 'the child's parents are the birth mother and the child's biological father' (FLA, s 26(1)), thus reinforcing the sexual family. A male person is presumed to be a child's biological father in several circumstances, including marriage to the birth mother or marriage-like cohabitation with her within certain periods of the birth, or acknowledgement by him and the birth mother that he is the child's father. These presumptions of paternity do not apply if the contrary is proven, or if more than one person may be presumed to be the biological father. Parentage tests can be ordered and inferences drawn if a person refuses to comply (FLA, s 33). As is explained below, the fact that a person is a child's birth parent does not alone mean that he or she has guardianship rights, severing parentage from legal entitlement (Bainham 1999).

When children are born via assisted reproduction, a donor who provides human reproductive material or an embryo is not, by reason only of that donation, the child's parent (FLA, s 24). A donor is the child's parent only if determined to be so under Part 3, which normally requires a contractual arrangement or a court order. A strict, formal equality approach to legal parenthood based on biogenetic ties has thus been rejected in cases involving assisted reproduction. Moreover, the FLA takes the birth mother as the starting point in its definitions of parentage, recognizing the still highly gendered facts of reproduction, gestation and birth, as does the Human Fertilisation and Embryology Act 2008. To the extent that the birth mother typically takes care responsibility for the child, this approach somewhat echoes Fineman's (1995) proposal that the adult dyad be decentred in law in favour of the caretaker–dependant dyad, with other adults being able to opt in contractually.

If a child is conceived through assisted reproduction (apart from surrogacy), the child's birth mother is the child's parent. In addition, a person who was married to, or in a marriage-like relationship with, the birth mother when the child was conceived is also the parent, barring proof that, before conception, the person did not consent to be the parent or withdrew consent (FLA, s 27). This section provides a mechanism for recognition of parentage of both same-sex partners who agree to have a child together (as well as opposite-sex partners who agree to have a child using donated gametes, or via assisted reproduction), regardless of whether the non-birth parent provided genetic material. It also provides the opportunity for a partner to opt out, at least prior to conception, as does the Human Fertilisation and Embryology Act 2008. This provision departs from Fineman's proposal, because it assumes that an adult in a marriage or marriage-like relationship with the birth mother is a parent, absent evidence of intention to the contrary. Like the UK's legislation, the section remains premised on the sexual family (McCandless and Sheldon 2010). As we see below, it seems not to be intended that a single woman could agree with a sperm donor, with whom she is not in a sexual relationship, that he be a legal parent (FLA, s 30(1)). What McCandless and Sheldon call 'parental dimorphism', or a resistance to the notion that a child can have two 'mothers', can also be detected in the FLA's according of the term 'mother' only to the birth mother, thus emphasizing gestation. A lesbian co-mother, for instance, will be a 'parent', not a mother, even if she has donated genetic material.

With the FLA, British Columbia now legally regulates the parenthood aspects of surrogacy. If a written agreement made prior to conception between a potential surrogate and intended parent(s) provides that the surrogate will not be a parent and will surrender the child to the intended parent(s), then the intended parent(s) will be the child's parent(s) (FLA, s 29(2)). Protection is, however, given to the surrogate mother after the child's birth, because she must consent in writing to surrender the child, and the intended parent(s) must take the child into their care before the contractual arrangement takes effect (FLA, s 29(3)). Here, gestation trumps intention.

The most innovative provisions in the FLA, unlike anything in the Human Fertilisation and Embryology Act 2008, create the possibility of more than two parents, albeit only when assisted reproduction is used. If, prior to conception of the child, a written agreement is made between intended parent(s) (likely in a surrogacy situation) and a potential birth mother who agrees to be a parent together with the intended parent(s), then they all are the child's parents (FLA, s 30(1)). In addition, a potential birth mother can make such an agreement with her partner and a donor who agrees to be a parent with them, in which case all three will be parents. In all cases contemplated, the parents will either be in the adult dyadic relationship or they will be donors of reproductive material. Even if this donor does not reside with the child, it appears they will be a guardian (FLA, s 39(3)(a)). This section consecrates the importance of genetic parenthood by contemplating that only donors may be additional parents; for example, the donor's partner, if one exists, could apparently not be made a parent/guardian.

If a lesbian parent prefers a legalized scenario whereby a known sperm donor has a relationship with her child, but is not a full-blown parent/guardian, an intermediate situation sometimes preferred by lesbian mothers (Kelly 2011), she can make an agreement with him respecting 'contact' (FLA, s 58). Presumably, the donor's partner could also be granted contact.

The FLA also contains provisions empowering courts to declare whether a person is a child's parent if there is a dispute or uncertainty on that point (FLA, s 31). Although such orders are to give effect to the above rules respecting determination of parentage, there is a risk that judicial discretion may introduce variations contrary to statutory intention (Fielding 2011). For instance, heteronormative assumptions, notably that a child should have a father, might be made contrary to the pre-conception intention of lesbian parents (Harding, in this volume; Millbank 2008; Kelly 2011: 37–42). As Zanghellini has said, even if 'poly-parenting, when mutually chosen by the parties to a parenting project, is the model that has the greatest potential for offering truly innovative forms of relationality', it is quite another matter for a court to impose poly-parenting as a desirable outcome because of the supposed (and unsubstantiated) benefits of dual-gender, biological and genetic parenting (2012: 485). In the UK, some judges have imposed this model, despite the legislation's stating that, where a female parent is recognized as the legal parent, 'no man is to be treated as the father of the child for any purpose' (Human Fertilisation and Embryology Act 2008, ss 45(1), 48(2)). The FLA contains no such protective provision, which would run counter to the legislation's aim of opening the door to some degree of poly-parenting.

Other heteronormative assumptions are suggested by the fact that the FLA offers more options and protection to women who conceive via assisted insemination than to those who conceive via intercourse. First, as noted, when assisted conception is used, a third parent can be introduced via contract, but this option is not open when children are conceived 'naturally'. As such, a dyadic nuclear family model that conforms to the formal equality norm seems to be assumed, based on a notion that those who conceive 'naturally', who will more often be heterosexual, would not want anyone else involved in parenting. This affirmation of genetic ties and the dyadic opposite-sex family gives way in the FLA when assisted conception is used, as it often will be by gay men and lesbians. Here, the assumption seems to be that the legal system should permit gay men using surrogacy and lesbians using sperm donors to parent in threes (or more, if there is more than one donor of reproductive material), so that children will have a parent of each sex and access to their genetic origins. Arguably, then, the aura of formal equality of genetic mothers and fathers hangs over the new regime, no matter whether it concerns 'natural' or assisted reproduction.

Second, a sperm donor will not be defined as a parent unless further steps are taken by the birth mother to make an agreement with him. However, a child who is conceived via intercourse has both the birth mother and the biological father as her parents. Although this section may make intuitive sense for most heterosexual couples, it poses a challenge to single mothers, whatever their sexual orientation, who wish to parent without the biological father and who, for reasons such as poverty or lack of access to sperm, choose not to use assisted reproduction. In this sense, the FLA betrays a heteronormative assumption that biological parenthood prevails when intercourse leads to conception, privileging a symmetrical, formal equality approach to birth mothers and birth fathers in situations where such symmetry may not be warranted. That being said, if the birth mother does not reside with the biological father after the child is born, he will not automatically have guardianship rights (FLA, s 39(1)). To that extent, the FLA moves beyond formal equality, but not entirely, as we see in the next section.

Guardianship and parenting arrangements

The FLA replaces 'custody' and 'access' with a new concept of guardianship, which comes with parental responsibilities and parenting time (s 40). When parents who have lived together separate, each remains the child's guardian, creating a default of ongoing guardianship after separation (FLA, s 39(1)). An agreement or order can vary that default and provide that a parent is not the child's guardian (FLA, s 39(2)). A parent who has never resided with the child is not a guardian, unless an agreement has been made in an assisted reproduction scenario, or an agreement between the parent and all of the guardians makes this parent a guardian, or the parent regularly cares for the child (FLA, s 39(3)); 'care' is not defined. If a sperm donor makes an agreement with the birth mother and her partner, but does not reside with the child, he will nevertheless be a guardian (FLA, s 39(3)(a)). Guardianship of a child is thus linked, in most cases, to the fact of having resided with a child (and another parent, as a rule), or having signed an agreement reflecting the intention of all adults involved in a child's life. A person who is not a guardian may obtain 'contact' with a child through an agreement or order (FLA, ss 58,

59). Contact could, accordingly, be given to parents who do not fall within the category of 'guardian', as well as to grandparents, and so on.

The list of a guardian's parental responsibilities is extensive, and the default is that each guardian may exercise them in consultation with the other guardians, unless consultation would be unreasonable or inappropriate in the circumstances (FLA, s 40(1), 40(2)). Parental responsibilities include, to mention only some: making day-to-day decisions affecting the child and having day-to-day care, control and supervision of the child; making decisions respecting where the child will reside; making decisions respecting with whom the child will live and associate; and exercising any other responsibilities reasonably necessary to nurture the child's development (FLA, s 41). Without an agreement or court order allocating parental responsibilities differently, each guardian has day-to-day care and decision-making power. Although a mother who feels that consultation is inappropriate, for instance owing to a pattern of abuse by the other parent, might be able to resist the need to consult with the other guardian(s), if challenged, she will have to produce clear evidence to support her resistance to equal distribution and consultation, which could be difficult.

'Parenting time' is defined as 'the time that a child is with a guardian, as allocated under an agreement or order'. During parenting time, a guardian may exercise the parental responsibility of making day-to-day decisions affecting the child and having day-to-day care, control and supervision of the child. No default position as to parenting time is indicated, in contrast to parenting responsibilities (FLA, s 42(1), 42(2)). However, the default for parental responsibilities grants each guardian 'day-to-day care, control and supervision of the child'.

Guardians are ostensibly free to adjust the parental responsibilities and parenting time; agreements are to be made considering only a child's best interests (FLA, s 37(1)) and not, say, parental rights. In theory, then, there is no bias towards shared parenting or formal equality, and the government has stated repeatedly that there is no presumption in favour of equal parenting.[5] The FLA stipulates that parental responsibilities may be allocated under an agreement or order so that they are exercised by (a) one or more guardians only, or (b) each guardian acting separately or all guardians acting together (FLA, s 40(3)). Crucially, and in contrast to Australia's Family Law Act 1975 (Cth) (Rhoades 2010), no particular arrangement is presumed to be in the best interests of the child, responding to concerns that shared parenting is too often erroneously assumed to be best for a child. Section 40(4) specifies that it must not be presumed that parental responsibilities should be allocated equally among guardians, that parenting time should be shared equally among guardians, or that decisions among guardians should be made separately or together. The ability of guardians to alter the default position of ongoing parental responsibilities is, however, premised on the assumption that these parents are able to negotiate an allocation that departs from an equality principle of continuing guardianship. This assumption, in turn, could be said to rest on another assumption, that parents are equally situated – which often they are not.

The FLA default position marks a major change from that in the former legislation, which gave some power to the parent who usually has care and control of the child or with whom the child usually resides. The FRA did not prevent parents from agreeing to share parenting – many did – nor did it prevent orders for joint custody and guardianship (Boyd 2010b), but, under the old system, any parent arguing for a more shared arrangement had to ask for it, working against the default of sole custody to the parent with day-to-day personal care of the child. The new FLA default of ongoing guardianship on separation, regardless of the past history of parenting, places the burden on a parent resisting shared guardianship, posing a challenge given the normative climate in favour of shared parenting (Boyd 2010a).

By shifting the default for guardianship when parents separate, the FLA may generate serious problems for an unequally situated mother caregiver, for example, one who is dealing with a manipulative or abusive spouse or a spouse who has not demonstrated commitment to a child in the past. A mother attempting to leave an abusive relationship will be assumed to share ongoing guardianship with her ex-partner. She will have to try to negotiate another arrangement and, if the ex-partner resists (as can happen in a power-and-control scenario, where children are used as a way to maintain power), she will have to apply to court. Both negotiation and court applications can pose problems. For instance, a mother who does not have permanent residence status or who lacks language skills will be disadvantaged in any negotiation and is also likely to encounter barriers in her invocation of assistance from the judiciary. Ironically, resorting to court is precisely what the law reforms are trying to preclude (Ministry of Attorney General (British Columbia) 2010: 2–5; Treloar and Boyd 2014; see also FLA, s 4).

Equally ironically, the new FLA definition of the best interests of the child emphasizes factors such as family violence and care. Under this excellent provision, an agreement or an order will not be in the child's best interests 'unless it protects, to the greatest extent possible, the child's physical, psychological and emotional safety, security and well-being' (FLA, s 37(3)). This provision will benefit the woman in the above scenario, but only if she is able to marshal the social and legal supports to go to court, or to have an inappropriate agreement reviewed. Although a child's guardian must exercise his or her parental responsibilities in the best interests of the child, and parties must consider only the best interests of the child when making an agreement (FLA, s 43, 37), how these duties will be supervised is unclear.

In determining a child's best interests, 'all of the child's needs and circumstances must be considered', including several factors listed that reflect concerns raised by feminist scholars and advocates for abused mothers during the consultation process (FLA, s 37(2)). Among these is 'the history of the child's care', reflecting attention to the significance of care labour. Important in counteracting the disproportionate impact that an emphasis on maximum contact and 'friendly parents' has had in Canadian law (Cohen and Gershbain 2001; Kelly 2012b) is the following factor: 'the appropriateness of an arrangement that would require the child's guardians to cooperate on issues affecting the child, including whether requiring cooperation would increase any risks to the safety, security or well-being of the child or other family members' (FLA, s 37(2)(i)). This factor, if taken seriously, should temper the extent to which parental responsibilities should be shared and exercised in consultation (FLA, s 40(2)).

Another factor is 'the impact of any family violence on the child's safety, security or well-being, whether the family violence is directed toward the child or another family member' (FLA, s 37(2)(g)), signalling the risks that spousal abuse can pose to a child's safety, security or well-being (see also s 38(g)). In addition, in assessing family violence, a court must consider various factors, including 'whether any psychological or emotional abuse constitutes, or is evidence of, a pattern of coercive and controlling behavior directed at a family member' (FLA, s 38(d)). This provision reinforces the fact that family violence is defined as including, not only physical and sexual abuse (and attempts), but also psychological or emotional abuse, including intimidation, harassment, coercion or threats, including to other persons, pets or property (FLA, s 1 'family violence'). Family violence is also explicitly defined to include 'in the case of a child, direct or indirect exposure to family violence' (FLA, s 1(e)). These detailed provisions, although entirely gender-neutral, reflect consultation with experts on the complex dynamics of family violence.

These important definitions of family violence may not, however, be properly taken into account, owing to the equality default of ongoing guardianship. In addition to pointing parties towards desirable settlements from a policy perspective (Dewar 2000: 67–8), default rules apply if there is no agreement between the parties. One key question is which system best prevents abuses in conflict situations. The FLA default overlooks the extent of situations where serious conflict characterizes the relationship between separating parents and overestimates the extent to which cooperation and negotiated departures from ongoing guardianship can happen on a non-level playing field.

Reconciling norms in heterosexual and same-sex parenting: a focus on care

As detailed above, the FLA introduces innovative concepts that depart from an approach rooted in strict equality of mothers and fathers. For example, it permits three people to be parents of children born of assisted conception and severs guardianship rights from parentage. These norms can be read, not only as opening the possibility of legally recognizing non-normative families, but also as reflecting a healthy combination of (a) a focus on care and its significance to a child's well-being and to what defines parenthood and (b) a focus on intention. Biogenetic ties are relevant, but sometimes can be overridden in light of evidence on care and intention.

Much research on parenting law addressing the disputes between heterosexual partners has emphasized the significance of care to legal parenthood and to awards of custody. This emphasis has grown out of feminist research on the sexual division of labour (Boyd 2012; Herring, in this volume), but it also rests on a notion that the labour that an adult puts into parenting should be relevant to determining rights and resolving disputes. Nedelsky has written about the nexus between routine physical care-taking and the bonds of connection with children (1999: 320–2). The material element of care, still more often performed by mothers, also reflects and generates an emotional component. These insights echo work on conceptions of parenthood that emphasize the labour that is put into parenting, which creates 'a deep relational attachment' between an adult and a child, sometimes regardless of genetic or gestational ties (Austin 2007: 27). Moreover, recent research with fathers (notably, mostly fathers *not* involved in parenting disputes) shows that they have a greater appreciation of the significance of care labour to concepts of parenthood than may previously have been realized. The fathers, by and large, felt that a man can be a 'good father' only by being a 'father-as-carer', that is, by earning the right to be involved in a child's life through care labour (Ives *et al.* 2008: 79; but, see Kershaw *et al.* 2008: 199).

Arguably, the FLA's emphasis on guardianship usually flowing from the fact that a parent has resided with a child is premised on a notion that this parent will more likely have engaged in a care relationship with the child than one who has not. As well, if a non-residential parent regularly cares for a child, he or she can be a guardian (FLA, s 39(3)(c)). The problem, however, is that, in heterosexual families, fathers who reside with children may not, in fact, share the care responsibilities for the child. As a result, the default position of ongoing guardianship grants such fathers formal rights of authority, without accompanying responsibilities. It may, thus, generate difficulties for mothers attempting to leave relationships, especially those characterized by abuse or manipulation. Although Herring (in this volume) suggests that parents might lose their parental rights through non-care, it is not clear that judges would be inclined to apply this model where parents have previously co-resided with a child. Another potential problem is that the word 'care' is not defined in the FLA, opening up the possibility that evidence that a parent 'cares about' a child, combined with some time spent, will be interpreted as 'regularly cares for the child', opening a route to guardianship rights being ordered by a court (Smart 1991).

Applying this analysis rooted in care to same-sex parenting is more challenging, because it reveals the limits of a gendered lens that positions women and men oppositionally (even if that opposition is theorized by reference to the gendered division of labour, rather than essentialized gender roles: Boyd 2012). When disputes arise involving separating lesbian parents, the birth mother often is favoured over a social mother without a genetic tie to the child, premised on a biological definition of parenthood and ignoring the social mother's care relationship and intention to parent the child.[6] The FLA's assumption of ongoing guardianship upon separation arguably gives important recognition to the social mother in this scenario. To the extent that same-sex couples share domestic labour, including childcare, more often than do opposite-sex couples, the assumption of ongoing guardianship may be more apt for lesbian co-parents than for heterosexual parents. That said, not all same-sex couples adopt less strict gender roles than straight couples, with an unequal division of labour often being observed (Carrington 1999; Barker 2012: 154–8). The external pressures to provide privatized caregiving within the family remain constant in capitalist societies such as the United States and Canada (Fineman 2004), meaning that many parents reach an arrangement where one spends more time on childcare. The studies differ on whether most lesbian mothers perceive both partners as the parents of the child, or whether a significant number depart from this perception of equality, with some prioritizing the birth mother (Leckey 2011: 593–4).

In considering parenthood within lesbian families, we might return to Gavigan's question, 'What makes a lesbian a mother?' (2000: 103). Interviews with lesbian mothers about the relative weight to be placed on care versus biogenetic ties for the purposes of determining parenthood reveal that active involvement in daily care is key to being viewed as a parent (Kelly 2011: 90). As a result, the emphasis placed on care by scholars such as Herring (in this volume) may be apt even for same-sex parents: the adult who provides day-to-day care for the child is likely to know the child best and, therefore, to be able to make the best decisions for the child. If one lesbian co-mother engages more closely in the care relationship with the child than the other, might the FLA's default position of ongoing guardianship be as misguided as it would be for a straight couple, in its assumption of formal equality? As Leckey (2013: 13) cautions, 'now that two women may become legal spouses and that a child may have two mothers, might judges too readily interpret facts from the diverse ecology of queer kinship through the script of two equal mothers?'

Finally, owing to its embodiment of heteronormative assumptions that (at least) two parents exist, the FLA sits uncomfortably alongside the phenomenon of single mothers by choice (Kelly 2012a). Because single motherhood departs from the normative expectation that children should have two legal parents and, especially, a father, it presents a clear challenge to formal equality. The FLA, however, is ambivalent about embracing this challenge to heteronormative parenthood. On the one hand, the legislation is clear that a sperm donor is not a parent without more evidence (FLA, s 24), affirming that, at least in assisted reproduction, a genetic connection per se is not sufficient to establish parenthood, and emphasizing instead a combination of intention and caregiving (Boyd 2007; Zanghellini 2009). This provision ostensibly protects a single mother who has used assisted insemination from having another parent imposed on her family against her will. On the other hand, mothers who conceive via intercourse are not similarly protected, as it is stated that the child's parents are the birth mother and the biological father (FLA, s 26(1)). Consequently, a single mother who intends to parent alone may be left insecure in the legal status of her family.

Conclusion

Family law generally, and laws on parenthood in particular, have moved over the past three decades towards enhancing the formal legal equality of mothers and fathers. This trend, although reflecting important initiatives to undermine the sexual division of labour and to encourage engaged fatherhood, has had unintended consequences for mothers who take primary responsibility for care of their children, for same-sex partners who wish to co-parent, and for women who attempt to parent autonomously of a genetic father.

I have argued that a focus on care and, to some degree, intention has the capacity to undermine the excesses of this formal equality approach to parenting laws and to recognize gender differences. British Columbia's new FLA goes some distance towards displacing some assumptions related to formal equality and the sexual family and moves tentatively towards a post-equality position on parenthood. It does so by moving away from rights-based or 'natural' parenthood based on biogenetics, while still emphasizing care and the gendered processes of conception and birth. In the case of assisted reproduction, it lays considerable emphasis on a pre-conception intention to be a parent. Whether the FLA is interpreted in ways that are sensitive to the still-gendered terrain of parenting, and that resist heteronormative assumptions, however, remains to be seen. The legislation reproduces an assumption that there will normally be two parents (especially in cases of 'natural' reproduction), and it contains a default in favour of ongoing guardianship for both separating parents. As such, this innovative legislation remains wedded to problematic aspects of the sexual family and 'parental dimorphism' (McCandless and Sheldon 2010), limiting its potential to recognize the less normative, and more hidden, stories of parenting (Monk, in this volume) that perhaps most challenge our conceptions of equality.

Acknowledgements

Thanks to Gillian Calder, Rachel Treloar and Robert Leckey for constructive comments on earlier drafts, to the SSHRC for funding, and to Jennifer Flood for editing assistance.

Notes

1   SBC 2011, c 25.
2   RSBC 1996, c 128.
3   Law and Equity Act, RSBC 1996, c 253, s 61(1)(a).
4   'Assisted reproduction' is defined as 'a method of conceiving a child other than by sexual intercourse': FLA, s 20(1).
5   See, e.g., British Columbia Debates, 21 November 2011, p 8946 (Hon. S. Bond).
6   See, e.g., *Buist v Greaves* (1997) 72 ACWS (3d) 301, [1997] OJ No 2646; *KGT v PD* 2005 BCSC 1659, 21 RFL (6th) 183.

References

Austin, M.W. (2007) *Conceptions of Parenthood: Ethics and the Family*, Aldershot, UK: Ashgate.

Bainham, A. (1999) 'Parentage, parenthood and parental responsibility: Subtle, elusive yet important distinctions', in A. Bainham, S.D. Sclater and M. Richards (eds) *What Is a Parent? A Socio-Legal Analysis*, Oxford: Hart.

Barker, N. (2012) *Not the Marrying Kind: A Feminist Critique of Same-Sex Marriage*, Houndmills, UK: Palgrave MacMillan.

Boyd, S.B. (2003) *Child Custody, Law, and Women's Work*, Don Mills, ON: Oxford University Press.

—— (2007) 'Gendering legal parenthood: Bio-genetic ties, intentionality and responsibility', *Windsor Yearbook of Access to Justice*, 25(1): 63–94.

—— (2008) 'Is equality enough? Fathers' rights and women's rights advocacy', in R.C. Hunter (ed.) *Rethinking Equality Projects in Law: Feminist Challenges*, Oxford: Hart.

—— (2010a) 'Autonomy for mothers? Relational theory and parenting apart', *Feminist Legal Studies*, 18(2): 137–58.

—— (2010b) 'Joint custody and guardianship in the British Columbia courts: Not a cautious approach', *Canadian Family Law Quarterly*, 29(3): 223–52.

—— (2012) 'Still gendered after all this time? Care and autonomy in child custody debates', in N. Priaulx and A. Wrigley (eds) *Ethics, Law, and Society, Vol. V: Ethics of Care, Body Politics, Theorising the Ethical and Governance*, Aldershot, UK: Ashgate.

Brownridge, D.A. (2006) 'Violence against women post-separation', *Aggression and Violent Behavior*, 11(5): 514–30.

Carrington, C. (1999) *No Place Like Home: Relationships and Family Life Among Lesbians and Gay Men*, Chicago: University of Chicago Press.

Cohen, J. and Gershbain, N. (2001) 'For the sake of the fathers? Child custody reform and the perils of maximum contact', *Canadian Family Law Quarterly*, 19: 121–83.

Collier, R. and Sheldon, S. (2008) *Fragmenting Fatherhood: A Socio-Legal Study*, Oxford: Hart.

Dewar, J. (2000) 'Family law and its discontents', *International Journal of Law, Policy, and the Family*, 14(1): 59–85.

Duxbury, L. and Higgins, C. (2012) *Revisiting Work–Life Issues in Canada: The 2012 National Study on Balancing Work and Caregiving in Canada*. Online. Available at: http://newsroom.carleton.ca/wp-content/files/2012-National-Work-Long-Summary.pdf (accessed 14 June 2013).

Fehlberg, B., Millward, C. and Campo, M. (2009) 'Shared post-separation parenting in 2009: An empirical snapshot', *Australian Journal of Family Law*, 23(3): 247–75.

Fehlberg, B., Smyth, B., Maclean, M. and Roberts, C. (2011) 'Legislating for shared time parenting after separation: A research review', *International Journal of Law, Policy, and the Family*, 25(3): 318–37.

Fielding, N.G. (2011) 'Judges and their work', *Social & Legal Studies*, 20(1): 97–115.

Fineman, M.A. (2004) *The Autonomy Myth: A Theory of Dependency*, New York: New Press.

—— (2001) 'Fatherhood, feminism and family law', *McGeorge Law Review*, 32(4): 1031–49.

—— (1995) *The Neutered Mother, the Sexual Family, and Other Twentieth Century Tragedies*, New York: Routledge.

Gavigan, S.A.M. (2000) 'Mothers, other mothers, and others: The legal challenges and contradictions of lesbian parents', in D.E. Chunn and D. Lacombe (eds) *Law as a Gendering Practice*, Don Mills, ON: Oxford University Press.

Ives, J., Draper, H., Pattison, H. and Williams, C. (2008) 'Becoming a father/Refusing fatherhood: An empirical bioethics approach to paternal responsibilities and rights', *Clinical Ethics*, 3(2): 75–84.

Kelly, F. (2011) *Transforming Law's Family: The Legal Recognition of Planned Lesbian Motherhood*, Vancouver: UBC Press.

—— (2012a) 'Autonomous from the start: Single mothers by choice in the Canadian legal system', *Child and Family Law Quarterly*, 24(3): 257–83.

—— (2012b) 'Enforcing a parent/child relationship at all cost? Supervised access orders in the Canadian courts', *Osgoode Hall Law Journal*, 49(2): 277–309.

Kershaw, P., Pulkingham, J. and Fuller, S. (2008) 'Expanding the subject: Violence, care, and (in)active male citizenship', *Social Politics: International Studies in Gender, State & Society*, 15(2): 182–206.

Kirouack, M.C. (2007) 'La jurisprudence relative à la garde: Où en sommes-nous rendus?', in Service de formation continue, Barreau du Québec (ed.) *Développements récents en droit familial*, Cowansville, QC: Yvon Blais.

Leckey, R. (2011) 'The practices of lesbian mothers and Quebec's reforms', *Canadian Journal of Women and the Law*, 23(2): 579–99.

—— (2013) 'Two mothers in law and fact', *Feminist Legal Studies*, 21(1): 1–19.

Lessard, H. (2004) 'Mothers, fathers, and naming: Reflections on the law equality framework and *Trociuk v. British Columbia (Attorney General)*', *Canadian Journal of Women and the Law*, 16(1): 165–211.

McCandless, J. and Sheldon, S. (2010) 'The Human Fertilisation and Embryology Act (2008) and the tenacity of the sexual family form', *Modern Law Review*, 73(2): 175–207.

Millbank, J. (2008) 'The limits of functional family: Lesbian mother litigation in the era of the eternal biological family', *International Journal of Law, Policy, and the Family*, 22(2): 149–77.

Ministry of Attorney General (British Columbia) (2010) *White Paper on* Family Relations Act *Reform: proposals for a new* Family Law Act. Online. Available at: www.ag.gov.bc.ca/legislation/pdf/Family-Law-White-Paper.pdf (accessed 14 June 2013).

Nedelsky, J. (1999) 'Dilemmas of passion, privilege, and isolation: Reflections on mothering in a white, middle-class nuclear family', in J.E. Hanigsberg and S. Ruddick (eds) *Mother Troubles: Rethinking Contemporary Maternal Dilemmas*, Boston: Beacon Press.

Rhoades, H. (2008) 'The dangers of shared care legislation: Why Australia needs (yet more) family law reform', *Federal Law Review*, 36(3): 279–99.

—— (2010) 'Revising Australia's parenting laws: A plea for a relational approach to children's best interests', *Child and Family Law Quarterly*, 22(2): 172–85.

Shaffer, M. (2007) 'Joint custody, parental conflict and children's adjustment to divorce: What the social science literature does and does not tell us', *Canadian Family Law Quarterly*, 26(3): 285–313.

—— and Bala, N. (2003) 'Wife abuse, child custody and access in Canada', in R. Geffner, R.S. Igelman and J. Zellner (eds) *The Effects of Intimate Partner Violence on Children*, New York: Haworth Press.

Smart, C. (1991) 'The legal and moral ordering of child custody', *Journal of Law and Society*, 18(4): 485–500.

—— (2004) 'Equal shares: Rights for fathers or recognition for children?', *Critical Social Policy*, 24(4): 484–503.

Smyth, B. (2009) 'A five year retrospective of post-separation shared care research in Australia', *Journal of Family Studies*, 15(1): 36–59.

Statistics Canada (2011) *Family Violence in Canada: A Statistical Profile* (Catalogue no. 85–224-X), Ottawa: Statistics Canada, Canadian Centre for Justice Statistics. Online. Available at: www.statcan.gc.ca/pub/85–224-x/85–224-x2010000-eng.pdf (accessed 14 June 2013).

Treloar, R. and Boyd, S.B. (2014) 'Family law reform in (neoliberal) context: British Columbia's new Family Law Act', *International Journal of Law, Policy and the Family*, 28(1): 77–99.

Trinder, L. (2010) 'Shared residence: A review of recent research evidence', *Child and Family Law Quarterly*, 22(4): 475–98.

Zanghellini, A. (2009) 'Who is entitled to parental responsibility? Biology, caregiving, intention and the Family Law Act 1975 (Cth): A jurisprudential feminist analysis', *Monash University Law Review*, 35(1): 147–82.

—— (2012) '*A v B and C* [2012] EWCA Civ 285 – Heteronormativity, poly-parenting, and the homo-nuclear family', *Child and Family Law Quarterly*, 24(4): 475–86.

Chapter 4

Men, gender and fathers' rights 'after legal equality'

New formations of rights and responsibility in family justice

Richard Collier

A rich body of scholarship has sought to engage with contemporary fathers' rights activism within the field of family law reform.[1] Drawing on an array of sources and methods, this work has encompassed sociological and psychological studies of fathers, empirical research in the field of family studies and socio-legal analysis of legal texts and parliamentary debates. It has drawn on interviews with the participants in these debates, including fathers' rights activists and those who seek to counter their claims. Against the backdrop of scholarship concerned with how fatherhood has evolved as a distinctive object of legal regulation at particular historical moments (e.g., Dowd 2000; Collier and Sheldon 2008), there is some agreement within academic literature that a vocal, visible and, in terms of strategy, increasingly militant fatherhood lobby has succeeded over the past decade or so in influencing the direction of legal policy and practice. It has done so to varying degrees and in different ways, depending on country (Collier and Sheldon 2006). In England and Wales, as elsewhere, this is especially the case in legal debates around law reform towards shared parenting following separation (Maclean 2007; Collier and Sheldon 2008: Ch. 5; Jordan 2009; Diduck and Kaganas 2012: 465).

This chapter does not rehearse familiar debates for or against reform of the law in relation to shared parenting, as they have been advanced by a range of fathers' groups and shared parenting organizations, and countered by critics within both the family justice sector and legal academy (see, e.g., Fehlberg *et al.* 2011a, 2011b). Rather, notwithstanding this rich, interdisciplinary research base on contemporary fathers' rights activism, the chapter will suggest that important questions about gender and equality remain under-explored in this context.

More specifically, and by drawing on this international, interdisciplinary research base on fathers' rights activism and law and recent studies of fatherhood and law, the chapter makes three claims. First, understanding of the political terrain around fathers' rights and shared parenting law can gain much from a richer and more nuanced engagement with the interconnections between fatherhood, law and gender. Of particular relevance are social and legal changes that have, I argue elsewhere, reconfigured normative ideas of 'good' post-separation fatherhood (Collier 2010a). The chapter here considers the rhetorical force of fathers' love for their children within a political terrain in which the formulation of claims in terms of rights to recognition in the post-separation context is pervaded by contradictions and tensions around what it means to be a 'good dad'.

Second, approaching fathers' rights and law through a lens of masculinity politics casts considerable light on contemporary debates about fathers' rights and family justice in terms of the formation of identity as a fathers' rights activist (Crowley 2008a). Third, and finally, it is important to locate debates about fatherhood and law 'after legal equality' within a wider reconfiguration of gender and care under the political, economic and cultural conditions of neo-liberalism (Leckey, in this volume). The focus of the discussion is on developments in the UK (and particularly England and Wales). These concerns, however, have transnational resonance in understanding family law and gender 'after legal equality', raising questions within the context of family justice about what equality means and how it might develop.

Family law, shared parenting and the critique of fathers' rights

The development of UK fathers' groups in relation to equality in family law from the early 1970s to the present has been discussed in detail both within the academic literature and in accounts published by participants (e.g., Harris 2006). These debates encompass diverse organizations and concerns. It is post-separation shared parenting, however, that has become a 'touchstone' issue for fathers' activists internationally. Not only do recent developments in family justice in England and Wales suggest that there continues to be considerable 'pressure from fathers' groups for legislation to promote substantially shared parenting as a presumption, even when both parents do not agree' (Fehlberg et al. 2011a: 16), but it would also appear that the 'myth' (Trinder 2012) of the 'father as victim' of family law remains highly resonant (see also Chunn et al. 2007; Boyd 2008). In short, a substantial interdisciplinary research base on post-separation parenting (see Trinder 2010; Fehlberg et al. 2011a, 2011b; Newis 2011) suggests that reforming the law in the way fathers' groups advocate may have potentially deleterious consequences for mothers and children (Trinder 2012). Notwithstanding the fact that their arguments often rest on anecdotal evidence and assertion (Graycar 2000), rather than evidence-backed research, fathers' claims as to *in*equality in law certainly appear to have found a receptive audience among certain parts of government and the judiciary (Maclean 2007; Wallbank 2007: 3; Department for Education 2012).

These concerns align with a wider, feminist-inflected sociological and legal literature on fathers' rights groups and fathers' activism around law.[2] In this work, three themes recur that further question father activists' claims about men, gender and inequality in family law in relation to separation.

First, fathers' groups misread the gendered nature of law's regulation of shared parenting historically (e.g., Smart and Sevenhuijsen 1989; Boyd 2003; Newnham 2008) and the different constructions in law of the 'good' post-separation mother/father, not least with regard to obligations in 'making contact work' (Wallbank 2009a; Kaganas 2010, 1999) and the contradictions between trends towards formal equality and gendered patterns of care (Boyd, in this volume). Particular concern is expressed about how, within a dominant 'pro-contact' legal culture around post-separation parenting (Smart and Neale 1999), questions about domestic abuse, risk and safety (Featherstone and Peckover 2007) are marginalized (Kaganas and Piper 1999), as within the context of the policy push to mediation (Greatbatch and Dingwall 1999; see further, below).

Second, fathers' groups trade in regressive and questionable, yet politically resonant, gendered images (Collier 2005). Such images include, on the one hand, 'implacably hostile' mothers, resistant to contact without reason (Rhoades 2002a), 'alimony drones' (Kaye and Tolmie 1998a: 185), 'mendacious and vindictive' (Boyd and Young 2002: 58) and 'unruly' and 'irresponsible' mums (Berotia and Drakich 1993: 603; also Berotia 1998), and, on the other, 'safe' fathers discursively positioned as seeking contact and 'sharer[s] of responsibilities' (Smart and Neale 1999b: 123; Rhoades 2002a, 2002b). Broader ideas of masculine crisis and a crisis of fatherhood (Collier 1998) shape the fathers' rights literature, linking to a highly negative depiction of women within a strand of fathers' rights activism that is aligned with a particularly virulent anti-feminism, if not misogyny, within certain parts of men's movement politics (Messner 1997; Kimmell 2010).

Third, fathers' claims to inequality in law misunderstand, critics suggest, the drift of family law itself in relation to post-separation parenting. This is particularly the case in England and Wales regarding law's apparently increasing desire in policy, legislation and case law not to *disavow* but to symbolically *affirm* the importance of a father figure (Reece 2009a; Kaganas 2010). Studies have tracked, for example, a repositioning of the father in law and heightened concern with paternal validation in respect of parental responsibility orders (Reece 2009a, 2009b) and legal developments around shared parenting and shared residence orders (Newnham 2008; Harris and George 2010). Reforms of the law in relation to parental responsibility and unmarried fathers (e.g., Sheldon 2009; Wallbank 2009b), along with legislation on assisted reproduction (McCandless and Sheldon 2010; Smith 2010), have each been read as illustrating aspects of the 'tenacious hold' of traditional sexual divisions and the '(hetero)sexual family' in law (Fineman 1995; see also, in this volume, Herring; Harding; Boyd), a family in which the role of the father is still deemed pivotal to symbolically 'completing' 'law's families' (Diduck 2003). As Harding observes (in this volume), a broader reinscription of heteronormativity in family law itself appears to have shaped parliamentary and judicial discourse 'after equality' in some far-reaching ways (see Leckey 2013).

Framing the above developments in England and Wales, Kaganas (2010) has identified a heightened concern within the family courts to adopt therapeutic approaches to family conflict, redrawing the traditional role of the courts in relation to ideas of justice and equality (see also Reece 2009b) and, indeed, reshaping ideas of how equality may be achieved via law in this area. This must be seen in the context of a wider normative reconstruction of fatherhood across social and legal policy (Collier 2010a: Ch. 5); a multilayered 'fragmentation' of legal fatherhood (Collier and Sheldon 2008), as previously coextensive family practices around marriage, parenthood and sexuality become disaggregated in legal systems (Diduck 2008; Diduck and Kaganas 2012); and, importantly, as social, demographic and economic changes transform understandings of the structure and the functioning of families and households (see, e.g., Office for National Statistics 2012) in ways that have implications for understanding legal/gender formations.

The above processes are enmeshed, I argue in the following section, with new normative legal ideas about gender neutrality, gender equality and parental responsibility, redrawing the terms of political debate around fathers' rights and shared parenting.

Casting a 'gender lens' on fathers' rights activism 'after legal equality'

In this section, I consider the apparent disconnect between the formal gender equality claims of official law, the arguments about men's *in*equality advanced by father's rights activists and what research suggests are the realities of gendered caring labour and family practices 'on the ground'.

Reading fathers' rights as a masculinity practice

A growing body of family research and family law literature draws attention to the need to recognize the experiential significance of the situated, gendered aspects of emotional agendas between disputants in the context of the dynamics of highly conflicted cases (Day Sclater and Richards 1995; Day Sclater and Yates 1999; Vallance-Webb 2008; Barnett 2009a, 2009b). These are the very cases that research suggests tend to be part of the experience of separation for many fathers' rights activists (Crowley 2008a; Jordan 2009). Such recognition places the (gendered) emotional dynamics of separation centre stage, while seeking, at the same time, to recognize how not all conflicted separations are the same, how, for example, divorce-related parenting interventions must be sensitive to the parenting practices of individual mothers and fathers situated in specific contexts (Philip and O'Brien 2012). At the same time, in ways that curiously map to these concerns, a growing sociological literature on men and masculinities has sought to develop more nuanced accounts of men's identities *as men*, that is, as gendered subjects (Hearn 1998, 2004), including in relation to law and legal regulation (Collier 2010a, 2010b; Dowd 2010; Rudy Cooper and McGinley 2012; Fineman and Thomson 2014).

Taken together, these bodies of scholarship can advance, rather than replay, existing understanding of fathers' rights activism 'after legal equality' in several respects. It is possible, for example, to read contemporary fathers' activism around shared parenting law as a distinctive kind of (often anti-feminist) 'masculinity practice'. The process of becoming 'a man' has been historically and culturally associated within Western (and, more specifically, anglophone) psychological literature with a form of masculinity that is enmeshed with normative assumptions about particular interconnections between men, heterosexuality and fatherhood (Rosh White 1994). At its simplest, this involves a process of male maturation and a fatherhood ideal (as normative 'family man': Collier 1995; Coltrane 1996) that has connected cultural forms of (specifically heterosexual) masculinity to ideas of male suppression of emotion, denial of vulnerability and proscription against the sharing of inner experiences, in particular with other men. It is a cultural idea of masculinity that remains resonant transnationally (although not without qualification: see below), correlated with an ideology of 'masculinism' seen as informing men's responses to certain emotionally challenging life events, such as separation.

It is not difficult, therefore, to connect these kinds of association between men and gender to one interpretation of fathers' rights group activism in which men adopt a particular gendered (masculine) response to the position in which they find themselves within the emotional terrain of highly conflicted separation. A body of research on men and separation suggests, for example, that the 'depth of [individual] psychic injury accrued from damaging external realities' can frequently be 'denied or underestimated' (Garde 2003: 14; also Wilkins 2013) by many men, and often projected on to outside bodies (whether individuals, organizations or, indeed, entire legal systems), which are then seen as being to 'blame' for what has happened. The very form that much contemporary fathers' activism takes can be viewed as reflecting this desire on the part of some men to 'take action' and 'take control' of a situation, to 'act' rather than just stand by and let things happen (O'Brien *et al.* 2005; see also, on this 'need to exert power and control . . . when . . . masculinity has, in some way, been threatened', the reading of Yardley *et al.* 2013).

Complicating the picture: beyond 'angry dads'

In seeking to move beyond a dominant cultural imagery of 'angry fathers', 'dangerous dads' and 'malicious mothers' (Trinder 2007), however, and to rethink the relationship between law and gender 'after equality', it is important to also consider the limitations of this approach. Four points are of particular significance in regard to understandings of equality within the new politico-legal terrain of fathers' rights.

First, as I have argued in other work (Collier 2009a, 2009b, 2010a), fathers' rights activism cannot be reduced to, or understood in terms of, any unitary model of a gendered (masculine) subject or a singular notion of masculinity. Studies of contemporary fatherhood, fathering practices (e.g., Dienhart 1998; Doucett 2006; Dermott 2008; Miller 2010) and fathers' rights groups (Crowley 2009; Collier 2010a, 2014) draw attention, rather, to the importance of recognizing, at an experiential level, and engaging politically with, the heterogeneity and psychological complexity of the processes whereby individual men may 'take up' (or not take up) what are culturally seen, at particular moments, as distinctive gendered identities in relation to fatherhood (Beasley 2008). This aligns with the call for a more nuanced account of the emotional dynamics of separation in recent family law and masculinities scholarship, as above. Far from suggesting a simple elision between fathers' rights activists and the experience of men post-separation, the aim is to highlight the dangers of generalizing about gender formations in this area and the importance of specificity and context.

Second, and building on the above, both historical and sociological research reveals a richness and diversity to fathering practices in ways mediated, importantly, by issues of class, race, ethnicity, sexuality, health and locale. That is, fatherhood itself has a multidimensional and heterogeneous nature (Broughton and Rodgers 2007; Ives 2013), as do men's 'personal lives' (Smart 2007), and fathers' rights activism within transnational frames has a complexity that broad-brush, abstract approaches to paternal masculinity can easily miss out on (Collier and Sheldon 2006). In appreciating what men themselves may see as the 'special' quality of fatherhood, meanwhile, it is necessary to move beyond narrow formulations of fathers either as failing to contribute to contemporary family life or as sidelined from it (Dermott 2008: 143; see also Doucet 2006; Miller 2010). Rather, it is important to ground gendered ideas of fatherhood within specific situated, material contexts in which individual men and women parent in ways that recognize the significance of these experiential dimensions to fathering practices and, with it, the plurality of the ideas of masculinity that shape contemporary fatherhood.

Third, it is important to also consider how particular (often culturally specific) ideas about gender, vulnerability and emotion themselves intersect with individual men's subjective experiences of degrees of power and powerlessness within the process of separation. Interdisciplinary studies of men's health, for example, as well as work on fathers and divorce, male friendships and experiences of loss and belonging over the life course (e.g., Bank and Hansford 2000; Men's Health Forum 2007; MIND 2009; Wilkins 2010; Wilkins and Kemple 2010; White 2011; Health and Social Care Information Centre 2012), suggest that questions of gender, emotion and vulnerability in the context of separation can inform the social dynamics of fathers' activism in various ways (Collier 2009a, 2009b). Men's well-documented reluctance to seek help at times of emotional difficulty (Wheeler 2003; O'Brien *et al.* 2005) has been seen to connect to wider gendered questions about public health (Robertson 2007) and the provision of relationship support (Wilkins 2013; see further, below) in terms of understanding men's engagement (or lack thereof) in therapeutic and medical intervention (Ramm *et al.* 2010). These issues, significantly, can shape individual and organizational perceptions of, and responses to, men's health, as in relation to approaches to depression, suicide (Wylie *et al.* 2012) and assessments of service provision (Conrad and White 2009; MIND 2009).

Thus, summarizing this literature, a recent UK-based review of research on men, separation and relationship support (Wilkins 2013), funded by the charity Relate and the Men's Health Forum, concludes that policymakers must take these gendered dynamics of separation more seriously, in ways that can inform wider approaches to men's health within the context of separation and the shifting political terrain of fathers' rights. It is striking, for example, how the loss of intimacy experienced by many separated and divorced men within the process of separation (Jones *et al.* 2012) can raise difficult 'questions for men about gendered identity', emotional expressiveness and emotional support (Robertson 2007: 98; see further, Crowley 2008a). Within the context of the highly conflicted separations experienced by many fathers' rights activists, these issues can be seen to take on particular significance, with research indicating that depression and/or other psychological and physical health problems are commonplace. This finding corresponds with the testimonies of non-resident fathers, who appear more likely to become actively involved in fathers' groups (Gouldstone 2008; Jordan 2009), as well as with family and parenting studies that suggest that prolonged conflict can have a significant impact on the well-being of both mothers and fathers (Trinder *et al.* 2006: 39, 85; Trinder and Kellett 2007: 30).

Fourth, and finally, these concerns, therefore, lead to practical questions about gender and the provision of relationship support in seeking to develop understanding of fathers' rights activism, *beyond* the framework of formal equality claims in law through which fathers' rights activism is usually understood. Evidence from international studies of fathers' groups indicates, for example, that many men, and some women, turn to these organizations to access practical and emotional assistance at a time when they are experiencing psychological distress, and when they see support from other quarters as lacking (Crowley 2008a; Collier 2009a; Jordan 2009). If it is the case that many men have limited access to emotional support and less experience of it more generally, as discussed above (Wilkins 2013), it is important that socio-legal analysis does not lose sight of the wider service–welfare dimension to fathers' rights organizations. This, research suggests, can have experiential significance for some men and wider family members, such as second partners and grandparents (Collier 2010a). Crucially, fathers' activism can encompass an opportunity to experience a shared affirmation of identity *as* a 'good father' (or other relative) via interaction with others, when such an identity is itself seen as threatened by separation.

There is, it is necessary to remember, currently very limited provision available to support and engage non-resident parents, women and men (Coalition on Men and Boys 2009; Wilkins 2013). Despite the growing international literature on divorce-related parenting interventions, claims about their effectiveness remain modest, and little is actually known about if and how such programmes offer support to individual men as fathers (see further, Philip and O'Brien 2012). As observed, there also exist an array of fathering practices on the part of divorced or separated fathers, ranging from those who sustain co-parenting arrangements to those who have limited or intermittent parental contact (Dermott and Gabb 2012). Each, importantly, raises rather different questions about fatherhood, vulnerability and care, calling for different kinds of gender-sensitive support and intervention (O'Brien *et al.* 2005).

The limits – and possibilities – of reading fathers' rights 'after legal equality'

A proviso: constructing the 'father as victim' by another name?

Before concluding, it is important to consider the limits of this reading of fathers' rights, law and gender 'after legal equality'. What may appear at first sight to be 'lost' in the above are the structural contexts, the gendered nature and materiality of men's and women's lives, as well as, importantly, consideration of how gendered ideas of parenthood are historically grounded within social contexts shaped by relations of *power*. The affective domain of the mother, for example, is not part of the above analysis, let alone any consideration of her financial–economic position post-separation. Men's public displays of emotion, of the kind well illustrated by the protests of Fathers 4 Justice in the UK, appear to attract a culturally redemptive value (and, with it, media and legal–judicial attention) not accorded to women. The targeting of women ministers and judges by some fathers' rights activists in the UK, and the practices of certain activists more generally, raise further and troubling questions about the wider interconnections between men and gender (Collier 2014), aggression (Eagly and Steffen 1986), power, control, masculinity and men's violence (see, e.g., Yardley *et al.* 2013).

These concerns acquire additional salience in the context of neo-liberal cultural and political–economic frames and a logic of privatization that have seen a policy shift away from the promotion of ideas of *responsibility* in law (a particular hallmark of New Labour governments in the UK prior to 2010) to, increasingly, a focus on notions of individual *autonomy* and a recalibration of the role of law in family justice (Kaganas 2010). This has seen a gendered realignment in terms of how mothers and fathers are understood as particular kinds of vulnerable subject requiring assistance and remedy, as individuals deserving, or undeserving, of the support of the state. Significantly, in the UK, a neo-liberal 'politics of austerity' has had, in the years since 2010, an explicitly gendered dimension (see also, on ideas of economic justice after legal equality, Jakobsen, in this volume). It is mothers, not fathers, who face the harshest consequences of a neo-liberal redrawing of the market state and of the abolition of legal aid in private family cases. It is mothers who disproportionately suffer from the loss of jobs in the public sector due to government-imposed cuts (Toynbee and Walker 2012).

On such a reading, focusing on the experiential dimensions of fathers' rights activism 'after legal equality' may appear a distraction from a particularly regressive moment in the history of gender-equality projects in law and a backlash triggered by feminist gains in the field of family law (Chunn *et al.* 2007). Further, as noted, fatherhood is not being devalued in law; it is being *reconstituted* (Collier and Sheldon 2008), subjected to a different form of law's governance of personal lives (e.g., Lee 2009), as a new model of the 'responsible father' itself emerges as a distinctive object of intervention in law (see also Reece, in this volume). A new focus on fatherhood in social policy has itself served to marginalize mothers, writing mothers *out* of policy (Featherstone 2010), while failing to engage with the implications of contemporary critical debates on men and masculinity for such policy (Hearn 2010).

Beyond gender difference and equality?

It is possible, nonetheless, I have argued in this chapter, to read fathers' activism in a way that does not lose sight of the above questions. Drawing attention to the complexity and gendered dimensions of men's experiences does not by itself detract from recognition of how power relations remain fundamental to critical engagement with fathers' rights politics. As Dowd (2010) suggests, 'taking masculinity seriously' can be part of a wider project seeking to contribute to contemporary feminist engagements with law by addressing precisely these questions of men and masculinity (see also Rudy Cooper and McGinley 2012; Fineman and Thomson 2014). Thus, understanding contemporary fathers' rights politics and seeking to engage with its many challenges to legal ideas of equality – and, with it, appreciating the present nature of obstacles to, and support for, shared parenting – requires recognition of the multi-layered, gendered dimensions of the emotional factors that impel participants on all sides of this debate. It also entails recognizing how these factors are shaped within nationally specific social and legal contexts. It is not, as noted, to elide fathers' rights activism with the experiences of all men. Highlighting the situated, often contradictory, investments individuals can have in gender categories at particular moments in their life course makes it possible to see, rather, how contingent ideas about fatherhood can be understood *as* the effects of power, while, at the same time, having the potential to produce oppositional practices and resistances (Ashe 2007).

It is within the context of this shifting political terrain 'after equality', therefore, that, at a discursive level, the material aftermath of fathers' groups' efforts to reform the law has become increasingly significant in shaping the gendered politics of family justice internationally. The embrace of formal equality claims (see further, Boyd, in this volume) aligns a concern to protect or defend the (heterosexual) family from the social ills of 'father-absence' with the present direction of legal policy in relation to fatherhood (and the promotion, in particular, of a form of post-separation 'engaged' fathering: Collier and Sheldon 2008). However, it is in the disconnect between fathers' rights claims and family policy that the 'cracks in the argument' and contradictory consequences of these reconfigurations of the rights and responsibilities of parents 'after legal equality' become visible. It is here, for example, that fathers' rights activism runs both *with* and *against* the grain of contemporary family policy around parenting and equality (Collier 2014). Such policy entails beliefs about fatherhood that emerge from a complex nexus of social, economic, cultural, political and legal changes that have resulted in 'a new set of norms for fatherhood' in law (Fineman 2004: 195). In the light of the above discussion, and in this context, it is unsurprising that fathers' rights activists should have had some success in 'refashion[ing] and reposition[ing] fatherhood' within this 'legal and cultural imaginary' (Smart 2006a: 123).

Finally, it is worth noting how, just as it is hard, as Tina Miller (2010) puts it, to 'un-do gender', the cultural demands of the normative 'new parenthood' contained in law and policy, marked by ideas of gender equality and gender neutrality, can themselves confound the expectations of equality on the part of many individuals as they encounter law (often for the first time, and often at considerable and unforeseen expense). Tensions may exist between the emotional *experiences* of separation considered above and cultural–legal *ideas* around 'divorcing responsibly' within the post-separation context (see Reece 2003; van Krieken 2005). These ideas can run against the grain of deeply embedded gendered beliefs on the part of both women and men (Kaganas and Day Sclater 2004; Barnett 2009b; Collier 2009a) and the intersubjective nature of ideas of fairness and equality (Reece, in this volume), highlighting again the dangers of falling prey to the legal rationality mistake (Barlow 2009). In the case of fatherhood, studies of fathers' rights groups suggest that fathers' experiences and expectations of law are translated into practices precisely within the wider contexts of these gendered normative constraints (Miller 2010) and via an awareness of the political and cultural force of equality claims within law; the sense that we, indeed, live our lives 'after (legal) equality'.

This chapter's reading suggests, ultimately, that we may well have reached the limits of traditional gendered categories and concepts in terms of understanding the complexities of the emotional dynamics of separation in the context of fathers' rights activism. In seeking to move beyond the discourse of 'gender wars', for example, and to recognize the limitations of equality discourses on the contours of intimate obligations (Glennon 2010), we may need to move beyond considerations of gender differences. Although they can shape some parents' discourses around equality and legal rights within the context of separation, it is important to also acknowledge, as Liz Trinder (2007) has observed, the *common* problems that can face both parents, mothers and fathers (not least in relation to levels of distress that appear broadly similar for men and women involved in high-conflict court proceedings: Trinder *et al.* 2006: 106). The interconnected nature of the personal lives of women, men and children (Smart 2007), and the diverse set of social relationships involved in processes of separation (encompassing second partners, children, grandparents, friendship networks) further suggest that fathers' rights activism cannot be understood simply in terms of a 'gender wars' framework or reduced to questions of fathers' legal claims to gender equality. In this context, there is a pressing need to advance new kinds of argument rather than to repeat old ones, to focus on 'the intimate, the archival and the micro', to transcend the barriers that so often confine legal scholarship (Leckey, in this volume: 8).

What we see in this political terrain 'after legal equality' are ideas about the contingent and shifting nature of men's role in families; questions of the potential and limits of social recognition via rights claims, issues of history, subjectification, voice and political strategy; ideas about the discursive role of emotions and of love especially (such as, in this case, a father's love for his children) in social movements concerned with legal reform, as well as the shifting place of emotions such as love in judicial and parliamentary discourse (see also Harding and Donovan, both in this volume); and issues of how fathers have, and have not, been understood as familial subjects at particular moments via reference to particular gendered ideas of economics, care and responsibility. The arguments of fathers' rights groups and their diverse critics can each draw on contingent cultural conceptualizations of a (male) gendered subject, a subject that contemporary masculinities research suggests is far more complex than may at first seem. It is, thus, unsurprising that calls for law reform around shared parenting justified by claims of equality should have proved so controversial and so able to provoke opposition – and indeed support – from multiple constituencies. For, in a sense, fathers' rights activism can itself be seen as an example of a new kind of political engagement around law that is being shaped by the new and evolving ideas of equality discussed in this volume.

Notes

1   See, e.g., Boyd 2001, 2003, 2004a, 2004b, 2008; Gavanas 2002, 2004; Smart 2004, 2006a, 2006b; Kennedy 2005; Berns 2006; Crowley 2006a, 2006b, 2008a, 2008b, 2009; Rhoades 2006; Collier 2009a, 2009b, 2010a, 2010c; Featherstone 2009; Jordan 2009, forthcoming; Ruxton and Baker 2009; see also Collier and Sheldon 2006.
2   In addition to work cited above, see, e.g., Featherstone 2010; Boyd and Young 2002; Coltrane and Hickman 1992; Graycar 1989, 2000; Melville and Hunter 2001; Menzies 2007; Berotia and Drakich 1993; Kaye and Tolmie 1998a, 1998b, 1998c; Rhoades and Boyd 2004.

References

Ashe, F. (2007) *The New Politics of Masculinity: Men, Power and Resistance*, London: Routledge.

Bank, B. and Hansford, S. (2000) 'Gender and friendship: Why are men's best same-sex friendships less intimate and supportive?', *Personal Relationships*, 7: 63–78.

Barlow, A. (2009) 'Legal rationality and family property: What has love got to do with it?' in J. Miles and R. Probert (eds) *Sharing Lives, Dividing Assets: An Interdisciplinary Study*, Oxford: Hart.

Barnett, A. (2009a) 'The welfare of the child revisited: In whose best interests? Part I', *Family Law*, 39(1): 50–4.

Barnett, A. (2009b) 'The welfare of the child revisited: In whose best interests? Part II', *Family Law*, 39(2): 135–41.

Beasley, C. (2008) 'Rethinking hegemonic masculinity in a globalising world', *Men and Masculinities*, 11(1): 86–103.

Berns, S. (2006) 'Musings on the legal scene: Law, populism and the politics of ressentiment', *Australian Feminist Law Journal*, 25: 19–40.

Berotia, C. (1998) 'An interpretative analysis of the mediation rhetoric of fathers' rightists: Privatization versus personalization', *Mediation Quarterly*, 16(1): 15–32.

Berotia, C. and Drakich, J. (1993) 'The fathers' rights movement: Contradictions in rhetoric and practice', *Journal of Family Issues*, 14(4): 592–615.

Boyd, S.B. (2001) 'Backlash and the construction of legal knowledge: The case of child custody law', *Windsor Year Book of Access to Justice*, 20: 141–66.

——— (2003) *Child Custody, Law, and Women's Work*, Don Mills, ON: Oxford University Press.

——— (2004a) 'Backlash against feminism: Canadian custody and access reform debates of the late twentieth century', *Canadian Journal of Women and the Law*, 16(2): 255–90.

——— (2004b) 'Demonizing mothers: Fathers' rights discourses in child custody law reform processes', *Journal of the Association for Research in Mothering*, 6(1): 52–74.

——— (2008) 'Is equality enough? Fathers' rights and women's rights advocacy', in R. Hunter (ed.) *Rethinking Equality Projects in Law: Feminist Challenges*, Oxford: Hart.

——— and Young, C.F.L. (2002) 'Who influences family law reform? Discourses on motherhood and fatherhood in legislative reform debates in Canada', *Studies in Law, Politics, and Society*, 26: 43–75.

Broughton, T. and Rogers, H. (eds) (2007) *Gender and Fatherhood in the Nineteenth Century*, London: Palgrave Macmillan.

Chunn, D.E., Boyd, S. and Lessard, H. (eds) (2007) *Reaction and Resistance: Feminism, Law and Social Change*, Vancouver: UBC Press.

Coalition on Men and Boys (COMAB) (2009) *Man Made: Men, Masculinities and Equality in Public Policy*, London: COMAB.

Collier, R. (1995) *Masculinity, Law and the Family*, London: Routledge.

—— (1998) *Masculinities, Crime and Criminology*, London: Sage.

—— (2005) 'Fathers 4 Justice, law and the new politics of fatherhood', *Child and Family Law Quarterly*, 17: 511–33.

—— (2009a) 'The fathers' rights movement, law reform and the new politics of fatherhood: Reflections on the UK experience', *Journal of Law and Public Policy*, 20: 65–110.

—— (2009b) 'Fathers' rights, gender and welfare: Some questions for family law', *Journal of Social Welfare and Family Law*, 31(4): 357–71.

—— (2010a) *Men, Law and Gender: Essays on the 'Man' of Law*, London: Routledge.

—— (2010b) 'Masculinities, law and personal life: Towards a new framework for understanding men, law and gender', *Harvard Journal of Law and Gender*, 33(2): 431–77.

—— (2010c) 'Fatherhood, law and fathers' rights: Rethinking the relationship between gender and welfare', in J. Wallbank, S. Choudhry and J. Herring (eds) *Rights, Gender and Family Law*, London: Routledge-Cavendish.

—— (2014) 'On masculinities, law and family practices: a case study of fathers' rights and gender', in M. Fineman and M. Thomson (eds) *Exploring Masculinities: Feminist Legal Theory Reflections*, Farnham, UK: Ashgate.

—— and Sheldon, S. (eds) (2006) *Fathers' Rights Activism and Law Reform in Comparative Perspective*, Oxford: Hart.

—— (2008) *Fragmenting Fatherhood: A Socio-Legal Study*, Oxford: Hart.

Coltrane, S. (1996) *Family Man: Fatherhood, Housework and Gender Equality*, Oxford: Oxford University Press.

—— and Hickman, N. (1992) 'The rhetoric of rights and needs: Moral discourse in the reform of child custody and support laws', *Social Problems*, 39: 400–20.

Conrad, D. and White A. (2009) *Promoting Men's Mental Health*, Oxford: Radcliffe Publishing.

Crowley, J. (2006a) 'Adopting "equality tools" from the toolboxes of their predecessors: The fathers' rights movement in the United States', in R. Collier and S. Sheldon (eds) *Fathers' Rights Activism and Law Reform in Comparative Perspective*, Oxford: Hart.

—— (2006b) 'Organizational responses to the fatherhood crisis: The case of fathers' rights groups in the United States', *Marriage and Family Review*, 39(1): 99–120.

—— (2008a) *Defiant Dads: Fathers' Rights Activism in America*, Ithaca, NY: Cornell University Press.

—— (2008b) 'On the cusp of a movement: Identity work and social movement identification processes within fathers' rights groups', *Sociological Spectrum*, 28(6): 705–24.

—— (2009) 'Fathers' rights groups, domestic violence, and political countermobilization', *Social Forces*, 88(2): 723–55.

Day Sclater, S. and Richards, M. (1995) 'How adults cope with divorce – Strategies for survival', *Family Law*, 25: 143–7.

Day Sclater, S. and Yates, C. (1999) 'The psycho-politics of post divorce parenting', in A. Bainham, S. Day Sclater and M. Richards (eds) *What Is a Parent? A Socio-Legal Analysis*, Oxford: Hart.

Department for Education (DfE) (2012) *Co-operative Parenting Following Family Separation: Proposed Legislation on the Involvement of Both Parents in a Child's Life: Summary of Consultation Responses and the Government's Response*, London: DfE.

Dermott, E. (2008) *Intimate Fatherhood: A Sociological Analysis*, London: Routledge.

—— and Gabb, J. (2012) *Fragile Fathering: Negotiating Intimacy and Risk in Parenting Practice*, British Academy-funded pilot project.

Diduck, A. (2003) *Law's Families*, London: LexisNexis.

—— (2008) 'Family law and family responsibility', in J. Bridgeman, H. Keating and C. Lind (eds) *Responsibility, Law and the Family*, Aldershot, UK: Ashgate.

—— and Kaganas, F. (2012) *Family Law, Gender and the State: Text, Cases and Materials*, 3rd edn, Oxford: Hart.

Dienhart, A. (1998) *Reshaping Fatherhood: The Social Construction of Shared Parenting*, Thousand Oaks, CA: Sage.

Doucet, A. (2006) *Do Men Mother? Fatherhood, Care and Domestic Responsibility*, Toronto: University of Toronto Press.

Dowd, N. (2000) *Redefining Fatherhood*, New York: New York University Press.

—— (2010) *The Man Question: Male Subordination and Privilege*, New York: New York University Press.

Eagly, A. and Steffen, V. (1986) 'Gender and aggressive behaviour: A meta-analytic review of the social psychological literature', *Psychological Bulletin*, 100: 309–30.

Featherstone, B. (2009) *Contemporary Fathering: Theory, Policy and Practice*, Bristol, UK: Policy Press.

—— (2010) 'Writing fathers in but mothers out!', *Critical Social Policy*, 30(2): 208–24.

—— and Peckover, S. (2007) 'Letting them get away with it: Fathers, domestic violence and child welfare', *Critical Social Policy*, 27(2): 181–202.

Fehlberg, B., Smyth, B., Maclean, M. and Roberts, C. (2011a) 'Caring for children after parental separation: Would legislation for shared parenting time help children?', in *Family Policy Briefing* 7, Oxford: Department of Social Policy and Intervention.

—— (2011b) 'Legislating for shared time parenting after separation: A research review', *International Journal of Law, Policy, and the Family*, 25(3): 318–37.

Fineman, M. (1995) *The Neutered Mother, the Sexual Family, and Other Twentieth Century Tragedies*, New York: Routledge.

—— (2004) *The Autonomy Myth*, New York: Free Press.

—— and Thomson, M. (eds) (2014) *Exploring Masculinities: Feminist Legal Theory Reflections*, Farnham, UK: Ashgate.

Garde, J. (2003) 'Masculinity and madness', *Counselling and Psychotherapy Research*, 3(1): 6–15.

Gavanas, A. (2002) 'The fatherhood responsibility movement: The centrality of marriage, work and male sexuality in reconstructions of masculinity and fatherhood', in B. Hobson (ed.) *Making Men into Fathers: Men, Masculinities and the Social Politics of Fatherhood*, Cambridge: Cambridge University Press.

—— (2004) *Fatherhood Politics in the United States: Masculinity, Sexuality, Race and Marriage*, Champaign: University of Illinois Press.

Glennon, L. (2010) 'The limitations of equality discourses on the contours of intimate obligations', in J. Wallbank, S. Choudhry and J. Herring (eds) *Rights, Gender and Family Law*, London: Routledge-Cavendish.

Gouldstone, S. (2008) 'Family law survey update', *McKenzie: The National Magazine of Families Need Fathers*, 82: 5.

Graycar, R. (1989) 'Equal rights versus fathers' rights: The child custody debate in Australia', in C. Smart and S. Sevenhuijsen (eds) *Child Custody and the Politics of Gender*, London: Routledge.

—— (2000) 'Law reform by frozen chook: Family law reform for the new millennium?', *Melbourne University Law Review*, 24(3): 737–55.

Greatbatch, D. and Dingwall, R. (1999) 'The marginalization of domestic violence in divorce mediation', *International Journal of Law, Policy, and the Family*, 13(2): 174–90.

Harris, M. (2006) *Family Court HELL*, London: Pen Press.

Harris, P. and George, R. (2010) 'Parental responsibility and shared residence orders: Parliamentary intentions and judicial interpretations', *Child and Family Law Quarterly*, 22(2): 151–71.

Health and Social Care Information Centre (HSCIC) (2012) *Routine Quarterly Improving Access to Psychological Therapies Dataset Reports*, Leeds: HCSIC.

Hearn, J. (1998) 'Theorizing men and men's theorizing: Men's discursive practices in theorizing men', *Theory and Society*, 27(6): 781–816.

—— (2004) 'From hegemonic masculinity to the hegemony of men', *Feminist Theory*, 5: 49–72.

—— (2010) 'Reflecting on men and social policy: Contemporary critical debates and implications for social policy', *Critical Social Policy*, 30: 165–88.

Ives, J. (2013) *The Moral Habitus of Fatherhood: A Study of How Men Negotiate the Moral Demands of Becoming a Father: March/April 2013 Briefing Report*, Birmingham: MESH/University of Birmingham. Online. Available at: www.esrc.ac.uk/my-esrc/grants/RES-000-22-3964/outputs/Read/6e85a38a-d0d6-43c2-ab7c-cf45b0cffc54 (accessed 25 July 2013).

Jones, R., Burgess, A. and Hale, V. (2012) *The Fathers' Journey: A Survey of Help-Seeking Behaviour by Separating and Recently Separated Fathers*, All Party Parliamentary Group on Fatherhood.

Jordan, A. (2009) '"Dads aren't demons. Mums aren't Madonnas." Constructions of fatherhood and masculinities in the (real) Fathers 4 Justice campaign', *Journal of Social Welfare and Family Law*, 31(4): 419–33.

—— (forthcoming) '"Every father is a superhero to his children": The gendered politics of the (real) Fathers 4 Justice campaign', *Political Studies*.

Kaganas, F. (1999) 'Contact, conflict and risk', in S. Day Sclater and C. Piper (eds) *Undercurrents of Divorce*, Aldershot, UK: Ashgate.

—— (2010) 'When it comes to contact disputes, what are family courts for?', *Current Legal Problems*, 63(1): 235–71.

—— and Day Sclater, S. (2004) 'Contact disputes: Narrative constructions of "good" parents', *Feminist Legal Studies*, 12(1): 1–27.

—— and Piper, C.D. (1999) 'Divorce and domestic violence' in S. Day Sclater and C. Piper (eds) *Undercurrents of Divorce*, Dartmouth, UK: Ashgate.

Kaye, M. and Tolmie, J. (1998a) 'Discoursing dads: The rhetorical devices of fathers' rights groups', *Melbourne University Law Review*, 22(1): 162–94.

—— (1998b) 'Fathers' rights groups in Australia and their engagement with issues in family law', *Australian Journal of Family Law*, 12(1): 12–61.

—— (1998c) '"Lollies at a children's party" and other myths: Violence, protection orders and fathers' rights groups', *Current Issues in Criminal Justice*, 10(1): 52–72.

Kennedy, R. (2005) *Fathers for Justice: The Rise of a New Social Movement in Canada as a Case Study of Collective Identity*, 2nd edn, Ann Arbor, MI: Caravan Books.

Kimmell, M. (2010) *Misframing Men: The Politics of Contemporary Masculinities*, New Brunswick, NJ: Rutgers University Press.

Leckey, R. (2013) 'Two mothers in law and fact', *Feminist Legal Studies*, 21(1): 1–19.

Lee, E. (2009) 'Pathologising fatherhood: The case of male Post Natal Depression in Britain', in S. Robertson and B. Gough (eds) *Men, Masculinities and Health: Critical Perspectives*, Basingstoke, UK: Palgrave.

Maclean, M. (ed.) (2007) *Parenting After Partnering*, Oxford: Hart.

McCandless, J. and Sheldon, S. (2010) 'The Human Fertilisation and Embryology Act 2008 and the tenacity of the sexual family form', *Modern Law Review*, 73(2): 175–207.

Melville, A. and Hunter, R. (2001) 'As everybody knows: Countering myths of gender bias in family law', *Griffith Law Review*, 1(1): 124–38.

Men's Health Forum (2007) *Men and Long-Term Health Conditions: A Policy Briefing Paper*, London: Men's Health Forum.

Menzies, R. (2007) 'Virtual backlash: Representations of men's "rights" and feminist "wrongs" in cyberspace', in D.E. Chunn, S.B. Boyd and H. Lessard (eds) *Reaction and Resistance: Feminism, Law and Social Change*, Vancouver: University of British Columbia Press.

Messner, M. (1997) *Politics of Masculinities: Men in Movements*, London: Sage.

Miller, T. (2010) *Making Sense of Fatherhood: Gender, Caring and Work*, Cambridge: Cambridge University Press.

MIND (2009) *Men and Mental Health: Get it Off Your Chest*, London: MIND.

Newis, P. (2011) *Firm Foundations: Shared Care in Separated Families: Building on What Works*, London: Gingerbread/One Plus One.

Newnham, A. (2008) 'Law's gendered understandings of parents' responsibilities in relation to shared residence', in J. Bridgeman, H. Keating and C. Lind (eds) *Regulating Family Responsibilities*, Aldershot, UK: Ashgate.

O'Brien, R., Hunt, K. and Hart, G. (2005) '"It's caveman stuff, but that is to a certain extent how guys still operate": Men's accounts of masculinity and help-seeking', *Social Science and Medicine*, 61(3): 503–16.

Office for National Statistics (ONS) (2012) Census 2011, London: ONS.

Philip, G. and O'Brien, M. (2012) *Supporting Fathers after Separation or Divorce: Evidence and Insights*, Norwich, UK: Centre for Research on the Child and Family UEA.

Ramm, J., Coleman, L., Glenn, F. and Mansfield, P. (2010) *Relationship Difficulties and Help-Seeking Behaviour*, London: DfE.

Reece, H. (2003) *Divorcing Responsibly*, Oxford: Hart.

—— (2009a) 'The degradation of parental responsibility', in R. Probert, S. Gilmore and J. Herring (eds) *Responsible Parents and Parental Responsibility*, Oxford: Hart.

—— (2009b) 'Parental responsibility as therapy', *Family Law*, 39: 1167–71.

Rhoades, H. (2002a) 'The "non contact mother": Reconstructions of motherhood in the era of the new father', *International Journal of Law, Policy, and the Family*, 16(1): 72–113.

—— (2002b) 'The rise of shared parenting laws – a critical reflection', *Canadian Journal of Family Law*, 19(1): 75–114.

—— (2006) 'Yearning for law: Fathers' groups and family law reform in Australia', in R. Collier and S. Sheldon (eds) *Fathers' Rights Activism and Law Reform in Comparative Perspective*, Oxford: Hart.

—— and Boyd, S.B. (2004) 'Reforming custody laws: A comparative study', *International Journal of Law, Policy, and the Family*, 18(2): 119–46.

Robertson, S. (2007) *Understanding Men's Health: Masculinity, Identity and Well-being*, Buckingham, UK: Open University Press.

Rosh White, N. (1994), 'About fathers: Masculinity and the social construction of fatherhood', *Journal of Sociology*, 30(2): 119–31.

Rudy Cooper, F. and McGinley, A.C. (eds) (2012) *Masculinities and the Law: A Multidimensional Approach*, New York: New York University Press.

Ruxton, S. and Baker, H. (2009) 'Fathers' rights, fatherhood and masculinity/ies', *Journal of Social Welfare and Family Law*, 31(4): 351–5.

Sheldon, S. (2009) 'From "absent objects of blame" to "fathers who want to take responsibility": Reforming birth registration law', *Journal of Social Welfare and Family Law*, 31(4): 373–89.

Smart, C. (2004) 'Equal shares: Rights for fathers or recognition for children?', *Critical Social Policy*, 24(4): 484–503.

—— (2006a) 'The ethic of justice strikes back', in A. Diduck and K. O'Donovan (eds) *Feminist Perspectives on Family Law*, London: Routledge-Cavendish.

—— (2006b) 'Preface', in R. Collier and S. Sheldon (eds) *Fathers' Rights Activism and Law Reform in Comparative Perspective*, Oxford: Hart.

—— (2007) *Personal Life: New Directions in Sociological Thinking*, Oxford: Polity.

—— and Neale, B. (1999) *Family Fragments?* Cambridge: Polity.

—— and Sevenhuijsen, S. (eds) (1989) *Child Custody and the Politics of Gender*, London: Routledge.

Smith, L. (2010) 'Clashing symbols? Reconciling support for fathers and fatherless families after the Human Fertilisation and Embryology Act 2008', *Child and Family Law Quarterly*, 22(1): 46–71.

Toynbee, P. and Walker, D. (2012) *Dogma and Disarray: Cameron at Half Time*, London: Mount Caburn.

Trinder, L. (2007) 'Dangerous dads and malicious mothers: The relevance of gender to contact disputes', in M. Maclean (ed.) *Parenting After Partnering*, Oxford: Hart.

—— (2010) 'Shared parenting: A review of the research evidence', *Child and Family Law Quarterly*, 22: 475–98.

—— (2012) 'The Children Act is an act of kindness', *The Guardian*, 6 February.

—— Connolly, J., Kellett, J. and Swift, L. (2006) *Making Contact Happen or Making Contact Work? The Process and Outcomes of In Court Conciliation*, London: DCA.

—— and Kellett, J. (2007) *The Longer-Term Outcomes of In-Court Conciliation*, London: Ministry of Justice.

Vallance-Webb, G. (2008) 'Child contact: Vengeful mothers, good fathers and vice versa', *Family Law*, 38(7): 678–81.

van Krieken, R. (2005), 'The "best interests of the child" and parental separation on the "civilising of parents"', *Modern Law Review*, 68(1): 25–48.

Wallbank, J. (2007) 'Getting tough on mothers: Regulating contact and residence', *Feminist Legal Studies*, 15(2): 189–222.

—— (2009a) 'Parental responsibility and the responsible parent: Managing the "problem" of contact', in R. Probert, S. Gilmore and J. Herring (eds) *Responsible Parents and Parental Responsibility*, Hart Publishing: Oxford.

—— (2009b) '"Bodies in the shadows": Joint birth registration, parental responsibility and social class', *Child and Family Law Quarterly*, 21(3): 267–82.

Wheeler, S. (2003) 'Men and therapy – are they compatible?', *Counselling and Psychotherapy Research*, 3(1): 2–5.

White, A. (2011) *The State of Men's Health in Europe (Extended Report)*, Brussels: European Commission.

Wilkins, D. (2010) *Untold Problems: A Review of the Essential Issues in the Mental Health of Men and Boys*, London: Men's Health Forum.

—— (2013) *Try to See It My Way: Improving Relationship Support for Men*, London: Men's Health Forum/Relate.

—— and Kemple, M. (2010) *Delivering Effective Practice in Male Mental Health*, London: Men's Health Forum.

Wylie, C., Platt, S., Brownlie, J., Chandler, A., Connolly, S., Evans, R., Kennelly, B., Kirtley, O., Moore, G., O'Connor, R. and Scourfield, J. (2012) *Men, Suicide and Society*, London: Samaritans.

Yardley, E., Wilson, D. and Lynes, A. (2013) 'A taxonomy of male British family annihilators, 1980–2012', *Howard Journal of Criminal Justice*, doi: 10.1111/hojo.12033.

Chapter 5

Economic justice after legal equality

The case for caring queerly

Janet R. Jakobsen

I was recently in a meeting with an activist in New York City who was working on a feminist project on 'economic security'. 'Is "economic security" what we used to call "economic justice"?' I asked. She affirmed that it was, but that funders were more open to the term 'security' than 'justice'. Although there had been some greater openings since the election of Barack Obama in 2008, she reported, the problems that had been referred to as 'poverty' in the twentieth century were, in the twenty-first, referred to as 'failures of economic security'. The result is that the responses to these problems were now those of creating security rather than those of creating justice. She was critical of the language of security, insofar as one can hear in it the reverberations of the intensification of the national security state in the United States after 2001. But, she also thought that 'security' named something important about the effects of what is often called 'neo-liberalism': both public policies and economic practices that have, in conjunction with 'globalization', led to major shifts in the structure of contemporary nation-states and in economic relations around the world.[1] Importantly, the advent of neo-liberalism has meant world economic relations marked, not just by growing income inequality, but also by increasing precariousness for a wide range of people – pretty much anyone who finds themselves among the '99 per cent' – and building security might be a necessary (if not sufficient) way to address this precariousness.[2]

This conversation made me wonder how we might think about the more traditional ethical and social movement category of 'justice' in relation to neo-liberalism. Justice has its own problems of association; like the connection between economic security and the national security state, justice is associated, not just with material equality, fairness and well-being, but also with the 'criminal justice system'. In the United States in the twenty-first century, criminal 'justice' is another name for mass incarceration (Alexander 2012). So, it might be worth reconsidering the value of both justice and security as means of approaching the problems created by neo-liberalism.

Certainly, social movements must address the persistence of inequality 'after' the extension of legal equality. In the United States, at least, income inequality has increased during precisely the period since the 1960s when movements for legal equality won major victories (Chetty *et al*. 2013). It is important to note that some of these victories, such as the Voting Rights Act, have been recently undercut by the US Supreme Court in a decision that was released in a sequence including major decisions on affirmative action and same-sex marriage. The relations among the three high-profile decisions allowed the positive decision on sexual rights to reinforce a narrative in which the possibility of naming and addressing racism was narrowed. According to the Court, racial rights had been instituted half a century ago and so were no longer needed (or needed only in very specific circumstances), and, by extending similar rights to same-sex couples, the Court was also making the need for further struggle on behalf of sexual justice superfluous.[3] As Roderick A. Ferguson notes in this volume (160), the Voting Rights Act decision legitimates its reinforcement of racial injustice by segregating race from sexuality and using the supposed advance represented by the same-sex marriage decision as part of 'the conditions whereby sexuality could facilitate the state's racial exclusions'. And, as Richard Collier points out (in this volume: 67), the contemporary neo-liberal moment is also 'a particularly regressive moment in the history of gender-equality projects in law', even as it may be a moment when certain types of claim – for same-sex marriage or 'fathers' rights' – may move forward. Following critical race theorists such as Kimberlé Crenshaw *et al*. (1996), Ferguson's argument makes clear that, because legal equality within the liberal framework focuses on single sets of relations – race *or* sex *or* gender – legal equality cannot be sufficient for the achievement of *social* justice. Thus, developing an adequate vision of justice requires thinking after and beyond legal equality to complex sets of *inter*-relations.

Moreover, as my activist friend pointed out, with her focus on creating security in the face of precariousness, not only do questions of legal equality not fully cover the issues that social movements currently face, a traditional approach to social justice that focuses only on material inequality is also insufficient. When the world is organized by neo-liberalism, neither the rights-based movements that have extended legal equality nor movements for material redistribution can fully address the moral wrongs of the current moment.[4] As Robert Leckey's summary of Collier's work makes plain, it is important to locate contemporary debates within 'a wider reconfiguration of gender and care under the political, economic and cultural conditions of neo-liberalism' (in this volume: 14).

The idea of neo-liberal precarity signals a certain vulnerability that is not fully present in the idea of inequality. It's clear that inequality makes some people more vulnerable than others, but precarity also signals the differential distribution, not just of material goods, but also of life chances. Inequality in the United States, for example, is supposed to be acceptable and, in fact, part of a just society, because the opportunity for social mobility means, as Ronald Reagan so memorably put it in 1982, that America is a country in which 'people can still get rich'. On the one hand, recent studies have shown (not surprisingly) that, in fact, there is less opportunity for social mobility in the United States than in other developed countries (Jantti *et al.* 2006), which means that the likelihood is small that one will be able to 'move on up' from the conditions in which one was born. In fact, many things will have to go well in order for one not to fall down the economic ladder. On the other hand, material well-being – economic security – leads to other forms of security as well, to assurance that, even if one doesn't get into the college of one's choice, one will be accepted to a 'safety school'; that if one makes a mistake or becomes involved with the law as a young person, one will be able to overcome this 'setback'; or that, if one develops an illness, one will receive the best care available and have a chance to live a long life. For those who are on the economic margins of society – who have less cushion to begin with – accident or illness, certainly disabling accident or chronic illness, is likely to lead to a spiral of increasingly negative effects, from the loss of a job or an end to chances for education through financial hardship to greater stress-based illness, and on and on.

As Occupy Wall Street has emphasized, the past several decades have marked shifts towards increasingly precarious employment and decreasingly generous social safety nets, all of which create a sense of 'precarity' for the majority of people. These shifts have been part and parcel of the shift from industrialization to finance- and service-based economies, as economies around the world have become constituted by temporary, contingent, flexible, intermittent or otherwise casual forms of labour (Lee and Kofman 2012). Thus, jobs are no longer marked by the security or benefits of unionized, long-term contracts, but are individualized and temporary, so that no one can be certain of one's access to employment or, if employed, of the duration of one's job. However, precarity goes beyond the conditions of employment itself to forms of security that once accompanied employment, including health care, paid sick-leave, paid family leave and childcare (although many of these forms of care have always been less available in the United States than in other industrialized countries).

These forms of caring are also significantly related to what are generally considered 'non-economic' forms of social relations, including those of gender, sexuality, race and nation. In the United States, the very ability to use one's employment as a source of health-care benefits for those about (and for) whom one cares is often dependent on getting married. In other words, if one accedes to the government regulation of sexual relations through marriage, then maybe one can get access to health benefits for those whom one loves. The fact that caring labour is dependent on gender and sexual arrangements has caused policy analysts to worry, as liberal Thomas Edsall (2013) recently did in the pages of *The New York Times*, that shifts in gender and sexual relations will also shift costs for the state, which will have to pay for labour once done by wives, daughters and extended family members. And, when caring labour is provided through paid employment, it is driven by the race and gender segregation of US labour markets and the inducement and enforcement of economically motivated transnational migration, traced by scholars such as Saskia Sassen (1999) and activist groups such as the National Domestic Workers Alliance (Nadasen and Williams 2010).

All of these relations – gender, race, class, sexuality, nation and many more – come together to form the assemblage that allows for caring labour, which provides some measure of security in the midst of neo-liberal societies. The fact of this assemblage implies that something more than economics must be addressed if we are to hope for justice. And, if the conditions of injustice are organized by neo-liberal policies that make for precarity as well as inequality, should those who hope for justice expand the concept to include security as well as equality (whether of rights or of material well-being)?

In this chapter, I explore the assemblage of social relations that makes for both inequality and precarity as the analytic basis for creating greater justice in our contemporary world. I have chosen to explore these relationships through the concept of 'assemblage', because it allows for a dynamic approach to how social relations work together. I am particularly interested in how discontinuous (and even contradictory) relations nonetheless come together to produce a hegemonic social fabric. I have been influenced, not only by Jasbir Puar's (2007) convincing use of a Deleuzian version of assemblage in her book, *Terrorist Assemblages*, but also by Annemarie Mol's (2003) version of assemblage as detailed in *The Body Multiple*. Mol works within the actor–network-theory school of thought to produce an ethnography of the disease atherosclerosis. By carefully documenting her observations of atherosclerosis in different settings, Mol shows that the disease is different if one is in the clinic listening to descriptions of symptoms, or if one is in the operating room creating openings for the patient's veins, or if one is in the lab measuring the width of the veins. These differences create divergent versions of the disease – the symptoms might not be of the relative severity that would be indicated by lab results; or they may be more severe and not relieved by surgery; or the surgeon may well be surprised by what the lab reports from its tests. Mol then shows the various epistemological mechanisms by which these ontologically discontinuous versions of the disease are made to line up. Through each of these mechanisms, one indicator – symptoms, surgery, lab tests – becomes the leading indicator in relation to which others are brought into line. However, Mol suggests a more accurate rendering of the disease would acknowledge the multiple realities of illness. It is true that the disease exists in the body of one person – but that body is multiple: suffers pain, has blockages, might or might not be helped by surgery.

This view of how divergent realities are brought together in an assemblage that makes up the human body – in which these different realities can be divergent and yet also interrelated – is also helpful in thinking about the social body. In exploring sets of social relations in this chapter, I will also be exploring the ways in which the social body is, like the physical body, made up of interactive, yet divergent, relations. In other words, the social body is also a 'body multiple', and social analysis often works through various epistemological mechanisms to hide this fact. Ferguson's chapter, for example, delineates the way in which hegemonic historiography works to produce the modern nation-state as a singular body. The body of the nation-state may be understood to include internal inequalities (correctable through legal rights), but historiography works to ensure that these inequalities in no way disrupt the singularity of the nation. One way in which this singularity is maintained is by analysing social relations along singular axes divided from each other – be these axes of social difference, such as class, race and gender, or divisions of spheres, such as that between public and private.

The concept of assemblage, in contrast, allows for an analysis that recognizes the distinctions among class, race and gender, but that also understands these relations to be inseparable from each other. Moreover, assemblage similarly allows for a connected reading of public and private – one that not only connects these two spheres but also sees the public–private division as related to social differences. So, for example, we know that caring labour is often split off from analyses of economic relations through an assumption of a division between the public world of fiscal policy and the private sphere of caring labour. Even when liberal commentators such as Edsall can see connections between caring labour and federal budget deficits, the ways in which caring labour is implicated in race and gender relations or in international migration remain hidden.

When this split between public and private is given this kind of analytic force, the social body is treated, not as a 'body multiple', in which discontinuous – public and private – realities *work together*, but as a set of separable, mechanistic sectors. Not only would it be more accurate to analyse public and private as an assemblage of social relations than as divided sectors, but doing so would illuminate the fact that this assemblage is crucial to the development and maintenance of neo-liberal precarity and its attendant forms of injustice. The analytic assumptions dividing issues such as gender and sexuality from economics are part of the assemblage that makes for both economic systems and state power. Shifts in labour patterns towards service work, temporary labour and piecework are all part of the economic shifts that have come to define neo-liberalism, and yet these forms of labour are fundamentally raced and gendered, and they often involve work in the private sphere – whether home health care or other forms of domestic labour or home-based piecework. The labour that allows for precarity is thus part of a broader set of social relations. Private relations implicate, not only economic systems, but also shifts in state policy from the welfare state to the neo-liberal state, as well as shifts around immigration policy, nationalism and the international division of labour. Public and private may be discontinuous realms, but they are also interrelated and part of the assemblage that makes for neo-liberalism.

Caring labour stands at the centre of all of these relations, despite the fact that this form of work has been variously excluded from economic policies – whether through the assumption that caring labour is a non-economic labour of love, or through the literal exclusion of paid domestic labour from various legal protections. Caring labour is one of the categories of 'excluded labor' in the United States, which have been actively removed from the Fair Labor Relations Act. However, as the National Domestic Workers Alliance has argued, instead of understanding caring labour as anomalous – as a special kind of labour in the private sphere – we could understand it as the model for all kinds of labour under neo-liberalism (Nadasen and Williams 2010). Unlike the paradigmatic factory worker of the industrial economy, the domestic worker is a service worker who often finds work through transnational migration and labours under conditions of great vulnerability. As even professional jobs move towards consulting and freelancing done on a job-by-job basis and often across borders, the conditions of labour for domestic workers are extending to broader swathes of the economy as a whole.

Moreover, caring labour – both in families and in the market – is central to the ways in which the welfare state is organized. Efforts to cut the costs of care, whether those costs are borne by insurance companies or by the state, often depend on moving care from institutions such as hospitals to private homes, a move that saves money in part by allowing caring labour to take place in non-unionized settings, with few protections for the workers. Thus, tracing the ways in which caring labour, its displacement and treatment make neo-liberalism possible can help to illuminate, not just how gender and sexuality are central to economic and state policy, but also how precarity and injustice are produced through a split between public and private spheres.

If we seek to build possibilities for justice, then we need an analysis, not just of how private social relations such as those of gender and sexuality work with neo-liberal policy, but also of alternative relational understandings. The alternatives I will suggest are not just to assumptions about the relationship between public and private, economic and caring labour, but also to social relations, including those of gender and sexuality. In other words, by taking a queer approach to gender and sexuality, one can also shift, change, queer the relation between public and private. Such changes are part of the broader project of making social change on behalf of justice. In the contemporary moment, we need something other than legal equality, we need to care, and, as I will suggest below, we need to care queerly (whatever our 'sexual orientation').

Public/private neo-liberalism

The idea of a split between public and private has always been central to political and philosophical liberalism, in which caring relations are consistently relegated to the private sphere.[5] With the advent of neo-liberalism has also come a new or renewed emphasis on this split. Neo-liberal policies are often understood as enacted through 'privatization', through the movement of public goods and services from the public sphere of which the state is a part into the purview of private (and mostly for-profit) corporations.[6]

Feminist and queer scholars have developed a longstanding critique of the public/private split, in part because caring is very much a public matter. As Eileen Boris and Jennifer Klein (2012: 5) argue in their recent history of home health care in the twentieth-century US, it is possible to 'rethink the history of the American welfare state from the perspective of care work' (see also Jakobsen (2011)). As Boris and Klein show in great detail, state policies, including a 'state-subsidized medical sector', have produced an economy in which caring labour in public and private, institutional and home settings is a major growth industry. In other words, even when caring labour actually takes place in 'private' settings, it is still fundamentally intertwined with public policy.

The continuing reality of this interrelation suggests that 'privatization' may be a misnomer for what is happening in the enactment of neo-liberal policies and practices. Just as the presumption that caring labour is fundamentally 'private' in nature hides the intertwining of public policy and intimate lives, so also labelling as 'privatization' the movement of economic goods from the state to for-profit corporations obscures the intertwining of state and corporation in privatized relations.

It is worthwhile returning to the blurry and perhaps nonexistent nature of the boundary between public and private, in part because this boundary is a site for struggles over gender, sexuality, race and class that are themselves part of the ongoing battle over the institutionalization of neo-liberalism (Duggan 2003). Although periodizations vary, many scholars locate the beginning of neo-liberalism in the 1970s, during the very period when social movements dedicated to changing gender and race relations and sexual possibilities were extremely active and also highly contested. To give just one example of this convergence, geographer David Harvey locates the crystallization of neo-liberalism in the United States and Britain in 1978–80, declaring these years 'a revolutionary turning point in the world's social and economic history' (2007, 1), and, thus, pegging neo-liberalism to the same years in which the Moral Majority was founded in the United States (Harding 2001). Other theorists, such as Marcus Taylor (2006) and Naomi Klein (2007), would locate the advent of neo-liberalism earlier, with the overthrow of Salvador Allende as president of Chile in 1973 and the imposition of new economic policies promoted by the Chicago school of economic thought. In a complex feedback loop, ideas incubated in the United States become part of an experiment in Chile that is variously aided and abetted by the US and its security forces. The Chilean dictatorship of Augustus Pinochet then produces a set of practices and policies that help to form neo-liberalism in the United States.

Although commentators such as Harvey, Marcus or Klein rarely note the coincidence of the global development of neo-liberalism and major public arguments over social relations such as gender, race and sexuality, this coincidence is not merely accidental (on gender, sexuality and Chilean nationalism, see Fiol-Matta (2002)). It is widely accepted that the formation of the welfare state – the governmental formation against which neo-liberalism is posed – is fundamentally implicated in these non-economic social relations (Skocpol 1992; Fitzgerald 2006; Chappell 2010). If the welfare state was formed as an assemblage of gender, sexuality, race, ethnicity, religion and nationalism, then the movement of money and social power away from state provision of certain goods and services and towards market mechanisms for the distribution of virtually everything needed for living also implicates this assemblage. The movement of public monies and activity into the private sphere of the market is not a one-way shift in a single boundary, but a multidimensional shift in relations that is realigning the boundary itself, along with those social relations that are attendant to it.

Take the ways in which neo-liberalism is enacted through interrelated binary oppositions: the rationalization for privatization depends, not only on the public/private opposition, but also on an opposition between the supposed benefits of efficiency offered by market forces and the presumed inefficiency of government bureaucracies. These oppositions are mobilized to enable the movement of resources from liberal to neo-liberal institutions, to make it seem rational, and even natural, to move formerly public undertakings, such as schools and prisons, into corporate enterprises. For-profit schools are thought, for example, to be able to provide a better education for less money, because market competition among providers allows parents to choose the better school for their children, and the profit motive leads to containment of costs. This logic connects 'privatization' to 'marketization'. The public/private dichotomy becomes intertwined with a divide between government and the market and is, then, further connected to the binary inefficient/efficient. 'Private' is now made the equivalent of the market, which is presumed to be efficient, whereas 'public' is governmental and inefficient. One can begin to see how effective the rhetoric enabled by these binary networks might be. If public is the same as governmental and inefficient, then why wouldn't people be likely to see government as also tyrannous and wasteful?

The assemblage formed by these relations allows for dynamic movement among the different oppositions, so as to bolster the privatization logic at its weak points. When people question the idea of moving 'public goods' into the 'private sphere', the idea of the market as more efficient than government is brought in to justify the move. In fact, much of what is understood to be privatization is not a move towards market competition but is, instead, a use of public funds for private profit, and this profit is enabled precisely by the absence of market competition. Instead of a competitive marketplace, government contracts and funds may well go to those with connections to government officials, without the type of competition that is supposed to create efficiencies. (Whether competition does create efficiencies is another question.)

The tight connections that make neo-liberalism seem natural begin to unravel when the link is severed between the two binaries public/private and government/market. For example, the ways in which privatization works as an evasion of markets, as a means of using government funds for individual profit, became visible in the summer of 2012 when *The New York Times* published a series of articles on how halfway houses in the state of New Jersey had been 'privatized' and were run by companies with close ties to the governor of the state:

> At the heart of the system is a company with deep connections to politicians of both parties, most notably Gov. Chris Christie.
>
> Many of these halfway houses are as big as prisons, with several hundred beds, and . . . New Jersey officials have called these large facilities an innovative example of privatization and have promoted the approach all the way to the Obama White House.
>
> Yet with little oversight, the state's halfway houses have mutated into a shadow corrections network, where drugs, gang activity and violence, including sexual assaults, often go unchecked, according to a 10-month investigation by *The New York Times*.
>
> (Dolnick 2012)

In other words, in this example, none of the positive aspects of the binaries associated with 'privatization' holds true: there is no market competition, there are no increased efficiencies, and privatization does not provide for more functional institutions. And yet, this programme was widely touted at the highest levels of government as paradigmatic of what privatization could and should be. The use of public monies for profit by those with close ties to government officials is sometimes called 'corruption'. Importantly, when placed in the context of those binaries that enable neo-liberalism, however, the name of these activities is 'privatization', and they are not treated as 'illegal', but rather as a fair, and even exemplary, part of the current form of capitalism.

Accumulating value

One way to understand what's happening with neo-liberalism, then, might be to move away from the idea of 'privatization' and consider an analysis focused on capitalism itself. We could, for example, think of the entire move to neo-liberal policies as akin to what Marx (1976: 874) called 'primitive accumulation'. For Marx, primitive accumulation is the moment in capitalism when resources are appropriated into the capitalist system – when, for example, the commons are enclosed and can no longer serve as land for public sheep

grazing. Rather, those people who once sustained themselves off the commons
– through animal husbandry, hunting and fishing, gleaning and gathering –
must now get the subsistence goods that they could once obtain directly from
nature through the intermediary of the market. They must, for example, pay
for goods for which they once hunted. And they must also sell their labour
power for wages, so that they have money to pay for these goods. Marx saw
primitive accumulation as part of the origins of capitalism in the move from
a feudal, land-based system to a capitalist, market-based system.

Rosa Luxemburg took this analysis of primitive accumulation one step
further, by showing in detail how capitalism continues to depend on primitive
accumulation (1964; see especially Section II: 'The historical conditions
of accumulation'). In particular, colonialism as a means of providing raw
materials for capitalism has the same effects as the move from feudalism to
capitalism. Colonialism takes resources that were previously outside the
capitalist system, including land, labour and natural resources, and forcibly
integrates them into capitalism. In so doing, colonialism allows the material
base of capitalism to continue to expand. Several contemporary theorists
(Joseph 2002; Harvey 2003) have further built on this idea, arguing that
capitalism continually needs to expand its resource base through ongoing
originary (primitive) accumulation. In other words, not all capital accumulation comes from surplus value created by the exploitation of labour. In order
for the system as a whole to work, there also needs to be the appropriation
of sources of value on which labour can work – whether the commons of feudal
villages or the natural resources of colonized areas of the world.

In the contemporary, post-colonial moment, the question is where the
material for this primitive accumulation might be found, and how it may be
appropriated into capitalism. Saskia Sassen (2010) argues that, in today's
conditions of 'advanced capitalism', sources for primitive accumulation are
found in the destruction of more traditional forms of capitalism and their
subsequent reincorporation into the system as 'raw' materials. In particular,
she is interested in the ways in which land continues to be a source of value
for capitalism. She looks at a range of cases, including the imposition of
structural adjustment at the global level, which forces countries to make debt
service their most important economic priority. These policies can devastate
local economies in ways that push people off the land because it must be
turned from crops for local sustenance to crops that produce exports and dollars
(or other foreign currency) for servicing debt. As Sassen summarizes (2010:
23): 'At its most extreme, the ensuing devastation of traditional economies
and traditional states has made the land more valuable to the global market
than the people on it'. Similarly, the housing bubble in the United States
and the ensuing mortgage debt crisis have forced thousands of people from
their homes, making houses and land in places such as Detroit extremely cheap
to investors. The rebuilding of the economy can then proceed profitably for

those who have bought the land for a pittance, and another capitalist economic cycle can ensue.

What is called neo-liberal privatization has similar effects of taking value produced through relations other than those of the market and appropriating that value into the market. So, for example, the value that was produced in the US public school system from the nineteenth century through the twentieth century could, at the end of the twentieth century, be appropriated into the market and become part of the basis for the profits of charter school corporations. In the privatization of the public school system, schools were closed, and their students were effectively 'expelled' from the buildings, just as capitalism was instantiated by expelling people from the commons. These public school buildings could be given to charter school corporations, or leased to them for very little money. Charter schools are then paid from public funds to teach these students, and profits are further enhanced by the increased exploitation of teachers and other school workers, who, under the new, 'privatized' mode of production, are no longer provided with pension and other benefits, making the cost of labour much cheaper in the new enterprises. Additional public schools then face declining enrollments and are closed, further opening the possibilities for profit (Rich and Hurdle 2013). This renegotiation of the boundary between public and private – in which private schools operate on public property with public funding – is just one of the many forms through which 'privatization' is actually an appropriation into the market of value that has accumulated in non-market sites.

However, this 'privatization' of schools and other formerly public goods is, at the same time, increasing the dependence of private corporations on government contracts, expanding the government's 'industrial complex' beyond the military to schools, prisons and health care. In each of these instances, one way for corporations to make a profit is to be intertwined with the government – using government buildings and/or government monies. To call these economic shifts 'privatization' makes it seem as though these corporations are operating in a market setting, when, in fact, they may receive no private monies and face no external competition at all. All of the money they make may come from the government. So, rather than a simple movement of public goods to the private sphere, neo-liberalism creates increased corporate involvement with the government as part of what is called 'privatization'. Thus, under conditions organized by neo-liberalism, the public–private boundary refers, not just to a shift from public to private, but instead to the type of *reconfiguration* of relations that Collier also notes regarding parental rights and responsibilities. And, as he observes, this reconfiguration is potentially contradictory (68). In this case, 'privatization' may lead to more, rather than less, involvement between private enterprise and government.

Similarly, with social movements, during the time of neo-liberal privatization, the focus on the state may in certain ways have *increased*, not decreased. Movements that might have been focused on building alternative social relations have instead become focused on recognition by the state and engagement with state-based institutions. For example, radical homosexual and queer movements that once sought to foster alternative sexual practices and relational formations have become increasingly focused on lesbian and gay rights within the state-regulated institution of marriage. A number of scholars and activists have also documented the massive growth of non-governmental organizations, which are often dependent on government grants for their survival, and which can increasingly be understood as extensions of governmentality and, perhaps, directly of the state (Halley *et al.* 2006; INCITE! 2007; Ho 2008; for an interesting exploration of how to negotiate between activist commitments and the demands of governance, see Alvarez 1999). Moreover, certain private concerns are also increasingly the focus of public policy. The 'war on women', named as part of the 2012 election cycle, included a number of well-publicized controversies over questions of contraception and abortion, questions that had been named by the US Supreme Court as part of the private sphere since *Griswold v Connecticut* in 1965.[7] However, in the era of neo-liberal privatization, the very issues of gender and sexuality that had been named as definitively 'private' are once again the subject of massive public debate over action by the state.

In short, what we're experiencing is a renegotiation of a complex, multidirectional relationship, an assemblage of actions and interactions that make up the public and the private, rather than a shift in the location of a single, straight boundary line. There are both analytic and political effects to thinking of neo-liberalism as accomplished simply through 'privatization'. When doing so, we do not name the endeavours subject to 'privatization' as alternative uses of *public* funds. We speak as though private corporations are providing the funds, when often the opposite is true. Thus, the idea of 'privatization' can support rationalizations in which it appears that the public simply 'cannot afford' certain kinds of project, such as education or infrastructural improvements, rather than that government has chosen to put its funds towards other projects, such as contracts with private incarceration firms.

We could think differently, however. We could think about how government could support social relations that contribute to justice. We could, for example, think of how a more complex and dynamic view of public–private relations could enable a new vision of economic justice that incorporates relations of social difference, such as gender, race, sexuality and nation.

Caring queerly

Caring labour is one of the connecting points between the increased precarity of individuals and households under neo-liberalism and neo-liberal shifts in economic and state policy. So, for example, health care that was once provided in hospital settings in the USA – often in public hospitals, but sometimes also in for-profit settings – has been increasingly pushed towards private provision or 'at home' care. The expected hospital stay after women give birth has been reduced from nearly a week to as short a time as conceivably possible – often less than 24 hours. Hospital recovery times for serious injuries have been reduced from a matter of months to a matter of weeks. The expectation that people will now be cared for by the private individuals in their lives during relatively intense periods of recovery has now been fully incorporated into the 'health-care system', as health-care 'customers' do more of the needed labour, just as customers in other industries scan and bag groceries, manage commodity orders online and otherwise do the work of corporations. The burden on families of these increased expectations for care can be extreme. People often have to quit their jobs in order to care for family members who are ill or injured. These burdens and attendant vulnerabilities are only increased for those who – for whatever reason – do not have a 'family' to fall back on. Even if one has lived in a traditional family and remained married for a lifetime, the loss of a spouse may produce intense vulnerability, unless one's children can take on new responsibilities of care or can afford to pay wages for such help.

Here, we see the intersection between the broad system of neo-liberal political economy and the personal desires and relations that are (thought to be) appropriate to studies of sex, family and kinship. In particular, the labour done within the context of families is crucial to the neo-liberal economic system as a whole. In the United States, this work is structured so that it is bound to be exploitative in some form, either as unpaid housework or as paid employment that is subject to both the race and gender segregation of the US labour market and to the forces of transnational migration (Boris and Klein 2012: 7).

Just as goods and services are provided in 'private' in this system, so the negative consequences of the system are often felt in an intensely personal form, whether in the exhaustion of personally providing care that might be socially provided, the pain of broken relations that couldn't stand the strain, or the trauma of staying in an abusive relationship simply for the sake of survival.

Radical social movements, including those such as queer movements that are thought to be focused on 'personal' issues, have taken these negative consequences seriously and set them in the light of alternative social possibilities. These creative responses provide a means of building all kinds of relationships that meet both needs and desires. Such creativity also provides a means of building connections across issues, as, for example, when health care, economics and sexuality all come together at the nexus of caring labour and so-called 'private life'.

In order to illustrate some of these possibilities, I would like to turn to a project recently co-sponsored by the community-based organization Queers for Economic Justice and the Barnard Center for Research on Women. The project, called 'Desiring Change' (Hollibaugh *et al.* 2010), is based on a series of meetings that brought together activist groups who shared a commitment to the idea that the best defence of new social possibility is the creation of a positive vision.[8] Because this vision is so expansive, it requires cross-issue organizing. In this way, the 'Desiring Change' project explores the picture that emerges when a range of issues are brought together: alternative familial forms, immigration, incarceration, homelessness, poverty, urban development, 'welfare reform', the 'war on drugs', globalization and war. The project asks questions such as the following: What are the specific connections between queer lives, queer desires and social issues as diverse as adoption, incarceration and war? The project is based on awareness that the vulnerabilities created by neo-liberal privatization are potential sites for alliance, but they can also be exploited to divide groups. Clearly articulating the relational basis for social justice can help us to build a scaffolding of connection and to resist divisions among those whose interests and values might be actively aligned. 'Desiring Change' is dedicated to making positive connections between these struggles and the lives of queer and trans people who have created non-familial systems of support.

In my own life, my utter dependence on such a network of alternative relation became apparent when my lover was injured in a bicycle accident that produced a spinal cord injury and resulting paralysis. To take just one example from that experience, over the five months that Christina was in the hospital, I was literally fed, and, perhaps more importantly, my dog was regularly fed and walked, by a network of people who were certainly not my kin and who, as a group, met none of the usual definitions of a community. Many of these people I had never met, and some of them I still have not met. Because I was at the hospital all day through the fall and winter, they would simply drop food off on the back porch of the house, and I would eat it when I came home that night. Some of them were Christina's friends and colleagues, a work community and network with which we are all familiar in the academy. And some of them might be said to be members of the oft-invoked 'gay and lesbian community', the local, lesbian, obstetrician/gynecologist, whom I had once met, and the local crew coach, whom I did not meet until much later, but who, in the course of lesbian life in a relatively small city heard of our plight, and each pitched in. Some were members of Christian and Jewish congregations to which Christina's friends and colleagues belonged, but who did not know us personally. Some were simply friends of friends or people who had faced similar crises and knew what was needed, or people with particular skills or a particular love of dogs.

In other words, Babe the dog and I were sustained, not by a community – our religious congregation or a community defined by institutions of employment – but by a network of people who came to their contributions and connections through various means. Since that moment of initial hospitalization, the network has expanded to include paid caregivers, my friends and colleagues here in New York (some fifteen of whom recently helped us move into my newly accessible apartment) and a range of disability support services and social movements. And, while these relational networks may become most visible in extreme contexts, they may also form a crucial part of how people sustain themselves in various circumstances.

Just before Christina got hurt, I had been doing a lot of work with the American Academy of Religion's committee on the status of women in the profession on the issues surrounding what's frequently called 'work–family balance'. We set up childcare at the annual meeting and looked at other policies that might make it more difficult to participate fully in the profession and maintain a family life. I had always found it a little odd that these tasks had become part of my portfolio, as I've long participated in the queer critique of 'family' as a category of social policy, but I also began to see that, in fact, this queer critique and the needs of those who saw themselves as fundamentally 'about family' – married heterosexual people, with children and/or ageing parents to care for – were much more in line than one might have first guessed. As I noted in a short essay for the committee on my experience with Christina, social supports for relations of caring and friendship are crucial, whether or not one is married. For those who are married, such supports could relieve crucial and often crushing burdens on families and individuals within families, often, particularly, women. As became all too clear in my own experience, these protections are vital when one lives in a formation that can be made to look like a family, and they are even more important when one does not. Without the primary care that US policy presumes to be provided by families, many people with spinal cord injuries who could potentially live outside institutionalized care do not. Yet, the failure to recognize these networks of relation has important consequences for social policy.

Recognizing alternative relationality also has major implications for the level at which public policy is focused. The question is whether 'families', understood broadly, are best supported by family-focused policy, or whether we need to look much more seriously at 'public' supports. Given the analysis of alternative relationality, the question of fighting poverty ought not to be so much one of whether individuals marry and then stay married or not, as it so often is in policy discussion. Instead, the question should be more whether the support networks on which individuals depend can provide for something more than basic survival. In the end, perhaps the better question is not whether to marry, so much as under what conditions marriages take place, and whether those conditions support only those who are married or whether they equally support everyone in society. The greatest difficulty with gay marriage is not whether it should or shouldn't be favoured as opposed to civil unions, but the level of focus that it receives in relation to other policies that might actually make marriages, unions or partnerships more likely to succeed, and that might, moreover, make survival likelier, regardless of how people organize their relationships. This analysis provides a vision of the networks that support non-normative lives, but not just those lives. In fact, this shift in focus would support lives across a broad spectrum of persons.

The way in which a focus on how life is sustained under non-normative conditions can illuminate social relations and policies that are useful across the spectrum of normativity is one of the things that disability rights movements mean by 'universal access' or 'universal design'. Universal access presents quite a different claim from the traditional approach to universalism. An approach organized around universal access does not begin from the normative individual as the site from which to determine that upon which everyone can agree. Universal access presumes that, by looking to those who are excluded by this traditional approach, we can find ways to change social spaces, not just for purposes of inclusion, but also so as to improve life possibilities more generally.

The difference between these two methods of approaching broader inclusion can be seen by comparing kerb cuts in New York City and those in downtown New Haven, Connecticut. As all New Yorkers know, the kerb cuts in the city are special areas cut into the centre of each side of any given corner to make it possible to wheel across the street and back up onto the sidewalk (although the actual effectiveness and accessibility of the cuts vary widely). Although absolutely crucial for getting around the city in a wheelchair, they are also a royal pain. First of all, most of the walking people also walk through the kerb cuts, making it difficult for those who must use them. Why do people take this path? Because it's actually easier than stepping down off the kerb and back up. And this ease is one of the main points that disability activists make – our built environment is not particularly easy or healthful for those who understand themselves as able-bodied, which means that they often use the spaces and mechanisms created for people with disabilities, such as kerb cuts and ramps. The New York City kerb cuts also tend to pool water, and in the winter ice, right below the special cut outs. In parts of New Haven, by contrast, the entire kerb is gently sloped around the corner, so that a wheelchair user and a walking person can both traverse the entire corner. There is no specially marked zone of inclusion and no specially produced pool of water to curse during times of rain and snow. Rather than thinking of disability as the exception for which special provisions are made, universal access suggests that a universally inclusive built environment is better for all, or at least for more, people.

Universal access is a powerful metaphor for organizing, and it is methodologically suggestive. Taking the approach of universal access, the idea of the universal would have to be built up from multiple, and necessarily different, starting points, rather than built out from a singular normative point. Applying Mol's concept of a 'body multiple' to the social body can help with conceptualization of social policy that begins from different starting points, but works to produce connected possibilities for justice. In particular, universal access suggests that taking non-normative lives seriously as an already central part of social relations would open possibilities for making the lives of those who live closer to the mythical norm better as well.

However, justice does not require only that we attend to those needs that can, through this attention, improve the lives of others. There are cases where attention to non-normative lives will require accommodation that does not enrich the lives of everyone else, and this accommodation, along with changes for universal accessibility, is part of the work of justice. Given that we are all dependent in at least some ways, and, I would suggest, queer in at least some ways (as none of us actually meets the mythical norm in all respects), perhaps we should look to social cooperation as not just pointing to the ends of justice, but as the very condition of our existence. It is about the possibility of developing a world in which the rich and varied dependencies that make life possible can be sustained.

On this reading, the question is not whether economic security or economic justice is the more accurate terminology, as in my original question. The question is whether we can expand the idea of either security or justice well beyond economics and, in fact, well beyond their traditional meanings. If we have any hope of resisting the implication of these terms in assemblages that connect them to neo-liberalism and its unjust effects, then we must also find ways of articulating them into assemblages that support and sustain alternative possibilities: relationships that confound the premises of the divisions between public and private, normative and not. In other words, an expanded justice is the product of caring queerly.

Notes

1   The definition of neo-liberalism is widely debated. See, e.g., the debate in *Social Anthropology* engendered by Loïc Wacquant's (2012) article on the anthropology of 'actually existing neoliberalism' and responses to it in the following issues of the journal. For a range of critical definitions, see Bernstein and Jakobsen (2013).

2   'We are the 99%' became the slogan of the 'Occupy Wall Street' movement in autumn 2011, used in both press coverage (Seltzer 2011) about the movement and by activists online, particularly through the Tumblr site, 'We Are the 99%': wearethe99 percent.tumblr.com

3   *Shelby County v Holder* 133 SCt 2612 (2013). For an in-depth reading of this decision and its relation to decisions also released the week of 24 June 2013 on affirmative action (*Fisher v University of Texas, Austin* 133 SCt 2411 (2013)) and same-sex marriage (*United States v Windsor* 133 SCt 2675 (2013); *Hollingsworth v Perry* 133 SCt 2652 (2013)), see Jakobsen (forthcoming).

4   On the relation between recognition and redistribution, see Fraser and Honneth (2004).

5   The literature on the public/private split and on the feminist critique of that split is voluminous, stretching back to now feminist classics such as Elshtain (1981), who traces the public/private split back to Aristotle; Pateman (1988), who traces it through the liberal contract theories of the Enlightenment; and Duggan (2003), who connects the public/private split in liberalism to the development of neo-liberalism.

6   Harvey (2007: 3) identifies 'deregulation, privatization, and the withdrawal of the
    state from many areas of social provision' as key features of neo-liberalism.
7   381 US 479 (1965).
8   For copies of the report and all of the background on the project, go to:
    http://bcrw.barnard.edu/publications/desiring-change/. Much of the conceptual basis
    for the project can be found in Queers for Economic Justice's articulation of 'A New
    Queer Agenda' (DeFilippis *et al.* 2012).

References

Alexander, M. (2012) *The New Jim Crow: Mass Incarceration in the Age of Colorblindness*,
    New York: The New Press.
Alvarez, S.E. (1999) 'The Latin American feminist NGO "boom"', *International Feminist
    Journal of Politics*, 1(2): 181–209.
Bernstein, E. and Jakobsen, J.R. (eds) (2013) 'Gender justice and neoliberal transfor-
    mations', *Scholar & Feminist Online*, 11(1). Online. Available at: sfonline.barnard.edu
    (accessed 5 August 2013).
Boris, E. and Klein, J. (2012) *Caring for America: Home Health Workers in the Shadow of the
    Welfare State*, New York: Oxford.
Chappell, M. (2010) *The War on Welfare: Family, Poverty, and Politics in Modern America*,
    Philadelphia: University of Pennsylvania Press.
Chetty, R., Hendren, N., Kline, P. and Saez, E. (2013) 'The economic impacts of tax
    expenditures: Evidence from spatial variation across the United States', revised draft
    July 2013, *Statistics of Income White Paper*, The Equality of Opportunity Project. Online.
    Available at: http://obs.rc.fas.harvard.edu/chetty/tax_expenditure_soi_whitepaper.pdf
    (accessed 5 August 2013).
Crenshaw, K., Gotanda, N., Peller, G. and Thomas, K. (eds) (1996) *Critical Race Theory:
    The Key Writings that Formed the Movement*, New York: New Press.
DeFilippis, J.N., Duggan, L., Farrow, K. and Kim, R. (eds) (2012) 'A new queer agenda
    (Special issue)', *Scholar & Feminist Online*, 10(1–2). Online. Available at:
    http://sfonline.barnard.edu/a-new-queer-agenda/ (accessed 5 August 2013).
Dolnick, S. (2012) 'Unlocked: Inside New Jersey's halfway houses', *The New York Times*,
    17–19 June. Online. Available at: www.nytimes.com/2012/06/17/nyregion/in-new-
    jersey-halfway-houses-escapees-stream-out-as-a-penal-business-thrives.html (accessed 5
    August 2013).
Duggan, L. (2003) *The Twilight of Equality? Neoliberalism, Cultural Politics, and the Attack
    on Democracy*, Boston: Beacon Press.
Edsall, T. (2013) 'Now what, liberalism?', *The New York Times*, 16 January. Online.
    Available at: http://opinionator.blogs.nytimes.com/2013/01/16/now-what-liberalism/?
    hp (accessed 5 August 2013).
Elshtain, J.B. (1981) *Public Man, Private Woman: Women in Social and Political Thought*,
    Princeton, NJ: Princeton University Press.
Fiol-Matta, L. (2002) *A Queer Mother for the Nation: The State and Gabriel Mistral*,
    Minneapolis: University of Minnesota Press.
Fitzgerald, M. (2006) *Habits of Compassion: Irish Catholic Nuns and the Origins of New York's
    Welfare System, 1895–1920*, Champagne-Urbana: University of Illinois Press.
Fraser, N. and Honneth, A. (2004) *Redistribution or Recognition: A Political–Philosophical
    Exchange*, London: Verso.

Halley, J., Kotiswaran, P., Thomas, C. and Shamir, H. (2006) 'From the international to the local in feminist legal responses to rape, prostitution/sex work, and sex trafficking: Four studies in contemporary governance feminism', *Harvard Journal of Law and Gender*, 29(2): 335–423.

Harding, S.F. (2001) *The Book of Jerry Falwell: Fundamentalist Language and Politics*, Princeton, NJ: Princeton University Press.

Harvey, D. (2003) *The New Imperialism*, Oxford: Oxford University Press.

—— (2007) *A Brief History of Neoliberalism*, Oxford: Oxford University Press.

Ho, J. (2008) 'Is global governance bad for East Asian queers?', *GLQ: A Journal of Lesbian and Gay Studies*, 14(4): 457–79.

Hollibaugh, A., Jakobsen, J. and Sameh, C. (2010) 'Desiring change', *New Feminist Solutions*, 5. Online. Available at: http://bcrw.barnard.edu/publications/desiring-change/ (accessed 5 August 2013).

INCITE! Women of Color Against Violence (ed.) (2007) *The Revolution Will Not Be Funded: Beyond the Non-Profit Industrial Complex*, Cambridge, MA: South End Press.

Jakobsen, J.R. (2011) 'Perverse justice', *GLQ: A Journal of Lesbian and Gay Studies*, 18(1): 19–28.

—— (forthcoming) 'Visions of justice: New economies and solidarities', *Journal of the European Society of Women in Theological Reflection*.

Jantti, M., Røed, K., Naylor, R., Björklund, A., Bratsberg, B., Raaum, O., Österbacka, E. and Eriksson, T. (2006) *American Exceptionalism in a New Light: A Comparison of Intergenerational Earnings Mobility in the Nordic Countries, the United Kingdom and the United States*, IZA Discussion Paper Series, Discussion Paper No. 1938. Institute for the Study of Labor, Bonn, Germany. Online. Available at: http://ftp.iza.org/dp1938.pdf (accessed 5 August 2013).

Joseph, M. (2002) *Against the Romance of Community*, Minneapolis: University of Minnesota.

Klein, N. (2007) *The Shock Doctrine: The Rise of Disaster Capitalism*, New York: Henry Holt.

Lee, C.K. and Kofman, Y. (2012) 'The politics of precarity: Views beyond the United States', *Work and Occupations*, 39(4): 388–408.

Luxemburg, R. (1964) *The Accumulation of Capital*, New York: Monthly Review Press.

Marx, K. (1976) *Capital: Volume 1: A Critique of Political Economy*, trans. B. Fowkes, London: Penguin.

Mol, A. (2003) *The Body Multiple: Ontology in Medical Practice*, Durham, NC: Duke University Press.

Nadasen, P. and Williams, T. (2010) 'Valuing domestic work', *New Feminist Solutions*, 5. Online. Available at: http://bcrw.barnard.edu/publications/nfs-valuing-domestic-work/ (accessed 5 August 2013).

Pateman, C. (1988) *The Sexual Contract*, Stanford, CA: Stanford University Press.

Puar, J. (2007) *Terrorist Assemblages: Homonationalism in Queer Times*, Durham, NC: Duke University Press.

Rich, M. and Hurdle, J. (2013) 'Rational decisions and heartbreak on school closings', *The New York Times*, 8 March. Online. Available at: www.nytimes.com/2013/03/09/education/rational-decisions-and-heartbreak-on-school-closings.html?pagewanted=all (accessed 5 August 2013).

Sassen, S. (1999) *Globalization and Its Discontents: Essays on the New Mobility of People and Money*, New York: New Press.

—— (2010) 'A savage sorting of winners and losers: Contemporary versions of primitive accumulation', *Globalizations*, 7(1, 2): 23–50.

Seltzer, B. (2011) 'Camps are cleared, but "99%" still occupies lexicon', *The New York Times*, 30 November. Online. Available at: www.nytimes.com/2011/12/01/us/we-are-the-99-percent-joins-the-cultural-and-political-lexicon.html (accessed 5 August 2013).

Skocpol, T. (1992) *Protecting Soldiers and Mothers: The Political Origins of Social Policy in the United States*, Cambridge, MA: Harvard University Press.

Taylor, M. (2006) *From Pinochet to the 'Third Way': Neoliberalism and Social Transformation in Chile*, London: Pluto Press.

Wacquant, L. (2012) 'Three steps to a historical anthropology of actually existing neoliberalism', *Social Anthropology*, 20(1): 66–79.

Part II

States' reach

Chapter 6

Cameos from the margins of conjugality

Kim Brooks

Every discipline of academic study has something to say about the family: scientists, philosophers, social scientists, legal scholars, linguists, humanities scholars, ethicists, theologians, economists, public 'policy wonks', feminist theorists. We prod at the contours of the institution of the family; create taxonomies of alternative models of family; unfold histories of the evolution of family relationships in different regions of the world, over different periods, and in different social and economic classes; theorize the relationships of power between members of families; explicate the explicit and implicit rules of family life; identify stages in family development; delineate distinct language practices that follow from our understandings of family; and so on. All of this work requires that we identify something called the family (whether human or non-human) and then go to the work of observing its behaviour in some way (whether through direct study or through study by some indirect means, for example, by reviewing newspaper clippings or digging up pots).

One of the most significant socio-legal documents that prod at the contours of adult personal relationships is the 2001 Law Commission of Canada report, *Beyond Conjugality: Recognizing and Supporting Close Personal Adult Relationships*. That report speculated, and in some cases verified, that adult personal relationships were more diverse than reflected in our network of laws. The Commission sought, in the context of specific legal regimes (e.g., tax law, bankruptcy law, labour law), to identify the objectives of the legal regime, to determine whether the relationships invoked in that area of law mattered, to discern whether individuals could be relied upon to self-identify as being within those particular relationships, and, if self-designation wasn't possible, to consider whether there was a more sensible way to use the relationships. The report was a watershed in the development of thinking about the role of adult personal relationships in Canada and, to a lesser extent, in the United States. The timing of the release of the report is ideal, given the dual questions – one empirical and one analytical – asked in this book: How have reforms since 2000, designed to enhance the equality of families, played out, and how have they changed conduct? What problems, unintended consequences and injustices have resulted from equality-driven reforms, both for their intended beneficiaries and for others (see Leckey, in this volume)?

Beyond Conjugality reframed the way we think about the function of relationships in legal regulation, but it was forced to do so in the absence of a sense of the texture of those underlying relationships themselves. The report relied on a detailed review of the census data to present a picture of the diversity of adult personal relationships, although those data lack the rich texture of the kinds of empirical work undertaken by scholars who research the evolving nature of close personal relationships in disciplines outside law. As the report asserts, 'We know little about the characteristics of non-conjugal relationships between unrelated persons' (Law Commission of Canada 2001: 5).

This chapter uses the changes to the legislation in Canada's Income Tax Act,[1] implemented by the Modernization of Benefits and Obligations Act,[2] and the subsequent cases on the meaning of 'common-law partner' or unmarried spouse as a method of deriving evidence about the texture of the lives lived by adults in personal relationships. In this chapter, I refer to adults as having proximate relationships, a phrase I mean to indicate a relationship that might be intimate in a variety of ways, and that might, given the statutory definition of common-law partner, be thought to be at the margins of conjugality. From that evidence, I seek to contribute to the social history of the margins of conjugal relationships between adult members in a post-legal-equality world in Canada. I step off from the chapters in this book undertaken by Claire Young and, to a lesser extent, Rosie Harding. Professor Young's work provides a detailed and thoughtful review of the implications of the design of the Income Tax Act for lesbians and gay men, comparing the benefits and obligations of the legislative (and case law) changes between 1994 and 2013. She then draws some empirical and normative conclusions about the equality-shifting nature of those changes.

Here, I look at the same context as that described in Young's chapter, but attempt an entirely different intellectual exercise, one that hopefully contributes to the *Beyond Conjugality* project. In particular, this chapter is inspired by the notion that you can see something by looking at it directly, or you can study it through the lens of something else. The legislative changes in 2000 provide an opportunity to learn something about what post-legal-equality proximate adult relationships look like in Canada. What might be seen is far from a thorough view; instead, it is a view of proximate adult relationships through the refraction of Canada's federal income tax legislation and its judicial interpretation. It's a glimpse in a mirror that allows you to see an image in another mirror, which reflects the 'real thing' of the relationships people have when they reside at the legal margins of conjugality.

I focus in particular on what we might learn about relationships between cohabiting adults at the margins of conjugality because that is what has most squarely been the focus of the post-legal-equality project: spouses. In other words, the legislative changes in Canada, designed to reflect the push for equal treatment initiated primarily by same-sex couples and non-married, opposite-sex couples, have been dominated by adult relationship recognition claims. Less academic and advocacy time has been spent on the relationship status of adults with children who do (or do not) become the subject of the legal regulation of the family or on other non-conjugal adult relationships, although chapters in this collection centre those enquiries. To be perfectly clear, the project of this chapter is not to be prescriptive about how Canada's tax legislation should be changed. Rather, it is to use changes to Canada's tax legislation as a prism to see something about what proximate adult relationships in Canada at the margins of conjugality look like.

Spouses under the Income Tax Act

Married opposite-sex partners have always been considered spouses under Canada's Income Tax Act.[3] Opposite-sex common-law couples became spouses for tax purposes in 1993, when the definition of spouse was amended to include a person of the opposite sex who cohabited with the taxpayer in a conjugal relationship throughout a 12-month period, or who was the parent of a child of whom the taxpayer was a parent.[4] In 2000, the Parliament of Canada passed the Modernization of Benefits and Obligations Act. That legislation changed the definition of spouse in a long list of federal statutes, including the Income Tax Act. References in the Act to 'spouse' became references to 'spouse or common-law partner', and references to 'marriage' became references to 'marriage or common-law partnership'. In 2005, the Civil Marriage Act legalized same-sex marriage in Canada, with the consequence that married same-sex couples (like opposite-sex married couples) do not need to rely on the definition of common-law partner in the Income Tax Act for treatment as spouses; they simply rely on their marital status.

The addition of the common-law partner definition to the Income Tax Act enables an exploration of the parameters of which individuals consider themselves to be spouses (at least for purposes of the Income Tax Act).[5] As noted above, the definition requires that the taxpayer cohabit with the person in a conjugal relationship and have cohabited with that person for a continuous period of at least one year, or be the parent of a child of the taxpayer.

Tax legislation does not define what it is to 'cohabit in a conjugal relationship'. Case law informs this determination. The courts and the Canada Revenue Agency have adopted the articulation of what constitutes cohabiting in a conjugal relationship from the 1999 Supreme Court of Canada decision in *M v H*[6] and from the 1980 Ontario District Court judgment in *Molodowich v Penittinen*.[7] Determining whether parties cohabit in a conjugal relationship requires examining whether the parties lived in the same place, whether they slept together, whether anyone else occupied the accommodation, whether they had sexual relations, whether they maintained an attitude of fidelity, whether they communicated about personal things, whether they ate together, whether they assisted each other in illness, whether they bought each other gifts for special occasions, whether they prepared meals, washed clothes, shopped, maintained the house or did other domestic chores for each other, and whether they participated together in community activities. The courts also look at evidence of their feelings towards each other, the attitudes of their families, the attitude of the community to them as a couple, whether there were financial arrangements for the provision of necessities between them, how they acquired and owned property, and any other special arrangements. In other words, the Tax Court and Federal Court of Appeal, alongside the Canada Revenue Agency, apply a broad facts-and-circumstances test. The advantage of this approach, given this project, is that the cases provide a good deal of description about what relationships at the margins of conjugality look like in Canada.

Seventeen cameos: adults in relationships at the margins of conjugality

In attempting to discern what adult relationships at the margins of conjugality look like, I examined the tax cases where the courts have been compelled to weigh in on whether a particular arrangement is or is not a spousal one (for tax purposes). I focused on the cases decided after 2000, on the assumption that 2000 was the marker (almost, at least) of a post-legal-equality world. I chose only informal procedure cases, for reasons explained below, and I have provided details about a maximum of two cases for each year. Although there are some differences in treatment between married and unmarried spouses that remain, and same-sex couples could not marry in every province until 2005, the inclusion of same-sex couples in marriage does not appear to have had any effect on the evolution of the tax case law in the post-legal-equality period.

The records presented in the tax decisions I reviewed are wildly incomplete, of course, given that they are cases where the judge or judges have already reduced the available facts to a list that generally focuses on the kinds of factors identified in *Molodowich*. Nevertheless, a portrait of some adults in relationships at the margins of conjugality might be drawn from these facts. The tax context is particularly rich, given that, in fourteen of the seventeen decisions since 2000, the taxpayer was self-represented, and so was likely freer to describe his or her relationship in his or her own words to the judge. All of the cases reviewed in this chapter are decided under the informal procedure process, so that they have no precedential value, which presumably liberates somewhat the judges who render decisions in them. Additionally, in informal procedure cases, the rules of evidence are relaxed: the Tax Court is not bound by the technical rules of evidence, and appeals are to be dealt with as informally and expeditiously as fairness permits.[8] What follows is a presentation of the facts of these seventeen cases. For the chapter's purposes, whether or not the court decided the two parties to have been spouses is unimportant. The courts' holdings are, however, available in the notes. Meet the people at the margins of conjugality in tax law.

Ms Sykes and Mr Barnett (2000)[9]

Ms Sykes and Mr Barnett were both recently separated from previous partners. Ms Sykes owned a house in Sidney, British Columbia, and Mr Barnet contributed to the mortgage payments and utility costs in exchange for an entitlement to 50 per cent of the increase in equity in the period for which the arrangement stayed in place. Mr Barnett lived about 90 per cent of the time in hotels in Vancouver, where he was employed. They had separate telephones and Internet connections; they did not list each other in their employment benefits plans or pension plans. They had a joint account at the credit union and they appear to have shared some food costs. Each adult had some shares (indirect in the case of Mr Barnett) in a company owned by Ms Sykes' mother. They had sex, but perhaps not very often.[10] They did not take holidays together. They both had children from former relationships. Mr Barnett provided no emotional or financial support for Ms Sykes' daughter. Ms Sykes represented herself.

Ms Rangwala and Mr Rangwala (2000)[11]

Ms Rangwala and Mr Rangwala were married for almost twenty years when they separated. After they separated (and then divorced), they continued to live together in the same house, although in separate parts of the house. Ms Rangwala made some small contributions to household expenses, but otherwise did not contribute to the cost of maintaining the home. Ms Rangwala told her employer that she and Mr Rangwala were separated and changed the designation of beneficiary on her retirement account to name their son. They kept their food in separately labelled containers in the fridge and did not perform any domestic services for each other. When Ms Rangwala had surgery, her brother came to assist her. She did not attend to Mr Rangwala if he fell ill. There was no communication between Mr and Ms Rangwala, and, when they went to parties, they went to and from the party separately and did not speak to each other while at the event.

Ms Sigouin and Mr Déragon (2001)[12]

Ms Sigouin and Mr Déragon were parents of a child. Ms Sigouin worked as an administrative assistant, and she and Mr Déragon lived together in Blainville, Quebec. They wanted to live separately, but were unable to because of Mr Déragon's precarious financial position. Mr Déragon converted the family room into a place where he could work and sleep. He paid Ms Sigouin a monthly amount to cover expenses. Ultimately, Mr Déragon declared bankruptcy and was unable to rent accommodation or borrow money. The sexual relationship ceased. They severed links with each other's friends. They cooked separately. Each adult had his or her own car, social life and recreational activities.

Ms Trudel and Mr Gagné (2001)[13]

Ms Trudel separated from her husband in 1988 and retained custody of her three children. She had a child with leukaemia, and a babysitter helped her care for her sick child. Ms Trudel met Mr Gagné, who used the same babysitter for one of his two children. Ms Trudel had to take two years' sick leave from work to care for her son. She developed a relationship with Mr Gagné that, she later stated, confused love and friendship. In 1992, Ms Trudel moved in with Mr Gagné in Boucherville. The couple differed on a number of aspects of family life, including how to discipline the children, and Ms Trudel was unimpressed with Mr Gagné's irregular attachment to the workforce. Mr Gagné moved to Ste-Foy for work, and Ms Trudel continued to live in his house with her children; Mr Gagné put the house up for sale. Ms Trudel had engaged in an intimate relationship with a friend in Quebec City and planned to move to live with him in the future. When Mr Gagné lost his job in Ste-Foy, he returned to Boucherville and moved back into the house. Ms Trudel moved into another bedroom. She paid rent and her share of household expenses (including a house cleaner, electricity, telephone and cable). They bought a washer and dryer together. She took care of the children and did the grocery shopping for herself and the children. She kept track of the amount Mr Gagné owed each month for meals that he consumed with his children. They took the occasional trip together or as a family. They went out socially together and referred to themselves as housemates. They had sex about once a year, often after a birthday dinner or other special occasion. Ms Trudel represented herself.

Ms Uwasomba and Mr Uwasomba (2002)[14]

Ms Uwasomba, a night-shift health worker, who insisted at trial on being called Victoria, and Mr Uwasomba, a mechanic, were granted a divorce in 1996. They had six children. After the divorce, the adults continued to live together in Brampton in the family residence, owned by Mr Uwasomba, who paid the expenses of the house. They shared other expenses and parental responsibilities. Mr Uwasomba moved into the basement, for which he had the only key. Mr Uwasomba prepared meals in the kitchen, but had his own refrigerator. Ms Uwasomba made meals for herself and the children. They had the same arrangements for laundry and cleaning as they did for meal preparation. The parties did not have sex with each other; Mr Uwasomba had other sexual relationships. The parties quarrelled about the children and generally did not speak to each other. Although they each continued to buy gifts for the children, they did not buy gifts for each other. They attended separate churches. They had separate social lives and, when they attended the same social gathering, they did not do so together. Ms Uwasomba was listed as Mr Uwasomba's spouse in the beneficiary designations for his retirement account and life insurance plan. They had their own bank accounts and credit cards. They jointly appealed the Canada Revenue Agency's assessment, and they represented themselves.

Ms Henry and Mr Dean (2002)[15]

Ms Henry moved to Toronto from Jamaica with her ten-year-old in 1993, to live with her sister. When the arrangements with her sister were no longer workable in 1994, she moved into the apartment of a friend and paid a modest amount of rent. When her friend was deported, Ms Henry needed to find another living arrangement. She met Mr Dean on a bus and agreed to share accommodation with him. She moved into his apartment in 1995, paying half the rent. The two adults had a child the following year. Ms Henry described their arrangement as a rent-sharing arrangement and nothing more. For some time, they had a two-bedroom apartment and, when they did, they slept in the same room. When they moved to a three-bedroom apartment, Ms Henry shared a room with her daughter. Sex was irregular and, generally, only when Mr Dean forced Ms Henry. Mr Dean had other sexual partners, but they did not come to the apartment. Ms Henry prepared meals, which Mr Dean ate in his room. In exceptional cases, Mr Dean prepared a meal because his children from a previous marriage were over for dinner. Mr Dean gave Ms Henry one Christmas present in 1995, but no gifts were exchanged after that. The adults each did their own laundry; Ms Henry did the children's laundry. Ms Henry purchased the groceries, except for the occasional chicken or beef purchased by Mr Dean. Ms Henry or her son took care of maintenance issues in the apartment. Ms Henry and Mr Dean did not take any trips together and they did not socialize together. Ms Henry went to church without Mr Dean. Ms Henry paid for the food, clothes, furniture and entertainment. She also paid the utility bills. Eventually, Ms Henry forced Mr Dean to leave. She represented herself.

Ms Richard and Mr Dumont (2003)[16]

Ms Richard and Mr Dumont lived together in Hull. She had a son from a previous relationship, and they had a son together. They had a conjugal relationship until 1999. They would have ended their living arrangements after that; however, Ms Richard's older child started to have issues at school and committed several minor offences. As a result, Ms Richard and Mr

Dumont agreed that it would be best for the son if they continued to live together in a larger home, which they acquired jointly in 2000. In the new home, each child had his own room, and Mr Dumont had a room. The adults shared the expenses of living in the home. Ms Richard might have slept on a sofabed in the basement, or perhaps she shared a room with Mr Dumont. She prepared the meals and ate with her children. Mr Dumont cooked his own food and ate separately. If they shared food, they calculated with precision what one of them owed to the other. There was conflicting evidence about who did the laundry and cleaning. Ms Richard and Mr Dumont socialized together periodically, but ceased visiting each other's families. They did not have sex after 1999. After 2002, Ms Richard changed the beneficiary designation on her insurance to her children. Ms Richard remained as Mr Dumont's beneficiary. Ms Richard was covered by Mr Dumont's dental and medical coverage. Mr Dumont and Ms Richard went to some activities together with the younger child; for example, they attended a Scouts event. Ms Richard alleged that she had a new boyfriend, and that Mr Dumont was often away on weekends. Ms Richard represented herself.

Mr Bellavance and Ms Gendron (2003)[17]

The living arrangements between Mr Bellavance and Ms Gendron changed over time. In 1995 and 1996, the two lived together in Matane, Quebec; then, Mr Bellavance moved to a new address, and Ms Gendron joined him at that address in 1999. They filed as spouses in 1998 and as single in 1999. Apparently, Ms Gendron became ill in 1999, and that ended their spousal relationship. For the period in issue (2000–2), Ms Gendron looked after Mr Bellavance's house while he was at work. She rented a room in the house he owned and paid him $100 a month for rent and electricity. Ms Gendron went to live with her daughter when Mr Bellavance was away, because she was unable to be alone (presumably because of her illness). Mr Bellavance and Ms Gendron's income tax returns were prepared by the same firm. Mr Bellavance reported that they had not had sex since January 2000. Each person did his or her own laundry, shopping, housework and meal preparation. Ms Gendron owned her own car. Mr Bellavance had little contact with Ms Gendron's family. He purchased the washer and dryer without assistance from her. Ms Gendron's income was higher. Mr Bellavance represented himself at the court hearing.

Ms Hamel and Mr Crépeault (2004)[18]

Ms Hamel and Mr Crépeault purchased a piece of land together in Boischâtel, Quebec. (Throughout the decision, Judge Tardif refers to the two as friends, which is the language Ms Hamel sometimes used in describing the relationship.) Mr Crépeault built a house on the land as the prime contractor, without charging Ms Hamel for his services. Ms Hamel and her two children moved into the house on its completion. Mr Crépeault and Ms Hamel planned to live together eventually (and did move into the house together a couple of years later), but did not want to live together in the period under consideration. The adults each had children from previous relationships, and they consulted professional counsellors in the period in issue to support the integration of their children into a blended family. Ms Hamel and Mr Crépeault were in an exclusive relationship during that time. Ms Hamel represented herself.

Ms Chicheluk and Mr Oree (2005)[19]

Ms Chicheluk separated from Mr Chicheluk, and the post-separation relationship was massively disruptive: Mr Chicheluk harassed Ms Chicheluk with late-night phone calls, communicated with her employer and parents, and damaged her car. She changed the locks on the door to her house in Winnipeg four times, and the police intervened on several occasions. She got a restraining order. They went to court to deal with child custody and support issues, multiple times. When Ms Chicheluk started a relationship with Mr Oree, the abuse by Mr Chicheluk escalated. She sought counselling. Mr Oree moved in with Ms Chicheluk, but would regularly move out of the home in difficult periods when Mr Chicheluk's behaviour worsened. For example, in 2000, they lived apart three times: from the end of March until the middle of April, from May to the end of July, and for approximately ninety days from the middle of October until December. Ms Chicheluk supported herself and her two children throughout this period. She owned her residence and vehicle and paid all of her own expenses. She did all of the cleaning, cooking, laundry and shopping. He did not contribute to the care of the children or the daily decisions. He did maintain the car, lawn and home and do snow removal when he was living in the house. Ms Chicheluk represented herself.

Ms Savory and Mr Lamy (2008)[20]

Ms Savory had a restraining order against Mr Lamy, a man with whom she had two children. They lived together for a short time (several months) in Halifax, but Ms Savory was often not sure where Mr Lamy was for extended periods and would forward his mail to his mother. She described their relationship as on-again-off-again. Between 2001 and 2004, Ms Savory and Mr Lamy lived in the same apartment unit. However, there was some evidence that Mr Lamy also lived in other places between 2001 and 2004. They had a sexual relationship during this period. Ms Savory was committed to Mr Lamy, in the sense that, during this time, she did not see anyone else on a consistent basis. From September 2004 to 25 February 2005, they definitely lived in the same apartment, and Mr Lamy definitely moved out at the end of that period. Mr Lamy took almost no part in household or family responsibilities. He did not help with chores. They never exchanged gifts. When Ms Savory was ill, Mr Lamy did not care for her or the children. They did not eat together, and daily communication was not a characteristic of the relationship. Their friends and family considered them to be a couple, and Ms Savory communicated with Mr Lamy's mother on a regular basis. Ms Savory, a cook in a residential institution, was the primary income earner and provided for the children. Mr Lamy did not contribute towards food, clothing or shelter, but he did have some contact with the children. Custody of the children for the year following the 2005 separation fluctuated between the two adults, and, after a year or so, custody for both children was granted to Ms Savory. She represented herself.

Ms DeRepentigny and Mr Ravimi (2008)[21]

Ms DeRepentigny had four children as a result of a previous relationship and had custody of them. She began living with Mr Ravimi in Salaberry-de-Valleyfield in February 1999, and they married in 2000. Mr Ravimi was Israeli in origin, and Ms DeRepentigny served as his Canadian sponsor. They had a daughter. Mr Ravimi's brother came to live with them in July 2002, and Mr Ravimi became increasingly distant after his brother's arrival. Ms DeRepentigny could only reach Mr Ravimi on his mobile phone. Mr Ravimi stopped contributing to expenses. Ms DeRepentigny took care of the medical appointments for the children, along with the decisions about their education. She paid all of the household maintenance expenses and did the laundry. Mr Ravimi did the cooking. They separated in 2005, and Ms DeRepentigny required Mr Ravimi to take his brother and move out. They did not formally divorce, because Ms DeRepentigny did not want to disrupt Mr Ravimi's immigration application. Mr Ravimi continued to visit his daughter at Ms DeRepentigny's house after they were separated, and, when he visited, he and Ms DeRepentigny maintained their sexual relationship. Mr Ravimi had a sexual relationship with another woman in the post-separation period. Ms DeRepentigny stopped seeing Mr Ravimi's relatives and had his mail held for him at the post office. They continued to have a joint bank account, because Ms DeRepentigny had signed for his car and was unable to close the account. Ms DeRepentigny represented herself.

Ms Hendricken and Mr Curran (2008)[22]

Ms Hendricken and Mr Curran lived together for over twenty years and had four children. They had a sexual relationship and continued that relationship, although they had sex only occasionally throughout the period in question. They did not have sexual relationships with anyone else. The two adults owned three parcels of land as joint tenants. The house where they lived was registered in Mr Curran's name. Mr Curran operated a golf course and restaurant; Ms Hendricken operated a daycare, worked as a forest technician and cooked at the restaurant. He looked after the house and its maintenance and paid the electricity and heating bills. She purchased the groceries and clothing for the children. He generally ate at the restaurant and slept in his own bedroom in the house, with his door looked. They had separate bank accounts and their own vehicles. They went to most events separately; they attended wakes together. Ms Hendricken spent Christmas with her family. Mr Curran spent Christmas with his sister. One of their children had Down's syndrome, alongside hearing loss and a heart condition. Ms Hendricken took the child to medical appointments, and, if she was unavailable, Ms Hendricken's mother attended in her place. Mr Curran rarely provided support when any child required medical attention or was ill. Ms Hendricken attended school meetings alone. The two adults had separate phone listings and did not exchange any gifts. They characterized their relationship as one of friendship, respect and fidelity.

Ms Robertson and Mr Bear (2009)[23]

Ms Robertson lived in Saskatoon. She and Mr Bear lived together in 2001 and separated on 31 May 2002. Ms Robertson moved in with her cousin for three or four months and then with her mother for approximately six months. Ms Robertson and Mr Bear reconciled in 2003 and moved back in together. They lived together for about a month, and then Mr Bear moved out again; Ms Robertson had her first child after Mr Bear moved out. Ms Robertson and Mr Bear reconciled again in 2004 and lived together for three weeks, during which time Ms Robertson became pregnant with their second child. At the time, Ms Robertson was working at a gas station. After the birth of her second child, Ms Robertson entered into a nurse training programme. Following the 2004 separation, Ms Robertson did not know Mr Bear's contact information or address. Mr Bear occasionally used Ms Robertson's address as his own, which she knew because she had been contacted by the police, who were looking for him. Ms Robertson represented herself.

Ms Kateb and Mr Leblanc (2009)[24]

Ms Kateb had custody of her two children from a previous marriage. The separation from her husband was acrimonious, and Ms Kateb feared for her safety, calling the police on several occasions between 1998 and 2001. Ms Kateb met Mr Leblanc at his workplace in 2002 or 2003. For a time, Mr Leblanc would come to Ms Kateb's house to facilitate the access visits of Ms Kateb's former husband. Mr Leblanc gradually moved into Ms Kateb's basement. He initially stayed there for only a few weeks and then went to live with his parents, but, in March 2003, he eventually moved in. Ms Kateb and Mr Leblanc agreed that he would pay the cost of basement renovation and undertake lawn maintenance and snow removal. In 2004, Ms Kateb had the opportunity to sell her house and did so, in order to move to a different neighbourhood and to build a house there. She had insufficient financial capital to borrow money from the bank to support the home construction and land acquisition, and so Ms Kateb and Mr Leblanc agreed to buy the vacant lot as co-owners. They were unable to come up with the funds required to build the house, and so they sold the lot. In December 2004, they purchased a property in Blainville, Quebec, as co-owners. They signed an agreement allowing Ms Kateb the return of her principal contribution if the house was sold and committing them to contribute equally to maintaining and repairing the property. Each of the adults and each of the children had their own bedroom in the home. Ms Kateb and Mr Leblanc had separate washrooms. Ms Kateb did not shop for Mr Leblanc, nor did she prepare meals for him. Her father is the beneficiary of her life insurance policy; she kept her own bank accounts. The children consider Mr Leblanc to be Ms Kateb's friend. On most of the children's school forms, Ms Kateb is identified as the emergency contact, although, on one form, Mr Leblanc was identified as an emergency contact and spouse. Mr Leblanc sometimes drove the children places. Mr Leblanc is the only insured driver on his car, he has individual drug insurance and he maintains his own bank account. The adults represented themselves in the matter before the court.

Ms Perron and Mr Jacob (2010)[25]

Ms Perron was a secretary and bookkeeper. She and Mr Jacob lived together in a co-owned home in Saint-Eustache. They knew each other for about twenty years and lived together for ten. Ms Perron had a child from a previous relationship who lived with them. Although they separated, they decided to continue to live together to reduce the stress of separation. Mr Jacob suffered from depression, and they thought that they lacked financial stability. After separating, Ms Perron relocated her bedroom to the basement. There were no shared household tasks: the adults prepared their own meals and did their own laundry. They split household maintenance and other expenses. From time to time, Ms Perron lent her car to Mr Jacob. They occasionally had a meal together. Ms Perron took care of her daughter's education and sports engagements. They socialized separately and did not have a sexual relationship following the separation. They had a joint bank account for expenses. Ms Perron represented herself.

Ms Astley and Mr Overton (2012)[26]

Ms Astley and Mr Overton met on the Internet in 2003. Their relationship grew increasingly close and they decided to get married in 2008. Mr Overton returned to his home in Great Britain after the marriage to proceed with his application for immigration to Canada. The process took longer than they expected, over a year, and he did not return to Canada until 2009.

Looking in the mirror's mirror

What I want to draw from these cases, in which the characterization of a proximate, adult relationship is contested in the post-legal-equality world, is modest: what do conjugal relationships at the legal margins look like?

The cameos are uniform in some ways and divergent in others. In most cases, the taxpayer was arguing that he or she was not in a spousal relationship, because a holding that the relationship was a spousal one would reduce the taxpayer's access to child tax benefits, the goods and services tax credit or the equivalent-to-spouse credit, all of which require consideration of the income of the taxpayer's spouse. In other words, the incentive for the individuals before the court was to persuade the court that the adults were not in a cohabiting conjugal relationship. The context provides some information about the income class of the people under consideration: most of them are low- or modest-income taxpayers, which means their individual income is probably under $50,000. The tax benefits at issue also mean that almost every proximate adult relationship in the sample involves children.

The sample is geographically and racially diverse. From Halifax to Winnipeg to Sidney, the locations of the adults span the country. There are a disproportionate number of cameos from Quebec. This may be because more Quebecers live together without getting married, because the revenue authority in that province is more active, because Quebecers are more likely to dispute assessments, because of some combination of these factors or because of coincidence. The racial diversity of the sample is not explicit in any of the cases. Even if nothing can be said about any particular set of facts with confidence, however, there are facts – this is perilous, but even names – from which to draw reasonable inferences suggestive that the sample as a whole contains some racial diversity.

Some proximate adults do not appear in these cameos. On the surface at least, there are no stories about queers, or at least none about a same-sex couple. There isn't one tax case (not just in the determination of who is a spouse, but at all) that deals explicitly with a trans person or bisexual person. There are no cases in the sample that address explicitly people who are in multiple sustained sexual relationships at a given time. Significantly, there are no cases about wealthy adults in proximate relationships, although those kinds of relationship could surely give rise to tax disputes. For example, two wealthy taxpayers could each claim the principal residence exemption on properties they own and be denied the second exemption because they are spouses; or one wealthy taxpayer might try to direct income to a less well-off adult in an attempt to split income, which would raise the issue of whether they are spouses. However, those kinds of circumstance seem not to have given rise to cases about whether the adults are cohabiting in a conjugal relationship. That may be because wealthier adults with proximate relationships wish to avoid having to trot out the intimate details of their life arrangements and so may find ways to settle their tax disputes; because they have access to good tax-planning advice that allows them to comply with the tax rules or to design their affairs to avoid detection when they do not; or it may mean that the Canada Revenue Agency finds it harder to identify (and enforce) the tax rules around principal residences or income splitting, for example, than it does the rules that require taxpayers to make explicit claims to benefits.

These cameos enable some brief glances of the lives lived by adults in proximate relationships. Proximate adults might live together, but not necessarily. When they do live together, sometimes they co-own the home, sometimes one person owns the home and the other person lives without direct financial contribution to costs, and sometimes one person owns the home and there is an explicit payment of rent between the adults. Many of the women, at least at the margins of conjugality, do not change their last names. Their sexual relationship may be ongoing, ceased or ignored in the presentation of the facts of their lives together. (It seems fair to assume that, if the taxpayer led evidence of a sexual relationship (or not), that would likely have been reported by the court.) The adults seem to have multiple, serial adult sexual relationships. They may share some of the tasks of living (cleaning, cooking, laundry) or they may be precise in delimiting where their obligations end (for example, by labelling their food in the fridge). Many people move along the spectrum of relationship proximity over the course of their relationship, undertaking some responsibilities and engaging in some practices (e.g., sexual intimacy or living together) during some periods, and not undertaking those responsibilities or engaging in those practices during others. Most adults in relationships at the margins of conjugality keep their own bank accounts. The acquisition of a washer and dryer is viewed as a significant household expenditure, and the cost of its acquisition is often shared. Financial hardship (e.g., bankruptcy), extraordinary caring requirements (e.g., an ill child or a child who requires additional attention, or a sick or disabled adult) or immigration pressures often justify maintaining a proximate adult relationship. As the last cameo hints, the advent of the use of the Internet to build relationships may redefine what it is to be in a proximate adult relationship at the margins of conjugality.

This chapter makes three modest contributions. First, it looks at the question of whether scholars of the family might find something to learn from the evidence (not meant in its legal sense, but, rather, in a broader sense) available from tax case law. I hope that the chapter demonstrates that some questions might be answered using these texts as archival materials. In this respect, the chapter challenges our sense of the hierarchy of legal knowledges. We readily position the holdings as the important part of any judicial decision.

Authors of case headnotes rarely include much, if any, of the case's factual context. The methodology employed in this chapter, which privileges facts, in essence centring the refraction of the real people beneath the surface of legal decisions over what we understand in a formal sense to be 'law', challenges our notions of what decision-makers do that is valuable, and the purposes for which we read cases. More on that below.

Second, the chapter specifically looks at the question of what we might be able to learn about who lives at the margins of conjugality. In short, the core part of this chapter focuses on presenting some of the figures who find themselves, in the tax context, as living at the margins of the post-legal-equality understanding of the meaning of conjugality.

Third, the chapter concludes with some speculation about the ways that adults at the margins of conjugality arrange their lives. Hopefully, I've left the reader curious about what might be available if we were to read the Income Tax Act and the cases it gives rise to in the way we read a good novel: as enriching our understanding of who we are, what we do and why we might do it.

Acknowledgements

With thanks to the participants at the After Equality workshop in Montreal (April 2013) and to Constance Backhouse, Robert Leckey and Rod Macdonald for thoughtful comments on an earlier draft. I am indebted to the Social Sciences and Humanities Research Council of Canada for its support through the standard research grant programme. Thanks to Jacqueline Byers for her research assistance.

Notes

1 RSC 1985 c 1 (5th Supp) (as amended).
2 SC 2000, c 12.
3 See Income War Tax Act 7–8 Geo V c 28, s 4 (1917).
4 Then Income Tax Act RSC c 1 (5th Supp) s 252(4).
5 Ibid., s 248(1) 'common-law partner'.
6 *M v H* [1999] 2 SCR 3.
7 *Molodowich v Penttinen* (1980) 17 RFL (2d) 376. The Revenue interpretation is at Canada Revenue Agency, doc 2006–0198341E5 (14 June 2007) (French). This test from *Molodowich* has been imported into the tax case law. See, e.g., *Milot v R* [1996] 1 CTC 2247 (informal procedure).
8 See Tax Court of Canada Act RSC 1985 c T-2, s 18.15(4).
9 *Sykes v R* (2000) [2005] 3 CTC 2054 (informal procedure). Judge Rowe held that the two adults were not in a common-law partnership.
10 Ibid., para 23.
11 *Rangwala v R* [2000] 4 CTC 2430 (informal procedure). Judge Campbell concluded that Mr and Mrs Rangwala lived separate and apart.
12 *Sigouin v R* [2002] 1 CTC 2596 (informal procedure). Judge Lamarre Proulx held that the adults were living separate and apart.

13 *Gagné v R* [2002] 1 CTC 2666 (informal procedure). Judge Dussault held that the adults were in a conjugal relationship and were, therefore, spouses.
14 *Uwasomba v R* [2003] 2 CTC 2295 (informal procedure). Judge Beaubier held that the parties were living separate and apart.
15 *Henry v R* [2003] 1 CTC 2001 (informal procedure). Judge Little held that, in the first half of the years in issue, the relationship was a spousal one, but, in the second half, it was not.
16 *Richard v R* 2003 CCI 774 (informal procedure). Judge Lamarre held that the adults were spouses.
17 *Bellavance v R* [2004] 4 CTC 2179. Judge Angers held that, although the two lived in the same house, they had ceased being spouses.
18 *Hamel v R* 2004 TCC 315 (informal procedure). Judge Tardif struggled with whether the adults were spouses, but ultimately held they were.
19 *Chicheluk v R* [2005] 3 CTC 2446 (informal procedure). Judge Sarchuk held that Ms Chicheluk and Mr Oree were not spouses.
20 *Savory v R* [2008] 5 CTC 2033 (informal procedure). Judge McArthur held that the two adults were in a common-law partnership for 2004, but not for the 2002 and 2003 taxation years.
21 *DeRepentigny v R* 2008 TCC 304 (informal procedure). Judge Favreau determined that the adults were living separately after 2005.
22 *Hendricken v R* [2008] 5 CTC 2206 (informal procedure). Justice Webb determined that the two adults were living in a common-law partnership.
23 *Robertson v R* [2009] 1 CTC 2085 (informal procedure). Judge Beaubier, in a decision rendered in 2008, held that Ms Robertson and Mr Bear had not been in a common-law partnership since 31 May 2002.
24 *Leblanc v R* [2009] 1 CTC 2191 (informal procedure). Judge Angers held that the adults had a common-law partnership.
25 *Perron v R* 2010 TCC 547 (informal procedure). Judge Favreau held that the adults were not in a conjugal relationship.
26 *Astley v R* 2012 TCC 155 (informal procedure). Judge Webb held that the adults were cohabiting spouses.

Reference

Law Commission of Canada (2001) *Beyond Conjugality: Recognizing and Supporting Close Personal Adult Relationships*, Ottawa: Queen's Printer.

Chapter 7

Leaping without looking

Helen Reece

In England and Wales, as elsewhere, courts have a hotchpotch of powers in relation to cohabitants (for detail, see Herring 2013: 82–9); in contrast to the case with registered relationships, these do not include the power to redistribute assets on separation.[1] In 2007, the United Kingdom Law Commission recommended creating such a power in certain circumstances; the United Kingdom coalition government has rejected this recommendation, at least during the present Parliament.[2] The government's solution to this lacuna remains information for cohabitants on the general legal information website, Advicenow,[3] funded by the government from its 2004 inception until 2011.[4]

This informational response was made more pressing by the 2000 British Social Attitudes survey evidence that a staggering 59 per cent of cohabitants believed the common law marriage myth that they were in exactly the same legal position as married couples (Barlow *et al.* 2001),[5] coupled with the ever-increasing popularity of cohabitation as a family form (Beaumont 2011: 1).[6] Advicenow was initially part of a wider government-funded Living Together Campaign, with the main aims of dispelling the common law marriage myth, raising awareness of specific issues that could affect cohabiting couples, and helping cohabiting couples to protect themselves by pointing out practical steps they could take and where they could get help (Braverman 2010: 1).

Although Advicenow achieved some success in *informing* cohabitants, it failed to achieve its objective of *influencing* them to make cohabitation agreements about asset redistribution on separation (Barlow *et al.* 2005: 55, 79, 2008: 42). The legal policy literature regrets cohabitants' recalcitrance, interpreting their resistance as barriers to be overcome, but, in what follows, I reinterpret these barriers as sound justifications for not concluding such contracts. Although Advicenow assumes that formalizing cohabitation relationships is the best solution, the legal policy literature overestimates the benefits of having an agreement and ignores the costs of reaching one.

Advicenow

Informing cohabitants

> We must emphasise that there is no such thing as common law marriage
> in England and Wales. If people think they obtain rights by living
> together for a period of time they are wrong. They must be disabused of
> that.
>
> (Bridge, cited in Barlow *et al.* 2005: 52)

Theoretically, information provision is one of the least intrusive forms of
governmental action, 'and the goal (if not always the result) of this form of
"regulation" is surely among the least controversial: increasing the autonomy and liberty of the individual by increasing the information upon which
his decisions are based' (Baker 1990: 223–4). There is, however, a price to
be paid for even accurate and pertinent information, not just by the provider
but also by the recipient, the most obvious being information overload
(Jolls and Sunstein 2006: 214). Accordingly, a case still needs to be made for
government's correction of this particular error, especially given that people
commonly have little notion of how law regulates their actions (see, e.g.,
Ashworth 2011).

Baker makes a strong case in the closely related instance of a 1975 Lousiana
enactment by which application for a marriage licence would trigger a state
requirement to provide the applicant with information about the more pronounced economic consequences of marriage. She suggests that this example
met three conditions that imply disclosure, rather than simple publication,
of a law:

> First, we would expect knowledge of a law that is aggressively promul-
> gated to have some *ex ante* utility. Such knowledge should have the
> potential to affect an individual's decision making: ignorance of it would
> therefore entail certain risks and potential costs. Second, we would expect
> that the typical recipient of the aggressively conveyed information would
> neither already have it nor be likely to seek it out at the most appropriate
> time. Third, we would expect that the potential benefits of providing
> the ordinary person this information would exceed the costs.
>
> (Baker 1990: 223)

These conditions currently hold just as well, if not better, for cohabitation
in England and Wales. Cohabitants misunderstand their legal position and,
left to their own devices, are unlikely to self-correct, not least because they
don't know that they don't know (see ibid.: 238–40); moreover, information
could fundamentally affect decisions that could impact on them in profound
ways, determining, on occasions, whether they end up homeless or even
destitute.

The obvious measure of the success of an information campaign is the extent to which it informs, subjectively – in terms of how helpful people find the information – or objectively – in terms of people's enhanced knowledge or understanding (see further, Reece 2003: Ch. 5). Subjectively, cohabitants generally found Advicenow helpful and informative (Barlow *et al.* 2007). Objectively measured, the proportion of cohabitants who believed the common law marriage myth fell, though not dramatically, from 59 per cent in 2000 to 53 per cent in 2006 (Barlow *et al.* 2008: 42). To the extent that Advicenow can be understood as an information campaign, it is legitimate and relatively successful.

Influencing cohabitants

It is doubtful whether there ever could be a pure information campaign, because any information campaign will send signals, the most inescapable being that the information is relevant (see Baker 1990: 242). Writing in 1990, Baker asks why, given the strong justifications for aggressively promulgating the marriage contract, no state had followed Louisiana's 1975 lead (ibid.: 257–8). She finds the answer in the message that such promulgation inevitably sends, namely, that marriage may legitimately be, or even should be, considered a private economic deal, rather than a non-negotiable public institution (ibid.: 223, 259–60). Analogously, the unavoidable message of Advicenow is that cohabitants should heed their legal position.

In the case of Advicenow, this is not contentious: Advicenow is explicit about attempting to influence cohabitants' behaviour (Braverman 2010: 1). With regard to the absence of a legal power to redistribute resources on separation, this means cohabitants' legally resolving what would happen to their assets in the event of relationship breakdown. This normative stance is reflected in the government-funded policy research, which expresses regret that, despite 'good intentions' (Barlow *et al.* 2007: 5, 11, 13, 48), few cohabitants take legal action.

The directive stance is clear throughout Advicenow: '*Now you know it's a good idea to make a living together agreement*, you need to know how to do it'.[7] The 'Moving in' and 'Housing' web pages emphasize the importance of thinking through the legal position:

> Moving in with your partner may be one of the most exciting decisions you'll make in your life. So as [sic] it hardly seems right to be thinking about what would happen if anything went wrong.
> *But it is something you need to think about.*[8]
> If you own your home with your partner you *need to be sure* you own in the right way for you both . . . Similarly, if you rent your home, you *need to be aware* of what rights each of you would have if you split up or if one of you died, and *what you can do now* to improve them.

'My partner and I are buying a flat together. I'm really excited but my mum keeps asking if I've thought about what would happen if we split up. If we split up couldn't we just split the proceeds 50/50?'

'You could, yes, but it would be best if you agreed now that this is what you would do. I know it's annoying, but your mum is right – *you need to think* about what would happen if you split up.'[9]

The 'Moving in' web page emphasizes, not just thinking about, but also discussing, the legal rights position: 'It isn't the most romantic of conversations, but *it is important that you discuss* what your rights to the home will be, should you split up'.[10]

In sum, the further the cohabitants formalize their relationship, the better:

You can gain rights in the flat if you make an agreement to share it (*ideally this should be written down and signed by both of you*) or if you make a financial contribution that helps to pay for the flat on the understanding that you are going to get a share. *The clearer you are about this, the better.*[11]

Evidently, Advicenow is not so much concerned with setting cohabitants straight as it is with creating a universal obligation for cohabitants to think about, discuss and resolve their legal situation. Reasons that cohabitants don't do so are presented as *errors*, informational or cognitive. Top of the list is, of course, the false belief that protection automatically exists:

Moving in with John wasn't the hardest decision I've ever made but still, the fiercely independent part of me needed some convincing. I did some research and believed I'd covered all the scenarios. Except the worst case one it seems.[12]

However, other common errors involve misconceptions about the nature of agreements:

A Living Together agreement needn't be like a celebrity pre-nup where you don't want your partner to waltz off with your Beverly Hills mansion and a recording contract after 15 minutes of marriage. They aren't about 'this is mine, that is yours, and you're not getting a penny out of me'. Instead you can use a living together agreement to sort out the day to day workings of living together, and protect both you and your partner from whatever might happen to your relationship in the future. . . . An agreement that does set out what would happen if you split up isn't an admission that you might. . . . Suggesting to your partner that you make an agreement isn't a declaration of the fact that you're about to dump them, or a suggestion that your partner may try to rob you blind.[13]

The same message shines out of the funded policy literature, albeit more subtly: the reasons that cohabitants give to researchers for not sorting out legal niceties are conceptualized as *barriers* that *inhibit* legal action (Barlow *et al.* 2007: 10, 48). Advicenow presents no downside: sorting things out is cost free.

The cost of agreements

Literal cost

However, there is at least a literal cost to agreeing, direct in respect of legal fees, and indirect if not direct in terms of cohabitants' time and energy. It is no surprise that the policy research found this to be one of the most significant barriers (Barlow *et al.* 2007; Panades *et al.* 2007: 32, 37). Advicenow is Janus-faced on this issue. On the one hand, cohabitants are reassured that they will learn 'the *simple steps* they can take to protect themselves and their families from *whatever the future holds*'.[14] If cohabitants click on the 'Housing' web page, the message is reinforced: 'Whether you rent or own your home, there may be *simple things you can do now to ensure you and your partner will always have a roof over your heads*'.[15]

However, two short paragraphs down, the website confesses that 'housing law is very complicated'. Moreover, the 'simple steps' message is confounded by both the number and complexity of the steps set out on the website. The Living Together Agreements download alone is thirty pages long,[16] and this is only one of many steps that cohabitants are instructed to take. The policy literature conceptualizes this as just a barrier to be overcome, but cohabitants may prefer the advice that, 'time is the coin of your life. It is the only coin you have, and only you can determine how it will be spent. Be careful lest you let other people spend it for you'.[17] Advicenow seeks to persuade cohabitants to spend this currency on contracting on the basis that agreements always make things better, both practically and emotionally.

Emotional cost

> Making {a living together} agreement prompts you to discuss how your living together will work in practice and what your expectations of each other are. In fact many of the couples we've spoken to say that they found that *just making the agreement strengthened their relationship*.[18]

Openness and communication have acquired the status of taken-for-granted virtues (see Strathern 1999: Ch. 4; Smart 2010), but there is surprisingly little *evidence* about the emotional impact of the process of reaching agreement (see Straus 2010: 5–6). Certainly, the Living Together Campaign research found couples with negative experiences of negotiations, experiences unvoiced on the website (Barlow *et al.* 2007: 49). Advicenow holds out the promise that the contracting process will bring cohabitants closer together, with little, if any, evidential justification.

> I told my boyfriend I wanted him to put the house in both our names and, eventually, he did. We're fine now but I'm glad we did it anyway – in a funny way, *it actually made us feel like more of a family*.[19]
>
> An agreement that does set out what would happen if you split up isn't an admission that you might. In fact, *it can strengthen your relationship by helping both partners to feel happier and more secure*.[20]
>
> *It is best to know the score*.[21]

According to Advicenow, an agreement will usually glow warm, but the worst-case scenario is cost-neutral, because the agreement can always be 'locked away out of sight and forgotten about, and only dug out if things went wrong'.[22] But, as Straus (2010) again recognizes, the empirical evidence about the emotional impact of an agreement is almost as sparse as the evidence about the emotional effect of agreeing.

The notable exception is Rountree's 2000 Californian investigation. He interviewed two distinct groups: married couples who had contracted out of some of the economic terms of the marriage contract and same-sex couples who were at that point, in California, legal strangers to each other and so had contracted to give each other some of the rights and responsibilities of marriage. He found that 'contracting intimacy' had quite different emotional effects against these two distinct institutional backdrops. In his words, intimacy was contracted in different 'promissory moods' (Rountree 2000: 138). For the married couples, a contract generally sent a negative emotional signal, experienced as an attempt to renege on the marriage framework of sharing and commitment, creating a 'me versus you' mentality (ibid.: 12). In the marriages that successfully weathered a premarital contract, the couple had to do a lot of 'work' to manage and counteract the negative signalling (ibid.: 145, 165). In contrast, the lesbian and gay interviewees experienced intimate contracts far more positively, with both partners inside a contractual cocoon (ibid.: 138, 166).

We can only speculate about the glow that contract could throw on current United Kingdom cohabitants. For those cohabitants who see themselves – or feel concerned that the law sees them – as individuated legal strangers, contract could create an 'us'. However, many cohabitants already feel like family. Even those who know that the law doesn't impose a sharing norm on them may still believe they are 'as good as married' (see Barlow *et al.* 2008: 38–9). These cohabitants might be more like Rountree's married couples, experiencing agreement as contracting out of that initial norm and turning 'us' into 'me versus you'.

Although the above is speculative, we know that a principal reason that couples – married and unmarried – do not contract is that they commonly *assume* that this *would* have a negative emotional impact on their relationship (Lewis 2002: 183; Mahar 2003: 2; Barlow *et al*. 2005: 43; Douglas *et al*. 2007: 14, 50; Panades *et al*. 2007: 33; Barlow and Smithson 2012: 316, 318).[23] This is, of course, why Advicenow works so hard to combat this expectation. However, if competent adults believe that contracting will damage their relationship, in the absence of clear evidence, shouldn't we trust their instincts? Advicenow gives little if any space to the possibility that cohabitants might be right. Advicenow takes no cognizance of even the possibility of different 'promissory moods': an agreement is always good, and all agreements are good. The optimism bias strengthens the chance that cohabitants are right to be wary of agreements.

Optimism bias

Not only is the optimism bias 'one of the most robust and reliable findings in the study of the psychology of prediction' (Armor and Taylor 1998: 314), but Kahneman suggests (2011: 255), 'In terms of its consequences for decisions, the optimistic bias may well be the most significant of the cognitive biases'. Taylor (1989) postulated that most people have three pervasive, enduring and systematic positive illusions. First, they have an overly positive view of their own attributes; second, they are unrealistically rosy about their future; third, they have a distorted faith in their own ability to bring about positive outcomes.

According to Armor and Taylor, 'optimism in people's specific expectations has been held responsible for both positive and negative consequences' (1998: 315). The legal policy literature concentrates exclusively on the negative consequences (Barlow *et al*. 2007: 34): basically seen as 'a burial of the head in the sand' (ibid.: 48), the optimism bias is regarded as one of the main barriers that must be overcome (ibid.: 10). This 'glass half empty' approach is perhaps most vigorously promulgated by Weinstein, who is cited in the legal policy literature (ibid.: 34). He regards the optimism bias straight-forwardly as a cognitive error, and his chief concern is that it prevents people from realizing and, therefore, preparing for the objective risks of external threats such as relationship breakdown (Weinstein and Klein 1995: 132).

There is no doubt that the optimism bias is a principal reason that both married and unmarried couples do not make agreements (Mahar 2003: 2; Barlow *et al*. 2007: 5, 10, 11; Panades *et al*. 2007: 32). They are deterred by two optimistic beliefs: first, that their relationship will persist (see Baker and Emery 1993: 443, 448); second, that they will be able to resolve matters with their partner if the relationship does break down (see ibid.: 443; Barlow *et al.* 2007: 34). In relation to the former belief, the optimism bias may be more rampant here than in any other sphere (Rachlinski 2003: 1181).

Not only does the optimism bias inhibit agreements, it also makes cohabitants less concerned about the content of any agreement (see Barlow and Smithson 2012: 308, 317). Accordingly, many follow Weinstein and Klein (1995) in believing that it is important to correct the optimism bias. This proves more easily said than done, because, 'any attempt to change risk perceptions is hampered by the variety of strategies individuals can use to arrive at optimistic conclusions' (ibid.: 139). The most effective approaches combine a scary message about the consequences of doing nothing with a reassuring message about the effectiveness of taking precautions (Sunstein and Thaler 2003: 1183), an approach that Advicenow adopts, as we will later see.

> 'Doctor, doctor, my wife thinks she's a chicken.'
> 'That sounds serious. Why didn't you tell me before?'
> 'We needed the eggs.'

In contrast to Weinstein's negative approach, Armor and Taylor (1998: 314, 357) believe that the potential for negative outcomes to follow unrealistic optimism may have been overstated. Their positive approach, buoyant in the psychological literature, makes no appearance in the legal policy discussions of living together agreements. The mother of this 'glass half full' approach is Taylor, who sees positive illusions as healthy – not just typical, but highly adaptive. Writing with Brown, Taylor concludes that, 'the capacity to develop and maintain positive illusions may be thought of as a valuable human resource to be nurtured and promoted, rather than an error-prone processing system to be corrected' (Taylor and Brown 1988: 205).

With regard to romantic relationships, people are optimistic, but not mindlessly so. Because people heed their levels of love and satisfaction, they are *relatively* accurate about the future of their relationships (Buehler *et al.* 1995: 24–7): a lover is 'a flexible prognosticator who balances visions of the worlds as one would want it with an understanding of the world that is' (Armor and Taylor 1998: 315). Furthermore, a dose of realism would not necessarily enhance lovers' predictive accuracy, because the optimism bias significantly enhances outcomes (Armor and Taylor 2002: 341), functioning as a powerful self-fulfilling prophecy (Sharot 2012: 44). Although people's overly optimistic expectancies are only rarely completely fulfilled, they commonly get closer to their goal than if they had not been unrealistically optimistic (Armor and Taylor 2002: 341). This is partly because the optimism bias enhances motivation and persistence (Armor and Taylor 1998: 354).

Outcomes are also enhanced because unrealistic optimism tends to take an active form, with people regarding themselves as, not so much inherently, but *potentially*, invulnerable to risks and further believing that the determinants of that invulnerability lie within their own control (ibid.: 341). So a partner may base his overly optimistic prediction about the survival of his relationship on his tendency to help with the childcare or remember anniversaries (Gagné *et al.* 2003: 302), his unrealistic optimism functioning as both cause and effect of his gratifying behaviour (Armor and Taylor 1998: 341). Accordingly:

> Substituting relatively pessimistic (or conservative) assessments for unrealistically optimistic ones may simply make people more unhappy and less enthusiastic about their undertakings, less persistent in pursuing them, and more concerned about the future, without necessarily improving the accuracy of their assessments. . . . To the extent that unrealistic optimism enhances performance, persistence, and positive mood, and to the extent that unrealistic optimism is relatively, if not absolutely, accurate, it may have more self-regulatory benefits than costs, and more self-regulatory benefits than realism has.
>
> (Ibid.: 392–3)

On this view, 'the willingness to make a leap of faith – to possess hopes for a relationship that reality does not seem to fully warrant – is critical for satisfying dating and marital relationships' (Murray and Holmes 1997: 598).

It could be suggested that Advicenow does not aim to pull off partners' rose-tinted glasses, but just to enable a quick peer over the top. Maybe the message of Advicenow is the common-sense, 'assume the best but prepare for the worst' (see, e.g., Sharot 2012: 210). However, making a cohabitation agreement is far from a matter of signing on the dotted line. A cohabitation agreement involves a couple generating, chewing over and resolving a range of diverse, unpleasant, counterfactual scenarios, and this may damage the optimism bias.

Although diverse roots of the optimism bias have been suggested (see, e.g., Brenner *et al.* 2002; Kahneman 2011: 259), it is commonly accepted that at least part of the explanation is that we base our predictions on a mental simulation of ourselves engaging in the actions necessary for the outcome, and our simulation tends to dwell on the positive, not negative, possibilities (see, e.g., Buehler *et al.* 1995: 11; Armor and Taylor 1998: 322; Gilbert 2007: 18; Sharot 2012: xvi). Once we have conjured up a positive mental picture of the future event, we see that picture as more likely, especially because imagining that picture crowds out any other. 'Thus, by merely imagining a desired outcome people may become unrealistically optimistic about its likely occurrence' (Armor and Taylor 1998: 324). Moreover, our mental picture of a positive future event is rich and vivid (Sharot 2012: 88, 119), this clear picture reinforcing our belief that the positive event is probable (Armor and Taylor 1998: 323). In contrast, when Sharot (2012: 88) asked people to visualize separation from their partner, their mental picture was blurry. We make a close connection between clarity and probability and between fuzziness and improbability; we have a fuzzy picture of an event that we believe is unlikely, and, if our picture is fuzzy, then we believe that the event is unlikely.

Crucially, if we make ourselves conjure up clearer pictures of negative events, then we regard those negative events as more likely. Explaining a negative event makes for a clearer picture, to such an extent that explaining the negative event may affect us similarly to experiencing the negative event (Sherman *et al.* 1981: 146), altering our behaviour. In other words, 'explanations affect expectations, which in turn affect actual behavior' (ibid.: 150). Moreover, just like a positive picture, generating a negative picture also crowds out alternative, positive scenarios (Sherman *et al.* 1985: 119). Once cohabitants focus in on the potential failure of their relationship, they may believe their relationship is more likely to fail, which may, in turn, cause them to act as if the relationship is failing, causing the relationship to fail (see Williams 2009: 767).

Those who wish to persuade cohabitants to reach agreement may find it necessary to dent unrealistic optimism, with negative impact on cohabiting relationships. Moreover, the process of reaching cohabitation agreements may dent unrealistic optimism, with negative impact on cohabiting relationships. The more seriously cohabitants take this process, the more their optimism may be dented, and the more their relationships may be damaged. The less seriously cohabitants take the process, the less their optimism will be dented, and the worse an agreement they may make.

Advicenow construction of agreements

An obvious response is that any emotional price is worth paying: cohabitants end up homeless, and occasionally destitute, when their partner leaves them with nothing. Advicenow does not recognize an emotional cost, but, if it did, then this is no doubt the tack that it would take, for, according to Advicenow, an agreement is always good, and all agreements are good. Advicenow constructs this goodness in three ways: first, exaggerating how bad the legal position is in the absence of an agreement; second, using 'atrocity tales' (Best 1987: 106); and, third, emphasizing the beneficial practical effects of agreements.

Advicenow replaces the 'common law marriage myth' with a new 'no rights mantra'. The front page begins by correcting the 'common law marriage myth', before adding: 'Couples who live together have hardly any rights automatically'. Just below this, still on the front page, the introduction restates, even more strongly, that, 'couples who live together have hardly any rights compared with married couples or civil partners'.[24] At the top of the About Living Together web page, the common law marriage myth is reinscribed as 'the popular myth that people gain legal rights simply by living with their partner for a certain period of time',[25] which is, of course, not entirely a myth. Indeed, Probert (2012: Ch. 7) postulates that it was the 1970s development of a patchwork quilt of rights and remedies in the United Kingdom that gave rise to the common law marriage myth.

Advicenow reinforces this gloomy message with 'atrocity tales'. Katie's headline is 'Katie's costly mistakes':[26] cohabitants are warned, 'Don't live to regret things like Katie'.[27] Another headline tells of Rachel and her mistake, which meant that she and her son 'ended up on the streets'.[28] Then there is Orla, whose tag is that she 'had no idea':

> I was dumbfounded – less than 3 hours earlier he'd dumped me, and now he was making me homeless too! I told him that he couldn't do that! I had as much right to be there as he did. We'd been living together for years. I thought that meant I was his common-law wife and I had rights. He couldn't just kick me out! But I was wrong.[29]

Cohabitants meet Sandra with the headline that she 'hadn't considered what would happen if she and Adam split up':

> I suddenly had no home, but what was even harder was not having anything! We hadn't discussed how the furniture, crockery, cutlery, gardening equipment, cost of landscaping, curtains or even the rugs would be divided. Everything stayed in the flat with Adam.[30]

On Advicenow, there are no case studies of how easily partners separate when they have made living together agreements, but we do hear implicit, and sometimes explicit, 'if onlies' in respect of the atrocity tales above: 'If Sandra and Adam had made a living together agreement it could have been a very different story, with much less heartache and a fairer result'.[31] Notably, a living together agreement would not, in fact, have eased Sandra's travails. After separating, Sandra and Adam managed to negotiate an agreement that they would sell the house. However, on the day of the sale, Adam declared that he would not go through with the agreement. Sandra caved in, because enforcing the agreement to sell would have meant going to court.[32] The problem for Sandra was that Adam would not honour their agreement, and this would have been the same had they reached an agreement before separation. In the light of this, is Advicenow right that, in practical terms, living together agreements are always good?

Are agreements always good?

To answer this, we need to establish what makes a good agreement. The simplest conception of a good agreement for me is one that maximizes my assets. However, in every instance of division of assets on separation, couples are playing a zero-sum game. Every agreement is worse than no agreement for one and better than no agreement for the other. So, any cohabitant may make herself worse off by reaching an agreement, except the cohabitant with absolutely nothing, who is becoming rarer (see Bottomley 2006). Some of Advicenow is, indeed, based around this simple notion of a good agreement as one that leaves *you yourself* with more than you would otherwise have had; unsurprisingly, in this conception in which you act to protect *yourself*, *you* are always a woman.

More often, Advicenow has a more complex idea of a good agreement, based on fairness, sometimes for the *couple* – how to make sure things are fair for *you and your partner*, so that you both make sure you keep a roof over your heads[33] – and sometimes for your partner – so that you 'ensure your partner doesn't always get the fuzzy end of the lollipop'.[34] However, finding what is fair has proved elusive, even for courts deciding divorcing couples' assets (see, e.g., Law Commission 2012). If there were a social consensus or even a norm on fairness for cohabitants, then the 2007 Law Commission proposals would likely not have fallen by the wayside (see, e.g., Dey and Wasoff 2007).

By recommending cohabitation agreements, Advicenow settles for intersubjective fairness, involving one cohabitant in *ex ante* generosity, making himself worse off than his legal position dictates. Recognizing the inter-subjective nature of the fairness does not exhaust the enquiry though. Cohabitants are not being asked to decide what they think is fair in their current circumstances. Nor are they being asked to predict what they would think was fair on separation, because at least the richer one would be better placed to answer this question on separation: 'Let's not sit around speculating – let's see what I think is fair if and when we part ways – I'll still be here to tell you!' The question seems to be either, 'What does my current self think would be fair in a future hypothetical scenario?', or, 'What should my future self think is fair in that hypothetical case?'.

Cohabitants are being 'forced into the future' (Beck-Gernsheim 2002: 48). The optimal time to answer the question of fairness on separation is on separation, when all the facts and circumstances are known. No objective factor prevents a couple from agreeing at this point; no options are foreclosed by failure to agree earlier. The reasons to agree during the relationship lifespan lie purely in the subjective sphere; simply put, either you do not trust your partner to be fair on separation, or you do not trust yourself. Cohabitation agreements are pre-commitment contracts, an attempt to bind your partner's hands or your own hands, or the hands of both of you.

There are certainly times to bind, from placing the alarm clock out of reach to squirting washing-up liquid over the children's half-chewed fish fingers (see Scott 1990: 40–1). Scott (ibid.: 13, 40–1) suggests that pre-commitment strategies are useful when we predict that our short-term preferences (for example, more alcohol) may conflict with our long-term interests (in staying sober). Loewenstein (1996) adds the case where we predict that a later, visceral state will impede our decision-making. Although the presence of a certain amount of a visceral factor will not prevent, and may even enhance, rational decision-making, a higher level will dominate. The question is whether cohabitation is a time to tie.

Let's look first at whether this is a time to tie your own hands. The argument for binding yourself is that, without an agreement, you would end up being meaner on separation than you would have been in an agreement made during the relationship (I haven't come across the converse argument, that a cohabitation agreement is necessary to guard against being excessively generous on separation). So, cohabitation breakdown is not a time when short-term preferences might overwhelm long-term interests: quite the opposite, Advicenow is concerned to stop too *keen* concern with long-term interests.

The domination of visceral factors, such as anger, hurt and pain, seems a more promising reason to pre-commit. Not only do visceral factors cloud decision-making by dominating thoughts, but also, people are generally less altruistic when in a visceral state (ibid.: 275, 284). However, the impact of visceral factors does not point clearly in favour of pre-commitment. Although we overestimate the importance of current visceral factors, we under-estimate the importance to us of future visceral factors (ibid.). In a hot state, people find it difficult to act as if in a cold state, but, conversely, in a cold state, people cannot imagine how they would want to act if in a hot state (Loewenstein and Schkade 1999: 98).

Recognizing this necessitates filling in a little more the question that cohabitants are trying to answer when they make an agreement. Cohabitants may be answering one of two questions: 'What should my future self think is fair in case we separate, and I still feel for you as I do now?' or 'What should my future self think is fair in case we separate, and I hate your guts?' Given the tendency to under-estimate future visceral factors, it is likely that they are answering the first question. Just as it is hard for a hurt, bitter cohabitant to see past his anger, it is hard for a happy, loving cohabitant to imagine his anger.

It is even more likely that they are answering the first question, given the presentism bias. According to Gilbert (2006: 114), 'we find it particularly difficult to imagine that we will ever think, want or feel differently than we do now', so the way we decide how we will feel about future events is to 'imagine how we would feel if those things happened now, and then we make some allowance' (ibid.: 134).

Is this the question that they should be answering? This is difficult to ascertain in the absence of a norm about fairness on cohabitation breakdown. We do know, however, that your future self will not thank you for the agreement. If your future self wants to do what the agreement requires him to do, then the agreement was wasted effort. If your future self does not want to do what the agreement requires him to do, then the agreement will neither make your future self happy, nor accord with his sense of fairness. Maybe you should trust your future, hotter self?

Often, of course, if cohabitants pre-commit, then they are opting for the present hot self over a different, future hot self. Love and passion, like anger and pain, are visceral states that dominate decision-making; the optimism bias not only dissuades cohabitants from making agreements, but also affects the content of any agreement that they do make.[35] Social policy is unlikely to succeed if based on cohabitants' awaiting a cold visceral valve before agreeing. Moreover, the valve ends up back at a different cold point: just like passion and infatuation, the visceral states of anger, hurt and pain do not last forever, and there is nothing to prevent a cohabitant returning to the issue at a later post-separation point. That this seldom happens shows that the cohabitant is merely keeping what he would have contracted to keep, if, pre-separation, he had correctly predicted his post-separation sense of fairness. There is an argument for trusting the post-separation self: he certainly won't thank you for having given away his gold!

This leaves the simpler, and stronger, argument that it is wise to make an agreement on the basis that you do not trust your partner. Relatedly, the discussion above leaves out the crucial aspect of bargaining in the process of reaching agreement. Before, but not necessarily after, separation, the poorer partner has bargaining chips, the most fundamental being, 'I won't continue this relationship without this deal'. This is an important factor to weigh in the scales. Once we have stripped away all the groundless arguments for agreements, we are left with one strong reason to make an agreement, to bind one's partner. It is hard to see how this reason, stripped bare, could *avoid* creating a market mentality, a bargain struck between 'me' and 'you', because that is what it is:

> 'My girlfriend bought a flat a few weeks before we met. It's spacious enough for two and it's much more convenient for where I work. I've been practically living there for a few months, and we've now decided I should give up my flat and move in with her permanently.'
>
> 'Great, but you should bear in mind that you will not gain any legal rights over the home. If you are asked to leave, or if your partner decides to sell the property, you have no right to stay, and no rights to a percentage of the price. . . . If you aren't able to have this discussion, or if you have agreed that you will not gain a share in the home, *think carefully about what you are willing to contribute to and what you don't want to pay for.* If you pay for home improvements or contribute to the mortgage without an agreement that you will share the home in place, it will be very hard for you to get your money back. Better to consider it a gift, or *rent that you would paying if you lived elsewhere*' [sic].[36]

Conclusion

Although Advicenow achieved some limited success in informing cohabitants, it made little headway in influencing them. According to Barlow (2009: 305), in assuming that information would make a significant difference, government fell 'prey to the legal rationality mistake, whereby law assumes people act according to the logic of the law, whereas in reality they act in accordance with the social imperatives within their own lives'. Contrary to the stance taken in the legal policy literature, cohabitants' recalcitrance may be something to celebrate.

Acknowledgements

For helpful comments on earlier drafts, I am grateful to participants at a Law Department staff seminar at the London School of Economics and Political Science and at the seminar 'After equality: Family, sex, kinship', at McGill University, and John Gillott. I am grateful to Jennie Bristow for sparking the idea for this chapter.

Notes

1 In relation to England and Wales, see Matrimonial Causes Act 1973, Part 2, and Civil Partnership Act 2004, sch 5; in relation to Quebec, see arts 401–30, 432, 433, 448–84 and 585 of the Civil Code of Québec. Contrast Family Law (Scotland) Act 2006, s 28.
2 Hansard, 6 September 2011, Col 15WS-16WS (J. Djanogly).
3 Advicenow 2008, 'LivingTogether'. Online. Available at: www.advicenow.org.uk/living-together (accessed 17 March 2013).
4 'About LivingTogether 2013.' Online. Available at: www.advicenow.org.uk/about-us/about-advicenow/about-livingtogether,10016,FP.html (accessed 17 March 2013).
5 For similar findings in relation to Quebec, see *Quebec (Attorney General) v A* 2013 SCC 5, [2013] 1 SCR 61, para 373.
6 For similar findings in relation to Quebec, see ibid., para 377.
7 Advice Services Alliance 2004, 'livingtogether agreements'. Online. Available at: http://static.advicenow.org.uk/files/Living_Together_Agreements-867.pdf (accessed 17 March 2013; emphasis added).
8 'Housing 2010.' Online. Available at: www.advicenow.org.uk/living-together/housing/ (accessed 17 March 2013; emphasis added).
9 'Moving in FAQs 2010.' Online. Available at: www.advicenow.org.uk/living-together/moving-in/moving-in-faqs-html,178,FP.html (accessed 17 March 2013; emphasis added).
10 Ibid., emphasis added.
11 Ibid., emphasis added.
12 '"I'm his common-law wife" – Rachel's mistake 2010'. Online. Available at: www.advicenow.org.uk/living-together/moving-in/im-his-common-law-wife-rachels-mistake-html,204,FP.html (accessed 17 March 2013).
13 Advice Services Alliance 2004, 'livingtogether agreements'. Online. Available at: http://static.advicenow.org.uk/files/Living_Together_Agreements-867.pdf (accessed 17 March 2013).

14 Advicenow 2008, 'LivingTogether'. Online. Available at: www.advicenow.org.uk/living-together/ (accessed 17 March 2013; emphasis added).
15 'Housing 2010.' Online. Available at: www.advicenow.org.uk/living-together/housing (accessed 17 March 2013; emphasis added).
16 Advice Services Alliance 2004, 'livingtogether agreements'. Online. Available at: http://static.advicenow.org.uk/files/Living_Together_Agreements-867.pdf (accessed 17 March 2013).
17 The Quotations Page 2013, Carl Sandburg. Online. Available at: www.quotationspage.com/quote/2989.html (accessed 17 March 2013).
18 Advice Services Alliance 2004, 'livingtogether agreements'. Online. Available at: http://static.advicenow.org.uk/files/Living_Together_Agreements-867.pdf (accessed 17 March 2013; emphasis added).
19 'LivingTogether: Introduction 2010.' Online. Available at: www.advicenow.org.uk/living-together/livingtogether-in-a-nutshell,10010,FP.html (accessed 17 March 2013; emphasis added).
20 Advice Services Alliance 2004, 'livingtogether agreements'. Online. Available at: http://static.advicenow.org.uk/files/Living_Together_Agreements-867.pdf (accessed 17 March 2013; emphasis added).
21 Advicenow 2008, 'LivingTogether'. Online. Available at: www.advicenow.org.uk/living-together (accessed 17 March 2013; emphasis added).
22 Advice Services Alliance 2004, 'livingtogether agreements'. Online. Available at: http://static.advicenow.org.uk/files/Living_Together_Agreements-867.pdf (accessed 17 March 2013).
23 For similar findings in relation to Quebec, see *Quebec (Attorney General) v A* 2013 SCC 5, para 373.
24 Advicenow 2008, 'LivingTogether'. Online. Available at: www.advicenow.org.uk/living-together (accessed 17 March 2013). This phrase is repeated when the introduction is clicked on at 'LivingTogether: Introduction 2010'. Online. Available at: www.advicenow.org.uk/living-together/livingtogether-in-a-nutshell,10010,FP.html (accessed 17 March 2013).
25 'About LivingTogether 2013.' Online. Available at: www.advicenow.org.uk/about-us/about-advicenow/about-livingtogether,10016,FP.html (accessed 17 March 2013).
26 'Katie's costly mistakes 2010.' Online. Available at: www.advicenow.org.uk/living-together/breaking-up/katies-costly-mistakes-html,406,FP.html (accessed 17 March 2013).
27 Ibid.
28 "'I'm his common-law wife" – Rachel's mistake 2010'. Online. Available at: www.advicenow.org.uk/living-together/moving-in/im-his-common-law-wife-rachels-mistake-html,204,FP.html (accessed 17 March 2013).
29 'Orla had no idea 2010'. Online. Available at: www.advicenow.org.uk/living-together/housing/your-housing-rights-html,402,FP.html (accessed 17 March 2013).
30 Advice Services Alliance 2004, 'livingtogether agreements'. Online. Available at: http://static.advicenow.org.uk/files/Living_Together_Agreements-867.pdf, 1 (accessed 17 March 2013).
31 Ibid., 1.
32 Ibid., 1.
33 See above.
34 'Housing 2010'. Online. Available at: www.advicenow.org.uk/living-together/housing (accessed 17 March 2013).
35 See above.
36 'Moving in FAQs 2010'. Online. Available at: www.advicenow.org.uk/living-together/moving-in/moving-in-faqs-html,178,FP.html (accessed 17 March 2013; emphasis added).

References

Armor, D.A. and Taylor, S.E. (1998) 'Situated optimism: Specific outcome expectancies and self-regulation', in M.P. Zanna (ed.) *Advances in Experimental Social Psychology*, vol. 30, San Diego, CA: Academic Press.

—— (2002) 'When predictions fail: The dilemma of unrealistic optimism', in T. Gilovich, D. Griffin and D. Kahneman (eds) *Heuristics and Biases: The Psychology of Intuitive Judgment*, Cambridge: Cambridge University Press.

Ashworth, A. (2011) 'Ignorance of the criminal law, and duties to avoid it', *Modern Law Review*, 74: 1–26.

Baker, L.A. (1990) 'Promulgating the marriage contract', *University of Michigan Journal of Law Reform*, 23: 217–64.

—— and Emery, R.E. (1993) 'When every relationship is above average: Perceptions and expectations of divorce at the time of marriage', *Law and Human Behavior*, 17: 439–50.

Barlow, A. (2009) 'Legal rationality and family property: What has love got to do with it?', in J. Miles and R. Probert (eds) *Sharing Lives, Dividing Assets: An Interdisciplinary Study*, Oxford: Hart.

—— Burgoyne, C., Clery, E. and Smithson, J. (2008) 'Cohabitation and the law: Myths, money and the media', in A. Park, J. Curtice, K. Thomson, M. Phillips, M. Johnson and E. Clery (eds) *British Social Attitudes, 24th Report*, London: Sage.

—— Burgoyne, C. and Smithson, J. (2007) *The Living Together Campaign – An Investigation of Its Impact on Legally Aware Cohabitants*, London: Ministry of Justice.

—— Duncan, S., James, G. and Park, A. (2001) 'Just a piece of paper? Marriage and cohabitation in Britain', in A. Park, J. Curtice, K. Thomson, L. Jarvis and C. Bromley (eds) *British Social Attitudes: Public Policy, Social Ties, 18th Report*, London: Sage.

—— (2005) *Cohabitation, Marriage and the Law: Social Change and Legal Reform in the 21st Century*, Oxford: Hart Publishing.

Barlow, A. and Smithson, J. (2012) 'Is modern marriage a bargain? Exploring perceptions of pre-nuptial agreements in England and Wales', *Child and Family Law Quarterly*, 24: 304–19.

Beaumont, J. (2011) *Households and Families, Social Trends 41*, Newport, Wales: Office for National Statistics.

Beck-Gernsheim, E. (2002) *Reinventing the Family: In Search of New Lifestyles*, Cambridge: Polity Press.

Best, J. (1987) 'Rhetoric in claims-making: Constructing the missing children problem', *Social Problems*, 34: 101–21.

Bottomley, A. (2006) 'From Mrs. Burns to Mrs. Oxley: Do co-habiting women (still) need marriage law?', *Feminist Legal Studies*, 14: 181–211.

Braverman, R. (2010) *Living Together Project Report*, London: Advice Services Alliance. Online. Available at: http://static.advicenow.org.uk/files/lt-report-2010-96.pdf (accessed 11 July 2013).

Brenner, A.L., Koehler, D.J. and Rottenstreich, Y. (2002) 'Remarks on support theory: Recent advances and future directions', in T. Gilovich, D. Griffin and D. Kahneman (eds) *Heuristics and Biases: The Psychology of Intuitive Judgment*, Cambridge: Cambridge University Press.

Buehler, R., Griffin, D. and Ross, M. (1995) 'It's about time: Optimistic predictions in work and love', *European Review of Social Psychology*, 6: 1–32.

Dey, I. and Wasoff, F. (2007) 'Protection, parity, or promotion: Public attitudes to cohabitation and the purposes of legal reform', *Law and Policy*, 29: 159–82.

Douglas, G., Pearce, J. and Woodward, H. (2007) *A Failure of Trust: Resolving Property Disputes on Cohabitation Breakdown*, Bristol, UK: University of Bristol.

Gagné, F.M., Lydon, J.E. and Bartz, J.A. (2003) 'Effects of mindset on the predictive validity of relationship constructs', *Canadian Journal of Behavioural Science*, 35: 292–304.

Gilbert, D. (2006) *Stumbling on Happiness*, New York: Vintage Books.

Herring, J. (2013) *Family Law*, 6th edn, Harlow, UK: Pearson.

Jolls, C. and Sunstein, C.R. (2006) 'Debiasing through law', *Journal of Legal Studies*, 35: 199–242.

Kahneman, D. (2011) *Thinking, Fast and Slow*, London: Penguin.

Law Commission (2007) *Cohabitation: The Financial Consequences of Relationship Breakdown*, No. 307, London: Law Commission.

—— (2012) *Matrimonial Property, Needs and Agreements: A Supplementary Consultation Paper*, No. 208, London: Law Commission.

Lewis, J. (2002) *The End of Marriage? Individualism and Intimate Relations*, Cheltenham, UK: Edward Elgar.

Loewenstein, G. (1996) 'Out of control: Visceral influences on behavior', *Organizational Behavior and Human Decision Processes*, 65: 272–92.

—— and Schkade, D. (1999) 'Wouldn't it be nice? Predicting future feelings', in D. Kahneman, E. Diener and N. Schwartz (eds), *Well-being: The Foundations of Hedonic Psychology*, New York: Russell Sage Foundation.

Mahar, H. (2003) 'Why are there so few prenuptial agreements?', Discussion Paper, Cambridge, MA: Harvard Law School.

Murray, S.L. and Holmes, J.G. (1997) 'A leap of faith? Positive illusions in romantic relationships', *Personality and Social Psychology Bulletin*, 23: 586–604.

Panades, R., Corney, R., Ayles, C., Reynolds, J. and Hovsepian, F. (2007) *Informing Unmarried Parents about Their Legal Rights at Birth Registration*, London: OneplusOne.

Probert, R. (2012) *The Changing Legal Regulation of Cohabitation: From Fornicators to Family, 1600–2010*, Cambridge: Cambridge University Press.

Rachlinski, J.J. (2003) 'The uncertain psychological case for paternalism', *Northwestern University Law Review*, 97: 1165–226.

Reece, H. (2003) *Divorcing Responsibly*, Oxford: Hart Publishing.

Rountree, W.R. (2000) 'Contracting intimacy: The transformation of property and parenting in familial relations', unpublished thesis, University of California.

Scott, E.S. (1990) 'Rational decisionmaking about marriage and divorce', *Virginia Law Review*, 76: 9–94.

Sharot, T. (2012) *The Optimism Bias: Why We're Wired to Look on the Bright Side*, London: Constable and Robinson.

Sherman, S.J., Cialdini, R.B., Schwartzman, D.F. and Reynolds, K.D. (1985) 'Imagining can heighten or lower the perceived likelihood of contracting a disease: The mediating effect of ease of imagery', *Personality and Social Psychology Bulletin*, 11: 118–27.

—— Skov, R.B., Hervitz, E.F. and Stock, C.B. (1981) 'The effects of explaining hypothetical future events: From possibility to probability to actuality and beyond', *Journal of Experimental Social Psychology*, 17: 142–58.

Smart, C. (2010) 'Law and the regulation of family secrets', *International Journal of Law, Policy, and the Family*, 24: 397–413.

Strathern, M. (1999) *Property, Substance and Effect: Anthropological Essays on Persons and Things*, London: Athlone Press.

Straus, H. (2010) 'What's love got to do with it? A psychological exploration of prenuptial agreements', unpublished thesis, Pacifica Graduate Institute.

Sunstein, C.R. and Thaler, R.H. (2003) 'Libertarian paternalism is not an oxymoron', *University of Chicago Law Review*, 70: 1159–202.

Taylor, S.E. (1989) *Positive Illusions: Creative Self-Deception and the Healthy Mind*, New York: Basic Books.

—— and Brown, J.D. (1988) 'Illusion and well-being: A social psychological perspective on mental health', *Psychological Bulletin*, 103: 193–210.

Weinstein, N.D. and Klein, W.M. (1995) 'Resistance of personal risk perceptions to debiasing interventions', *Health Psychology*, 14: 132–40.

Williams, S.H. (2009) 'Sticky expectations: Responses to persistent over-optimism in marriage, employment contracts, and credit card use', *Notre Dame Law Review*, 84: 733–92.

Chapter 8

Taxing times for lesbians and gay men

Twenty years later

Claire F.L. Young

In 1994, I wrote 'Taxing times for lesbians and gay men: Equality at what cost?' (Young 1994), an article in which I discussed the fight by lesbians and gay men for equality. My focus was the demand by lesbian and gay couples in Canada for inclusion in the definition of 'spouse' in the Income Tax Act (ITA).[1] My conclusion was that, although such a demand could form part of an overall strategy for equality, the consequences of including lesbians and gay men as spouses for tax purposes were not, as many seemed to believe, all or even overwhelmingly positive. In particular, it was important for those seeking equality to recognize that this claim had profound class implications. Although the couple in which one partner was economically dependent on the other and, to a lesser extent, the couple in which both spouses had high incomes would benefit, the couple in which both partners had low incomes would pay more tax once included as spouses under the ITA.

At a general level, we have seen significant progress in terms of equality for lesbians and gay men in Canada, and elsewhere, since 'Taxing times' was written. For example, in 2000 the Modernization of Benefits and Obligations Act was enacted.[2] That statute changed the definition of spouse in sixty-eight Canadian statutes to include same-sex couples as spouses. More recently, in 2005, the Civil Marriage Act legalized same-sex marriage in Canada.[3] In this chapter, I revisit the issues raised in 'Taxing times' and my concerns about a strategy that argued for the inclusion of same-sex couples as spouses for tax purposes. What have the consequences of extending the definition of spouse in the ITA been for lesbians and gay men? Are the class implications raised in 'Taxing times' still a cause for concern? Has the change had a positive impact in terms of being progressive tax policy? What changes have been made in the last twenty years to the income-tax system that affect lesbian and gay couples, and have they been positive changes? My conclusion is that, although some lesbians and gay men have benefitted from inclusion, many others are bearing a higher tax burden. As I shall discuss, those paying more tax as spouses are those who can least afford that cost. The redefinition of spouse has simply exacerbated previous tax inequalities, and, looking beyond sexual orientation to family recognition more broadly, I argue that all tax provisions that take spousal status into account should be removed, and the integrity of the individual as the unit of taxation in Canada should be restored.

'Taxing times' in 1994

When 'Taxing times' was written, lesbians and gay men had endured a series of legislative and litigation defeats in their claims for equality and legal recognition of their relationships. At the time of writing, the Ontario legislature, in a free vote, had just defeated Bill 167, the Equality Rights Statute Amendment Act, which proposed to redefine 'marital status' in fifty-six pieces of legislation to remove any reference to 'opposite sex' (Young 1994: 534). Although seven provinces and Yukon had included sexual orientation as a prohibited ground of discrimination in their human rights legislation, sexual orientation had not yet been recognized as an analogous ground of discrimination for the purposes of section 15 of the Canadian Charter of Rights and Freedoms. As I noted in 'Taxing times', there had been a series of cases brought forward by lesbians and gay men involving,

> the right to marry, the right to sponsor one's partner for immigration into Canada, the right to a spouse's allowance under the Old Age Security Act, the right to conjugal visits with one's partner in prison and the right to spousal coverage under Medicare.
> (Young 1994: 536–7 (reference omitted)

In each case, the litigant was unsuccessful, and no discrimination was found to have taken place. In *Canada (Attorney General) v Mossop*, a case involving entitlement by a gay man to bereavement leave respecting a death in his partner's family, the Supreme Court of Canada refused to find discrimination on the basis of sexual orientation under the Canadian Human Rights Act.[4] The Court said that to do so would be to read a prohibition on the basis of sexual orientation into the legislation, something that Parliament had decided not to include.

In 1992, *Leshner v Ontario (No 2)* was a groundbreaking decision, in part, because it involved a challenge to the definition of spouse in the ITA, albeit in the context of the application of that definition to employment pension plans.[5] Leshner, a government employee, applied to his employer to change his benefit plan coverage from single coverage to family coverage so that it would include his male partner. His request was refused, and he appealed to the Ontario Human Rights Commission. The Board of Inquiry found that there was discrimination under the Charter and that Leshner's partner was eligible for survivor benefits under the pension plan. The tax connection was that pension plans are heavily subsidized by the tax system, with deductions for contributions and a sheltering of all income of the plan from tax.[6] In order to qualify for the preferential tax treatment, and thus be registered as a pension plan under the ITA, the plan must meet certain criteria. The federal government took the position that, because the definition of spouse in the ITA did not include same-sex couples, any pension plan that purported to extend survivor benefits to a lesbian or gay spouse would be deregistered and not receive the tax benefits. The Board of Inquiry held that, if changes were not made to the ITA within three years to permit registration of pension plans that gave survivor benefits to same-sex couples, the employer would be required to set up a separate plan for its lesbian and gay employees.

Meanwhile, the Canadian Union of Public Employees (CUPE) had changed the terms of its pension plan to permit its employees to designate same-sex partners for the purposes of survivor benefits. It was subsequently advised by Revenue Canada (as it then was) that the plan would be deregistered if it continued that practice. In *Rosenberg v Canada (Attorney General)*,[7] two lesbian employees of CUPE argued that the refusal by Revenue Canada to accept the change to the pension plan discriminated against them on the basis of sexual orientation, in contravention of the guarantee of equality in section 15(1) of the Charter. The federal government conceded that there was discrimination, but argued that the discrimination was justified as reasonable under section 1, the Charter's reasonable limitation clause. The Ontario Court of Appeal unanimously held that the discrimination could not be justified under section 1 and it ordered that the words 'same-sex' be read into the definition of spouse in section 252(4) of the ITA, as it applied to registered pension plans. This decision was a watershed in terms of redefining 'spouse' in the ITA, although the redefinition was only with respect to pension plans (Young 1998). The federal government did not appeal the decision, signalling that the full inclusion of lesbians and gay men as spouses under the ITA was imminent. In 2000, as already mentioned, the Modernization of Benefits and Obligations Act changed the definition of spouse in federal legislation, including the ITA, to include same-sex partners as spouses.

The litigation and equality claims described above led me to consider the implications of lesbians and gay men seeking spousal status under the ITA. In 'Taxing times', I identified a variety of problems with this strategy and argued that 'the tax system is not the place to start. The problems are too intractable and the costs too high' (Young 1994: 559). In the following part, I review those problems, all of which continue to exist today. Consequently, over the years, I have argued strenuously for the elimination of many of the tax rules that take spousal status into account and changes to other rules to make them operate in a more equitable manner (Young 2000, 2009a, 2009b).

The 1994 critique

Although the individual has always been the unit of taxation in Canada, there are a myriad of tax rules that take spousal status into account for a variety of purposes (Young 2000: 1). In 'Taxing times', I raised a number of concerns about the impact of expanding the definition of spouse to include same-sex couples. My main concern focused on the class implications. I considered the impact of spousal status for tax purposes on three differently situated couples. They were the couple in which both spouses were high-rate taxpayers, the couple in which both spouses were low-rate taxpayers and the couple in which one spouse was a high-rate taxpayer and the other had no taxable income. My conclusion was that the couple in which both spouses had low incomes and, therefore, were low-rate taxpayers would actually pay more tax when taxed as spouses. Meanwhile, the couple in which both spouses had high incomes would benefit from a tax perspective if they also had considerable wealth and capital. The couple in which one spouse was a high-rate taxpayer and the other had little or no income would also pay less tax when taxed as a couple. As I said in the article, 'In short there will be winners and losers and . . . the losers will be those least able to afford the loss' (Young 1994: 558).

Impact of the rules on differently situated couples

The following section analyses why some couples would pay less tax and others more tax, when treated as spouses for tax purposes, rather than as individuals. It is important to note that the provisions I discussed in 1994 apply in exactly the same manner, and the problems I identified in 1994 have the same impact today. The main reason that a couple with two high-rate taxpayers would benefit from spousal status is that sections 70(6) and 73 of the ITA allow spouses to transfer capital property, either *inter vivos* or on death, to each other on a tax-free basis. The consequence is that any capital gain that may have accrued to the property is deferred until the property is disposed of by the transferee spouse. Absent this relieving provision, tax would be paid on any accrued gain at the time of disposition of the capital property by the transferor spouse.

The couple that consists of a high-rate taxpayer with a spouse who has little or no taxable income can potentially benefit from several tax provisions. First, section 118(1)(a) of the ITA gives a spousal tax credit to an individual who supports their spouse. In addition, the spouse with no taxable income may transfer certain tax credits, including the tuition tax credit, the education credit, the age credit, the pension credit and the disability credit to the high-rate taxpayer spouse, resulting in a significant tax benefit, because the high-income spouse may use them to offset his or her taxes owing. Section 60(1)(iv) of the ITA provides another tax benefit to this couple: the ability of the high-rate taxpayer to contribute funds to a spousal registered retirement savings plan (RRSP) in the name of his or her spouse. Contributions made into any RRSP, individual or spousal, provide an immediate tax benefit, insofar as they are immediately deducted from the contributor's income. Another benefit is that income generated by the investment is not taxed, so long as it remains within the plan. The additional benefit of the specifically spousal

RRSP is that the funds become the property of the spouse. That is, the device serves to shift future retirement income from the high-rate taxpayer to the spouse with little or no income. The result is less tax paid when the funds are taken in retirement.

As I noted in 'Taxing times', basing entitlement to tax benefits on dependency is a privatization of economic responsibility for dependent persons. That is, the private family is encouraged, through the provision of a tax subsidy, to assume responsibility for the economic security of its members, thus, to a certain extent, relieving the state of its responsibility. Furthermore, the tax subsidy in each of the measures discussed above goes to the economically dominant spouse, not the spouse who needs the funds. Such a policy assumes a certain pooling and sharing of income in the relationship, and, as I noted in 'Taxing times', that is not always the case (Young 1994: 557). Furthermore, tax breaks that reward dependency can also be viewed as supporting the 'traditional' family, that is, one in which one spouse participates in the paid labour force and the other works solely in the home. As I discuss later, a recent change to the ITA and a proposed change both reinforce this policy of rewarding the traditional family through tax breaks.

In 1994, it was the couple in which both spouses had low incomes that stood to lose the most by any change that would treat them as spouses. Generally, the change meant that this couple paid more tax than it did when treated as two individuals, a situation that continues today. The primary reasons are the rules that require the combining of spouses' incomes for the purpose of computing the refundable Goods and Services Tax (GST) Tax Credit and the Canada Child Tax Benefit. Entitlement to both these tax credits depends on one's level of income, and, as income increases, the amount of the credit is reduced and eventually phased out completely. Certainly, the loss of these credits by the low-income couples contributed significantly to the tax windfall enjoyed by the federal government when same-sex couples were included as spouses. Kathleen Lahey has estimated, for example, that the overall loss for lesbian and gay couples with respect to the GST Tax Credit was somewhere between $37.3 million and $42.7 million, and the loss for lesbian and gay couples with respect to the Child Tax Benefit was estimated to be $12 billion. Given that over 90 per cent of those claiming the Child Tax Benefit are women, the requirement to aggregate income for the purposes of this benefit had a particularly adverse impact on lesbian couples (Lahey 2001: 63).

As I noted in 'Taxing times', any analysis of the impact of including lesbians and gay men as spouses for tax purposes cannot ignore the gender implications. My conclusion was that gay men would benefit more from inclusion as spouses than lesbians. The reason was, and continues to be, that women tended to earn less than men and have less wealth (Young 1994: 555). Consequently, the tax advantages accorded to high-rate taxpayers would be disproportionately enjoyed by gay men. In addition, because the value of tax deduction is tied to the rate at which a taxpayer pays tax, high-income earners would benefit more from any tax break that is a deduction in the computation of income, with the result that lesbians would not benefit to the same extent as gay men from those tax breaks that are deductions from income. The following example illustrates this point. Taxpayer A and taxpayer B both contribute $10,000 to a spousal RRSP. Taxpayer A has a high income and pays tax at an average rate of 40 per cent, whereas taxpayer B has a lower income and pays tax at an average rate of 10 per cent. Taxpayer A will save $4,000 in taxes owing, whereas taxpayer B will only save $1,000, even though they both contributed the same amount to the spousal RRSP. This effect is referred to as the 'upside-down' subsidy.

Another issue raised in 'Taxing times' was the potential difficulty faced by lesbians and gay men who would be required to designate their spouse on their tax return. They would be 'out' to Revenue Canada, even though they might not be 'out' in any other context, including to their family. Section 239(1)(a) of the ITA states that it is an offence to make a false or deceptive statement on a tax return, meaning that lesbians and gay men living in conjugal relationships had, and continue to have, no legal option in this matter. Given that section 241(4) of the ITA gives Revenue Canada the power to share information from tax returns with a variety of entities, lesbians and gay men who might not wish to be out faced a dilemma. Either they could risk their relationship becoming public or, if not prepared to take that risk, they would be committing an offence under the ITA. Furthermore, should they wish to take advantage of tax benefits associated with, for example, workplace pension plans, then of course they had to be 'out' to their employer, a situation that often exposed them to homophobic behaviour by their employer or fellow employees.

Twenty years on

I now move ahead twenty years to today. My focus again is the impact of rules that take spousal status into account on lesbians and gay men. At this juncture, I should note that Kim Brooks' chapter takes this part of my argument one step further by considering the issue of how adults in relationships at the margins of conjugality understand themselves, and how the ITA responds. My question, however, is different and builds on 'Taxing times' by asking the fundamental question of whether my concerns about the consequences of including lesbians and gay men as spouses were valid. I believe they were. The class and gender problems identified in 'Taxing times' exist unchanged today. Indeed, as I shall demonstrate, many of those concerns have been exacerbated by some recent changes to the income tax system, as well as a proposed further change.

All the provisions identified earlier in this chapter that privilege couples with high incomes and couples in which one spouse is economically dependent on the other remain. The GST Tax Credit and the Child Tax Benefit continue to look to 'family' income as a measure of entitlement, meaning that two low-income individuals who enter a spousal relationship will see the amount received as a tax credit either diminish or disappear altogether. From a gender perspective, women continue to earn less than men. Latest figures show that average earnings for women are $31,000, compared with $45,200 for men, meaning that women only earn 68 cents for every dollar earned by men (Young 2011: 664). Therefore, lesbian couples are more likely to have low incomes compared with gay male couples and, thus, are more likely to suffer the disadvantages related to the couple with two low-rate taxpayers discussed above. Furthermore, the Conservative government of Canada has introduced and proposed new tax measures that take spousal status into account. These measures include rules introduced in 2007 allowing spouses to split pension income and a proposal for further income splitting once the deficit has been erased. Both these measures reward the 'traditional' family and further privatize the responsibility for the economic security of citizens.

Privatization and economic dependency

I now turn to a discussion of the income-splitting measures. As long as income is subject to progressive tax rates, there is an advantage to taxpayers to split income. If income can be shifted from the person with the higher income, who pays tax at a higher marginal rate, to a person who has little or no income and who pays tax at a lower marginal rate, less tax is paid on that income than would otherwise be payable. Section 60.03 of the ITA permits individuals to allocate up to one-half of their pension income to their spouse, thus giving them the opportunity to have that portion of their income taxed as if it had been earned by that spouse. These rules are a significant departure from previous Canadian policy on income splitting in spousal relationships. First, they permit the splitting of investment income between spouses, albeit only if that income is generated by a pension. Second, unlike a spousal RRSP, which involves a transfer of ownership and control, pension income splitting is a fiction: it requires no transfer of funds from the individual to their spouse. The pension remains the property of the individual, even though the spouse is liable to pay the tax on the pension income. All that is required to split pension income is a joint election by the spouses in the year the pension is received.

One consequence of the introduction of pension income splitting is that we may well see the demise of the spousal RRSP. Why would taxpayers establish a spousal RRSP for their spouse, and thereby give the invested monies to their spouse, when they can obtain the same income-splitting result without giving up control of those funds? The new pension-splitting rules have a particularly negative impact on those who are economically dependent on their spouse. Those dependent individuals are liable for tax on the pension income attributed to them, even though they may not have control or ownership of it. Rather, they will have to depend on their spouse's actually sharing that income with them in retirement, a very private response to their economic needs. In addition, to the extent that individuals choose not to establish spousal RRSPs for their spouse, many lesbians and gay men who were the lower-earning partner in a couple and whose relationships end prior to the retirement of their spouse will no longer have their own spousal RRSP to provide some economic security in their retirement.

Reinforcing the traditional family

During the last federal election campaign, the Conservative Party of Canada (2011) announced that, once the deficit was erased, it would introduce legislation to amend the ITA to allow the splitting of up to $50,000 of income from any source by couples with children under the age of 18. The initiative was described as a 'Family Tax Cut' programme, and the main argument made in support of the proposal was that it is unfair for two couples with the same total income to bear different tax burdens simply because the split of the earnings between the individuals in the couples differs. However, there is clearly more to it than simply trying to achieve horizontal equity between the couples. As I shall discuss, this proposal has profound implications for lesbian and gay couples with children, providing a significant incentive to those couples who choose the traditional model of family, with one spouse as the breadwinner and the other remaining in the home, performing household chores and providing childcare. It is also important to note that, although other jurisdictions such as the United States and the United Kingdom treat married couples as one unit for various tax purposes, neither of these jurisdictions goes so far as to provide income splitting within the couple to this degree. Furthermore, in Canada, the income-splitting rules have a broad application, applying to common-law partners as well as to married couples.

The Conservative Party of Canada (2011) has stated that a main rationale for permitting spouses to split income is that couples with the same aggregate incomes should pay the same amount of tax, regardless of how much of that income is earned by one spouse or the other. Thus, for example, if each spouse in couple A earns $50,000, and one spouse in couple B earns $100,000 and the other spouse earns nothing, economic theories based on horizontal equity tell us that both couples should pay the same amount of tax, because they have the same aggregate incomes and, thus, the same level of well-being. Currently, however, couple B will pay more tax than couple A, because of progressive marginal tax rates that tax higher individual levels of income at higher rates. There are two significant problems with this rationale. The first, as Laurin and Kesselman (2011) have noted, is that we need to take account of other taxes, such as payroll taxes, when determining the overall economic status of each couple. Once taxes such as contributions to the Canada Pension

Plan and Employment Insurance are taken into account, the gap between the two couples is significantly reduced, and it may even be eliminated. The second problem with using horizontal equity as a justification for income splitting is that it looks to income as the sole measure of well-being, thereby ignoring other relevant factors. In fact, one can argue that couple B is just as well off as couple A, because, although the former couple may have less after tax income, couple B has significant benefits from the services provided by the non-income-earning spouse. These benefits include the services provided in the home by the stay-at-home spouse, including childcare and household labour. Couple A has to either pay for those services or give up leisure time to provide them.

As noted earlier in the discussion of splitting pension income, a proposal such as this has a negative impact on the autonomy of the spouse with little or no income. The income split is completely fictional. There is no requirement that individuals transfer to their spouse the income that is the subject of the split. To a certain extent, this policy appears to assume that income is pooled and shared within spousal relationships, but studies show that this is not the case for the majority of couples (Kesselman 2008). Another problem is that, although there may be an overall benefit for the couple, the marginal effective tax rate for the spouse with little or no income goes from zero or a low rate to a higher rate, and that spouse is responsible for paying the tax on income allocated to him or her, without necessarily having received that income. Again, the consequence is a reinforcement of the traditional family, in which one spouse controls the finances, and the other is dependent on that spouse for economic security.

For lesbians and gay men, this provision has the effect of encouraging heteronormativity. Despite the fact that they are in same-sex relationships, the tax system is pushing them towards adopting behaviours that mimic heterosexual couples, with a highly gendered division of labour. In this volume, Rosie Harding demonstrates how both parliamentary and judicial discourse in the United Kingdom continues to reinscribe heteronormative visions of the family into gay and lesbian households in the family law context. My point is that the same is true in the tax context. The income-splitting rules simply reinforce the heteronormative family, in which there is a breadwinner who works outside the home and a stay-at-home spouse. To the extent that including lesbians and gay men may have had, or might have in the future, a radicalizing impact on notions of 'family', this kind of proposal nullifies or severely counteracts that possibility.

As many have commented, income splitting is regressive in its impact because it favours those with high incomes over those with lower incomes (see Wooley 2007; Laurin and Kesselman 2011; Philipps 2011; Young 2011). As Laurin and Kesselman (2011: 10) concluded, more than $1 billion of the annual tax subsidy associated with this proposed income splitting, estimated to be just over $4 billion, would go to the 8 per cent of families in the top income quartile, in which the lower-income spouse earns less than 15 per cent of the family's income. The effect is an upside-down subsidy, with most of the tax subsidy going to the couples that need it least, that is, those with the highest income. As with other tax measures that take spousal status into account, this one has a gendered impact, with gay male couples more likely to be in the top income quartile than lesbian couples.

The limitation of this proposed tax subsidy to couples with children, rather than all spousal couples, tells us that the policy is about much more than simply ensuring that couples with the same aggregate income pay the same amount of tax. If the policy was based on horizontal equity concerns, then income splitting would be available to all couples, regardless of whether they had children or not. Clearly, the limitation of the subsidy to couples with children is about rewarding the 'traditional' family, the couple with children, in which one spouse stays at home to take care of the children. To the extent that one believes that tax subsidies should be given to families with children, it should be noted that the tax system is replete with tax subsidies available to families with children. The Child Tax Benefit and the Child Tax Credit are both intended to assist parents with children by defraying some of the costs associated with raising children. The Child Care Expenses Deduction is a deduction in the computation of income that provides a partial subsidy for the costs of childcare for parents participating in the paid labour force. More recently, the Conservative government introduced the Child Fitness Credit and the Child Arts Tax Credit, tax expenditures that give a tax credit for a portion of fees paid by parents whose children participate in sporting and artistic activities. Whether an additional tax subsidy for a couple with children, most useful for such a limited number of families, can be justified is questionable. Almost 16 per cent of families with children are single-parent families, and yet single-parent families are not eligible for the tax subsidy, a fact that again indicates that the intention is to reward those who live in a 'traditional' family consisting of two parents of asymmetrical earnings and their children.

What next?

In 2001, the Law Commission of Canada (2001: ix) launched a major research project titled *Beyond Conjugality: Recognizing and Supporting Close Personal Adult Relationships*, a project entailing a 'fundamental rethinking of the way in which governments regulate relationships'. The Commission concluded that governments rely too heavily on marital and common-law relationships in accomplishing state objectives. It suggested that the government re-evaluate the way in which it regulates relationships, and it devised a four-part methodology to facilitate this re-evaluation. One question posed by this new methodology was, 'Are the objectives of the legislation legitimate and, if so, are relationships relevant to achieving them?' (Law Commission of

Canada 2001: xix). The ITA was legislation that was reviewed in this report. Other than the report, there has been no consideration by the legislators of why we take spousal relationships into account for tax purposes, and whether such a policy can be justified. It is now time to revisit the issues raised by the Law Commission of Canada in the tax context.

Other than maintaining the status quo, it appears that there are three possible approaches to dealing with some of the problems associated with the tax rules that apply to spouses. First, one could substitute a criterion that does not take conjugality into account and have the current rules apply to a different group of taxpayers, one defined by reference to other factors that are more relevant today than spousal status. As I shall discuss, one suggestion is to look to relationships based on economic interdependence, rather than those based solely on spousal status. Second, one could change some of the tax rules so that they operate in a fairer and less problematic manner. At the same time, there may well be some rules that should simply be repealed. Third, one could maintain the integrity of the individual as the unit of taxation and repeal all rules that take spousal status into account for tax purposes. As already mentioned, my conclusion is that the third approach should be adopted.

Before turning to a discussion of the three options for reform, it is important to recognize that the tax measures under discussion are tax expenditures. Tax expenditures are defined as any deviation from the benchmark personal income-tax structure. They include measures such as deductions in the computation of income, tax credits, exemptions from tax and deferral of tax payable. Tax expenditures are the functional equivalent of direct government expenditures, with one main difference. Instead of being delivered as a direct grant to an individual, tax expenditures are delivered by the tax system. The distinction is significant. Whereas we tend to analyse the impact of a technical tax provision by reference to criteria such as horizontal and vertical equity, neutrality and simplicity, we apply different criteria to tax expenditures. As the Law Commission of Canada has asked, 'Could the objective be better served through the use of some other government policy instrument?' (2001: 65). To this question, I would add: Is the measure fair, or does it discriminate in an inappropriate manner against some taxpayers and in favour of others? I now discuss three possible options for reform.

Replace spousal status with another criterion

In 2010, Anthony Infanti published a groundbreaking article in which he argued that the USA should abandon the joint return and replace 'it with a system of mandatory individual filing that recognizes all economically interdependent relationships' (2010: 609). In so doing, he drew heavily on the work of the Commission, which had also recommended that economic interdependence replace conjugality for a variety of legal purposes. His argument, however, differs in one important respect. Unlike the Commission, which proposed to establish terms that would have to be met in order for individuals to qualify as economically interdependent taxpayers, Infanti recommended a system that would allow taxpayers to 'identify their economically interdependent relationships for themselves' (2010: 647).

Before moving to a general discussion of the appropriateness of substituting economic interdependence for spousal status, it is useful to consider this proposal in the context of one particular tax expenditure. In 2001, the Law Commission of Canada recommended that, 'the provisions that allow capital property to be transferred tax free between spouses . . . apply to all persons living together in economically interdependent relationships' (2001: 89). As discussed above, a transfer of capital property by an individual to his or her spouse takes place in a manner that defers any capital gain that may have accrued to the capital property until the spouse subsequently disposes of the property. The 'rollover' is available on both an *inter vivos* basis and on death. These rules serve a variety of purposes. From a practical perspective, if transfers between spouses were taxable events, the Canada Revenue Agency would have to trace all such transactions in order to ensure that any tax owing was paid. Given the informal context in which these transactions occur, such a task would be difficult. Another problem is that, because these transactions do not take place in the open market, there may be a liquidity problem, with no cash available to pay the tax. The rollover rules are also intended to encourage the redistribution of property within the relationship, especially from those with significant wealth to their less well-off spouse.

These rules can be critiqued on a variety of bases. First, it is questionable how effective they are at achieving their stated aims. There are many reasons why an individual may choose not to transfer property to their spouse on an *inter vivos* basis, including concern about transferring control of that property to the spouse. These rules are also affected by the operation of the attribution rules. Section 74.1 of the ITA provides that, if capital property that is transferred to a spouse at a less than fair market value generates income, that income is attributed to the transferor and not taxed to the spouse, thereby preventing income splitting with respect to income from property. Given that most of these transfers are presumably gifts, the attribution of income may well operate to deter taxpayers from entering these transactions. It is impossible to determine whether the rollover rules do encourage the redistribution of wealth on an *inter vivos* basis in spousal relationships. Second, they only benefit those couples with considerable wealth who own capital property. Canada does not have gift or estate taxes, and, consequently, these rules provide a huge benefit to those couples, because there is no taxation of any appreciation in the value of the capital property owned by the couple, as long as it is owned by either of the spouses. Third, although it may be difficult to trace *inter vivos* transfers between spouses, the same cannot be said of transfers on death, where the will or other documents relating to probate or intestacy will provide information about the transfer.

The Law Commission of Canada argued that, 'economic interdependencies that characterize close personal relationships are the very *raison d'être* of the rollover rules' (2001: 89).[8] Thus, rules that limit the rollover to those in spousal relationships are over-inclusive, because not all spouses are in economically interdependent relationships. At the same time, the rules are under-inclusive, because they exclude many who are in economically interdependent relationships, although not spouses.

I disagree with the recommendation of the Commission and believe, for two reasons, that the rules should be repealed outright. First, as mentioned, the application of the attribution rules may deter taxpayers from entering into these transactions, thereby obviating the need for the rollover rules. Second, tracing problems are not unique to intra-spousal transfers. Transfers to adult children or close friends can be difficult to trace. Furthermore, the ITA provides for a self-assessing system, in which taxpayers are required to declare a variety of transactions that cannot always be traced, including gifts to third parties.

At a macro level, taking economic interdependence into account for any tax purpose is highly problematic. If the ITA includes a definition of interdependence and ascribes that status to couples, then the current inequities in the ITA are being reinforced and continued, albeit with a different group. If couples are allowed to self-identify, then, presumably, the decision to self-identify or not will be driven solely by the tax advantages that may accrue. As we have seen, those advantages tend to benefit the couple in which at least one individual, and often both, has a high income.

Change some rules that take spousal status into account

An alternative to redefining the markers of entitlement to tax benefits and responsibilities is to consider each provision of the ITA that takes spousal status into account and determine if it could be amended in such a way that the problems identified above would be eliminated. If not, the provision could be repealed. So, for example, the Law Commission of Canada (2001: 82) recognized the problems for couples with low incomes that arise from the requirement to aggregate income for the purposes of the GST tax credit. Consequently, it recommended that, 'Parliament should amend the Income Tax Act so that the amount of the Goods and Services Tax credit to which individuals are entitled is not reduced if they are married or cohabiting in a conjugal relationship' (Law Commission of Canada 2001: 82). The difficulty with such a proposal is that the tax system is part of the broader social and economic policies in Canada. There are many social programmes that aggregate the income of spouses for the purposes of entitlement to benefits, including social assistance and student loans, among others. Tax expenditure analysis tells us that we should view tax expenditures such as the GST tax credit as the functional equivalent of a direct grant, such as social assistance. Therefore, it is difficult to treat these kinds of programme in isolation from one another.

Abolish spousal status as a marker for tax purposes

By redefining spouse in the ITA to include same-sex couples, we simply expanded the group to which provisions based on spousal status apply. The problems that I discussed in 'Taxing times' remained unchanged. In the years since, the federal government has signalled that it believes strongly that different tax rules should apply to those in spousal relationships and those who are not. That policy simply exacerbates the problems already embedded in the ITA. I believe that a strong argument can be made that the integrity of the individual as the tax unit should be restored in Canada, and all tax expenditures that are based on spousal status should be repealed. Although the opportunity to address the issue of why we take spousal status into account for tax purposes was not taken up when lesbians and gay men sought equality with heterosexual couples for tax purposes, surely it is time now to revisit the issue and expunge the tax rules that disadvantage those who can afford it least.

Conclusion

In this chapter, I have revisited my critique of efforts made in the late 1980s and 1990s to have lesbians and gay men included as spouses for tax purposes. My conclusion is that the critique remains as valid today as it was then. Indeed, new rules, such as those permitting pension splitting and proposals to extend income-splitting opportunities to couples with children, simply compound the problems I previously identified.

This state of affairs raises the question of why tax law and policy have been so impervious to an equality analysis. One reason is that our income tax system tends to be seen as a revenue-raising instrument, rather than, as I have discussed, a spending programme. When one focuses on the revenue-raising aspect, economic criteria are used to evaluate its effectiveness. Thus, we ask: Is the tax system efficient, or does it distort economic activity? Does the system violate horizontal equity by not treating equals equally for tax purposes? Is the system vertically equitable in treating people in differing economic situations differently in an appropriate way? Equality analysis is not part of this economically based method of evaluation. It is analysis from the angle of tax expenditure that allows us to focus on the spending side and to determine who benefits from particular measures and – perhaps more importantly – who does not. To date, such an analysis has been primarily the domain of feminist scholars (see, e.g., Lahey 1988, 2001; Young 2000, 2009a, 2009b; Philipps 2011) and, to a certain extent, the Law Commission of Canada (2001). Yet this work has not resulted in meaningful legislative reform, and, indeed, the Conservative government abolished the Law Commission of Canada in 2006.

From a political perspective, it is unsurprising that government tax policymakers have eschewed an equality analysis in any review of the impact of current tax measures and in the design of new tax policies. Since 2006, Canada has been governed by a Conservative government, one that has been committed to a policy of privatization of the responsibility for economic security and a return to the traditional family, at a general level and, more specifically, through tax measures. It was the Conservative government that introduced pension income splitting and that is proposing family income splitting. In 2011, after two terms as a minority government, the Conservative party won a majority in the House of Commons. There is every reason to believe that one consequence will be a continuation of the development of tax policy without reflection on its impact from an equality perspective.

The current political situation reinforces my opinion that it is time to remove all tax expenditures that take spousal status into account from the tax system and, to the extent that subsidies should be provided in certain circumstances, to deliver those subsidies directly. As we have seen, the tax system is too unwieldy a tool for accomplishing sophisticated social and economic policies. It is especially dangerous to use it in this manner when an equality analysis is totally absent from the development of the tax expenditures.

Acknowledgement

Many thanks to Rebecca Coad for her outstanding research assistance with this chapter.

Notes

1   RSC 1985, c 1 (5th Supp). In 1994, s 252(4) restricted the definition of spouse to a 'person of the opposite sex who cohabits with a taxpayer in a conjugal relationship and has so cohabited with the taxpayer for 12 months'. Married persons also qualified for spousal status under the ITA.
2   SC 2000 c 12. For tax purposes, a definition of common-law partner was added to the ITA. Section 248 defines common-law partner as 'a person who cohabits . . . in a conjugal relationship with the taxpayer and has so cohabited with the taxpayer for a continuous period of at least one year'. In addition, a married person is defined as a spouse for tax purposes. In this chapter, I use the term 'spouse' to refer to both married persons and common-law partners.
3   SC 2005 c 33.
4   [1993] 1 SCR 554; RSC 1985 c H-6.
5   (1992) 16 CHRR D/184 (Ont Bd Inq).
6   The value of this tax break is considerable, being approximately $23 billion for 2011 (latest figures available) (Department of Finance 2012).
7   38 OR (3d) 577 (CA).
8   Ibid.

References

Conservative Party of Canada (2011) *Here for Canada: Stephen Harper's Low-Tax Plan for Jobs and Economic Growth*, Ottawa. Online. Available at: www.conservative.ca/media/2012/06/ConservativePlatform2011_ENs.pdf (accessed 17 June 2013).

Department of Finance (2012) *Tax Expenditures and Evaluations, 2011*, Ottawa. Online. Available at: www.fin.gc.ca/taxexp-depfisc/2011/taxexp11-eng.asp (accessed 17 June 2013).

Infanti, A.C. (2010) 'Decentralizing family: An inclusive proposal for individual tax filing in the United States', *Utah Law Review*, 2010: 605–64.

Kesselman, J. (2008) *Income Splitting and Joint Taxation of Couples: What's Fair?*, Montreal: Institute for Research on Public Policy.

Lahey, K. (1988) *The Taxation of Women in Canada: A Research Report*, Ontario: Faculty of Law, Queen's University (unpublished).

—— (2001) *The Impact of Relationship Recognition on Lesbian Women in Canada: Still Separate and Only Somewhat 'Equivalent'*, Ottawa: Status of Women Canada. Online. Available at: http://publications.gc.ca/collections/Collection/SW21–82–2001E.pdf (accessed 17 June 2013).

Laurin, A. and Kesselman, J. (2011) 'Income splitting for two parent families: Who gains, who doesn't and at what cost?', *C.D. Howe Institute Commentary*, No. 335. Online. Available at: http://cdhowe.org/pdf/Commentary_335.pdf (accessed 17 June 2013).

Law Commission of Canada (2001) *Beyond Conjugality: Recognizing and Supporting Close Personal and Adult Relationships*, Ottawa: Queen's Printer.

Philipps, L. (2011) 'Income splitting and gender equality: The case for incentivizing intra-household wealth transfers', in K. Brooks, Å. Gunnarsson, L. Philipps and M. Wersig (eds) *Challenging Gender Inequality in Tax Policy Making: Comparative Perspectives*, Oxford: Hart.

Wooley, F. (2007) 'Liability without control: The curious case of pension income splitting', *Canadian Tax Journal*, 55: 603–25.

Young, C.F.L. (1994) 'Taxing times for lesbians and gay men: Equality at what cost?', *Dalhousie Law Journal*, 17: 534–59.

—— (1998) 'Spousal status, pension benefits and tax: *Rosenberg v. Canada (Attorney General)*', *Canadian Labour and Employment Law Journal*, 6: 435–53.

—— (2000) *What's Sex Got To Do With It? Tax and the Family*, Ottawa: Law Commission of Canada. Online. Available at: http://publications.gc.ca/site/eng/96865/publication.html (accessed 17 June 2013).

—— (2009a) 'Taking spousal status into account for tax purposes: The pitfalls and penalties', in A. Bottomley and S. Wong (eds) *Changing Contours of Domestic Life, Family and Law: Caring and Sharing*, Oxford: Hart.

—— (2009b) 'Tax and the family: The gendered impact of rules that take spousal status into account for tax purposes', in H.N. Scheiber and L. Mayal (eds) *Japanese Family Law in Comparative Perspective*, Berkeley, CA: Robbins Collection.

—— (2011) 'Pensions, privatization and poverty: The gendered impact', *Canadian Journal of Women and the Law*, 23: 661–85.

Chapter 9

The historiographical operations of gay rights

Roderick A. Ferguson

On 28 October 2009, US President Barack Obama signed the Matthew Shepard and James Byrd Hate Crimes Prevention Act, named after men who were, respectively, the victims of heinous, homophobically and racially motived hate crimes. In his remarks, Mr Obama drew the histories of anti-racist and anti-homophobic struggles together, saying,

> This is the culmination of a struggle that has lasted more than a decade ... Time and again we've been reminded of the difficulty of building a nation in which we're all free to live and love as we see fit.[1]

Mr Obama went on to suggest that legislation against hate crimes based on sexual orientation was inspired by the legacies of the civil rights movement:

> In April of 1968, just one week after the assassination of Martin Luther King, as our nation mourned in grief and shuddered in anger, President Lyndon Johnson signed landmark civil rights legislation. This was the first time we enshrined into law federal protections against crimes motivated by religious or racial hatred – the law on which we build today.[2]

The 2009 speech is significant because, two years before Mr Obama repealed 'Don't ask, don't tell', and three years before he endorsed gay marriage, he had revealed in the passage of the Shepard–Byrd Act that he was already a champion for and a subject of gay rights discourse, that is, its interpretation of anti-racist and anti-homophobic struggles and their relationship to the liberal nation-state.

In *Freedom with Violence: Race, Sexuality, and the US State*, Chandan Reddy discusses the Obama administration's use of anti-racism and anti-homophobia in the Act. He argues, 'For Obama, the Shepard–Byrd Act extended the antiviolence protections originally designed by the federal government to combat white supremacy and to promote race-neutral liberalism within the nation-state' (Reddy 2011: 5). Reddy goes on to note that leaders of GLBTQ national organizations lauded the bill, arguing that the Act was 'one of the building blocks to full equality – and [equal] treatment under federal law in all areas of our lives' (ibid.). The political 'genius' of the Shepard–Byrd Act, as he argues, was that it tied protections against hate crimes to a 'military appropriations bill that grew the military budget to its highest level in U.S. history' (ibid.: 3–4), hence neutralizing conservative and leftist opposition at the same time – neutralizing by tying anti-homophobia and anti-racism to the National Defense Authorization Act. In a related argument in his book, *Normal Life: Administrative Violence, Critical Trans Politics, and the Limits of Law*, Dean Spade (2011) has challenged the presumption that the state – through hate crimes legislation – is the realm of a political and legal Eden. He argues that hate crimes legislation has also fostered conditions of vulnerability for trans people, particularly for those marginalized by race and class.

Seen from the context of gay rights mobilization, the Obama administration's policies and stances around hate crimes, gay marriage and gay participation in the military are not the stand-alone gestures of a sympathetic presidential administration, but the effects of a gay rights discourse and its strategic investments in the histories and narratives of civil rights. In fact, the gay rights movement – as Reddy and Spade suggest – relies on a certain telling of the civil rights movement. For example, as hate crimes legislation such as the Shepard–Byrd Act demonstrates, and as Reddy has shown, gay rights re-narrate struggles over sexuality by re-narrating struggles over race. Specifically, they do so by constructing the state as the domain of resolution and by promoting rights-based practices as the *raison d'être* for political agency, making rights the point of political action and political transformation. Hence, gay rights discourse defines sexual freedom and anti-racist liberation as quests for equality under the state's terms. Yet, by seeing rights as the end of politics, the gay rights movement also erases the histories of how anti-racist and queer movements mobilized sexuality, gender and race to challenge and move beyond the logics and practices of the state.

As an exhibition of the historiographical agendas of the gay rights movement, the Obama address from 2009 illustrates the very phenomenon that this chapter investigates – that is, how gay rights are social formations with historiographical imperatives, ones that work to organize our historical understandings of minority difference, as well as political redress and agency. The Obama address and the National Defense Authorization Act are thus expressions of a contemporary political and legal moment in the US that shows – in Reddy's words – 'the law's unique dependence on historical narrative – on narrating the history of a social group as an inextricable aspect of the justice the law promotes' (2008: 2859). Reddy was speaking of *Loving v Virginia*,[3] the historic US Supreme Court case that overturned state laws prohibiting interracial marriage, now the legal victory that marriage equality advocates cite as their primary inspiration. As the gay rights movement re-narrates the *Loving* case, the movement reveals how the incitement to gay rights is a catalyst to historicize – rightly or wrongly – sexuality's relationship to race and to minoritized subjects' relationship to the state.

By reading the gay rights movement as a historiographical operation, this chapter observes how that movement has assembled and legitimized a mode of power, one that uses sexuality and race to make itself credible. As a historiographical enterprise, the gay rights movement reimagines the state and the civil rights era; it formulates rights-based actions and the state as the primary ways to achieve minority freedom. Finally, it produces certain disavowals and silences, disavowals and silences around revolutionary articulations of sexuality and race, articulations that challenged the notion that the state is the only domain of political agency, or even the presumptive one. In doing so, the gay rights movement exposes itself as a social formation that subjugates our knowledge of those very movements that articulated race and sexuality as critiques of the state and as levers for potentially transcending state logics and practices.

In the following, I engage historiography less as a matter of historical accuracy, although accuracy has its place. Rather, in this chapter, the critique of historiography is more a matter of which narrative illuminates agencies and conceptions of freedom beyond those prescribed by the state and counter to those that normalize the state as the addressee in matters of inequality. This critique attempts to illuminate how the gay rights movement is simultaneously a legal, social and textual formation – 'legal' in the sense that gay rights propose ways to mobilize the law to address inequality, 'social' in the sense that gay rights suggest – sometimes implicitly, often explicitly – relationships between minoritized subjects and the state, and 'textual' in the sense that they negotiate between various, often conflicting ways of narrating historical relationships between minoritized communities and the state. As a formation that aims for equality under the state, the gay rights movement shows how the pursuit of equality for minoritized groups always entails weighing and contriving relationships to the state, an effort that enlists the services of textuality, subjectivity and the law. In this historical moment, therefore, we can observe how gay rights – as a movement and as an emergent mode of law – help to naturalize a conception of history in which the state is taken as the legitimate mediator of minority freedom and satisfaction, a moment in which rights are seen as the primary resource for sexual, gender and racial liberation.

Gay rights: the writing of sexuality and race

In order to fully appreciate the historiographical properties of the gay rights movement, we need to have a developed sense of what historiography is as a mode of power/knowledge.

In *The Writing of History*, Michel de Certeau (1988) designates hegemonic historiography as an institutional expression of power/knowledge, an expression that is at once the constitution of a community and the delimitation of what belongs within and outside that community. He writes, for instance:

> All historiographical research is articulated over a socioeconomic, political, and cultural place of production. It implies an area of elaboration that particular determinations circumscribe: a liberal profession, a position as an observer or a professor, a group of learned people, and so forth.
>
> (de Certeau 1988: 58)

The writing of history, in other words, is not simply a scholarly practice. It also connotes practices of socialization, conventions that work to establish a community of interpreters. He goes on to argue, 'It is in terms of this place that its methods are established, its topography of interests can be specified, its dossiers and its interrogation of documents are organized' (ibid.). Historiography works, therefore, to establish certain orthodoxies around its fields and texts of interests and how they are analysed.

According to de Certeau, historiography also has a particular relationship with the state. As he says, 'Historiography takes the position of the subject of action – of the prince, whose objective is to "make history"' (de Certeau 1988: 7). As such, historiography assigns intelligence the role of determining how power can manoeuvre within and against certain realities and conditions. As he puts it, 'Its purpose is to construct a coherent discourse that specifies the "shots" that a power is capable of making in relation to given facts, by virtue of an art of dealing with the elements imposed by an environment' (ibid.).

Historiography thus attempts to turn people into state actors who will take up the cause of the state as they mediate challenges to and for the state. Turning people into state actors is the result of that normalization by which the state is taken as the ideal and final arbiter of justice, and as the most practical and judicious author of our agency. Part of the historiographical operation is, therefore, to develop within those people modes of intelligence that can provide tutelage to the state about how to strategize against conflict and turn it into a legible and manageable item. In such a context, laws and rights become primary mechanisms for developing those modes of intelligence, all the while producing a nexus between the state, the legal sphere and subjectivity/identity.

The gay rights movement takes up these historiographical aspects and, in doing so, becomes a way of writing history, making history and producing subjects. In this vein, gay rights mobilization attempts to establish a community of interpreters and social actors who will take sexuality and other modes of difference as ones that can be fulfilled by the state. Part of the historiographical exercise of the gay rights movement, therefore, involves producing social agents who will inform the state about how to manage potentially volatile and insurgent social differences. In doing so, the gay rights movement works to subjugate those histories of race and sexuality that became the occasions for insurgent rebellions against the state, histories that also provided models of subjectivity and community not limited by the prescriptions of citizenship and rights.

The disavowal of anti-statist liberation

To restate, the gay rights movement is only denotatively a social movement. It is also a social formation that encourages – in the name of gay identity and history – modes of intelligence consistent with state ideals. In addition, the gay rights movement is also a formation that promotes modes of subjugation, especially concerning those histories and practices that destabilize the state as the best technology for social transformation. More specifically, the histories that the gay rights movement and its ensuing legislation have to subjugate are precisely the movements around anti-racist and anti-homophobic liberation from the 1960s and 1970s – particularly the intersections of the black power and gay liberation movements. We can think of this subjugation as part of the conventions of civil rights and New Left historiography. As historian Peniel Joseph argues, the silencing of the black power movement, in particular, helps to constitute the field of civil rights historiography. As he states:

> Black power stands at the center of the declension narratives of the 1960s: the movement's destructiveness poisoning the innocence of the New Left, corrupting a generation of black activists, and steering the drive for civil rights off course in a way that reinforced racial segregation by giving politicians a clear, frightening scapegoat.
>
> (Joseph 2009: 707)

Discussing gay liberation organizations such as Gay Liberation Front, historian Terrance Kissack argues that New Left historiography is also characterized by a 'historiographical oversight' that diminishes the importance of movements after 1968, an oversight put in place by histories that,

> juxtapose the 'good sixties', or the early period of antiwar and civil rights activism, with the 'bad sixties', the final years of the decade characterized by the turn towards totalizing critiques of 'the system', a rejection of liberalism and electoral politics, and the advocacy of violent revolutionary action.
>
> (Kissack 1995: 106)

New Left and civil rights historiographies help to shape and inform the discursive contours of the gay rights movement as well. Inasmuch as the gay rights movement and its platform for anti-homophobia (i.e. hate crime legislation, marriage equality and military participation) silence the history of radical anti-racist and queer movements, they repeat a convention within the dominant historiography of civil rights and the New Left – that is, the marginalization of radical movements that challenged the prowess of liberalism, electoral politics and rights-based actions.

Although the narrative of political decline frames the black power and gay liberation movements as politically unviable and divisive, these movements were great inspirations to radical activists and organizations in the late 1960s and afterwards, inspiring people minoritized by class, racial, gender and sexual inequality to imagine and forge coalitions that could transcend the social and ideological restrictions of liberal capitalist states. The Black Panther Party, in particular, provided what black studies scholar Amy Ongiri describes as radical models of affiliation and identification that, 'created and provoked a radical affiliation among people . . . far removed from the African American struggle' (2009: 70). Indeed, the Gay Male Workshop for the 1970 Revolutionary People's Constitutional Convention (RPCC) – a meeting of radical activist organizations – credited the Black Panther Party with commanding the vanguard of all the oppositional movements. In the tradition of the Black Panther Party and the Young Lords, Third World Gay Revolution, a 1970s group of black and Latino queers who broke away from Gay Liberation Front, stated in their Sixteen-Point Program, 'All the colored and oppressed peoples of the world are one nation under oppression'.

Similarly, gay liberation activists and movements helped to promote sexuality as part of radical insurgency. For instance, the writer Jean Genet visited the US in 1970 and spent time with the Black Panthers and, in that time, advanced arguments about the revolutionary potential of sexuality. As Angela Davis (1991) states, 'It was Jean Genet who heightened the Black Panther awareness to the Homosexual Rights issue.'

One of the outcomes of that visit was Huey Newton's 1970 speech about women's and gay liberation at the RPCC. Newton used the speech to help foster a relationship between sexuality, feminism and black revolutionary politics. As a document, the speech records a moment in which new associations and modes of affiliation were being worked out between sexuality, race, gender and the critique of liberal capitalism. Newton began the speech by designating homosexuality as a social formation with the potential for revolutionary ruptures. As he states, 'During the past few years, strong movements have developed among women and homosexuals seeking their liberation. There has been some uncertainty about how to relate to those movements' (Newton 1970). Newton goes on to suggest that the radicalization of homosexuality and womanhood is part of a coalitional politics, an effort that is part of the labour of all radical actors, regardless of identity:

> Whatever your personal opinion and your insecurities about homosexuality and the various liberation movements among homosexuals and

women (and I speak of the homosexuals and women as oppressed groups) we should try to unite with them in a revolutionary fashion.

(Ibid.)

Newton's speech at the RPCC points to a new type of work that was being performed on gender, sexuality and race as modes of difference within the US, ones that would understand the radicalization and social productivity of those modes in terms of their imaginative departures from liberal ideologies.

Within this context, one of the areas designated for radicalization was the family as a social structure. As legal scholar Nancy Polikoff argues (2009: 530), 'The early gay rights movement stood squarely with those who supported diverse family forms and who saw the struggle for gay liberation as linked to the struggles of the other social justice movements of the late 1960s and 70s'. For radical queer activists, the main ideological obstacle to the diversification of the family was marriage. Polikoff goes on to state,

At the time, marriage was part of the problem, not the solution. Marriage was a problem because it channeled everyone into only one approved relationship, it regulated the lives of men and women along gender lines, and it policed the boundary between acceptable and unacceptable sexual expression.

(Ibid.)

In other words, critiquing marriage and developing alternatives to it were part of a coalitional experiment that attempted to simultaneously designate differences of gender, race, class and sexuality as the seeds for establishing forms of community and intimacy other than those offered by dominant institutions and imaginaries.

It is important not to romanticize the coalitional efforts of these organizations: there were dismaying internal struggles over racism, homophobia and sexism, struggles that occasioned the collapse of several organizations. Despite those failures, one must note that this was a moment in which radical social movements attempted to produce the conditions for radicalizing modes of difference and subjectivity, understanding part of that radicalization as an effort to address audiences other than the state and as a proposal to dis-embed forms of minority difference from the domicile of the state. Inasmuch as radicalization meant establishing modes of affiliation and identification across modes of difference, radicalization also meant disrupting hegemonic historiography's efforts to train our political and intellectual sights on the state as the never-ending location for social resolution.

This form of radicalization challenged what de Certeau refers to as the 'depoliticization' at the heart of hegemonic historiography. For de Certeau, history was depoliticized as it was institutionalized as a formal discipline, an institutionalization that – according to him – took place spatially as history was reorganized into the materially and spatially secluded and exclusive place of the seventeenth-century university. This seclusion not only provided the institutional conditions for history as a discipline, but helped to establish its ideological character as well. Summing up the ideological effects of this institutional and spatial seclusion, de Certeau argues,

> In the fashion of a withdrawal relative to public and religious affairs (which are themselves also organized in particular bodies), a 'scientific' place is established. A rupture provides the basis for a social unity which will then become a 'science'.
>
> (1988: 60–1)

For de Certeau, that rupture represents a historic and epistemological break from social complexity, and it accounts for the genealogical DNA of historiography in its hegemonic form. As a historiographical operation, the gay rights movement announces its own rise from this genealogy, disavowing and obscuring the very complexities that have shaped the histories that the movement interprets and claims to represent. In point of fact, the subjugation of the radical movements around race and sexuality illustrates how the gay rights movement as a historiographical enterprise attempts to suppress the social complexity of anti-racist and anti-homophobic struggles and their relationships to the US state. More specifically, the gay rights movement 'depoliticizes' those histories by removing them from discussions of how sexuality and race participated in histories that addressed the state as a contradictory domain characterized by irresolvable inequalities, silencing those histories in which sexuality and race were signs of an imaginative and critical flight from the seclusions and domiciliations of the state.

Placing race and sexuality

Domiciling modes of difference – that is, placing them within the restrictive parameters of liberal ideology – is constitutive of the US nation-state, in particular, and the liberal capitalist state, in general. Marx foreshadows this observation in 'On the Jewish question'. In that essay, Marx argues that political emancipation through the state – emancipation from restrictions caused by birth, rank and education – is the individual's way of emancipating him- or herself in a 'devious way, through an intermediary, however necessary this intermediary may be' (1978: 32). Under the state, the individual's emancipation is devious, because the state nominally abolishes potentially exclusionary qualifications (i.e. property ownership, birth, rank, race, education, etc.) as the basis for becoming citizens, electors and representatives. Yet, as Marx observes, the state allows those exclusions to 'act after their own fashion' and to 'manifest their particular nature' (ibid.: 33). In such a context, the political emancipation of sexual orientation – that is, with the state as intermediary – will allow social exclusions to act and manifest all the same.[4] Another way of stating this is to say that the state reveals itself as a historiographical formation as it narrates itself as the domain of political emancipation, by subjugating knowledge about how it promotes and develops systems of inequality.

The current context around marriage equality, gay participation in the military and hate crimes legislation within the US allows us to see political emancipation's historiographical deployment of histories of anti-racist and anti-homophobic struggle, *as well as* the 'deviousness' that Marx describes. In her discussion of *Loving v Virginia*, queer studies scholar Siobhan Somerville points out the legal heterosexism that undergirded the US Supreme Court's interpretation of that case. She writes,

> What activists fail to see when using *Loving* as a precedent for same-sex-marriage rights is that the case is not parallel to a history of homosexuality, as it is represented in the law; rather, it is embedded in the same history of sexuality that has determined the status of gay men and lesbians as excluded others.
>
> (2005: 357)

Rather than the *Loving* case possessing the ingredients for queer emancipation, it actually represents a pyrrhic victory where minority liberation is concerned, nullifying the racist basis of anti-miscegenation laws, while bolstering the state's then heterosexist bias. Somerville continues: 'By establishing a fundamental right to marriage regardless of race, the federal state in effect shored up the privileges of heterosexuality through a logic that was on the surface antiracist and anti-white supremacist' (ibid.). The gay rights movement's ideological investment in *Loving v Virginia* is, therefore, just one indication that the movement walks in step with political emancipation's constitutive subjugations and deceptions.

Polikoff approaches the deviousness of political emancipation when she notes that the attainment of gay marriage, under the US system, will only benefit same-sex couples with a particular economic profile. As she states, 'as it turns out, marriage won't produce higher benefits for most same-sex couples, because only married couples with one higher income earner and a stay-at-home or low-income-earning spouse are the winners under our current Social Security system' (2009, 548 (footnote omitted)). That deviousness – the reality that marriage equality will only represent some, even as it feigns to represent all – became part of the political intelligence of gay rights organizations. Discussing Gay and Lesbian Advocates and Defendants' use of couples who would fit the profile appropriate for the cause, she writes,

> GLAD [Gay and Lesbian Advocates and Defendants] could not use any married same-sex couples as plaintiffs but had to select those who met

the particular, gendered family profile for which Social Security was created – a couple with one primary wage earner.

(Ibid.)

In Marx's language, marriage equality would produce the conditions whereby exclusions will 'act after their own fashion' and 'manifest their particular nature' – even for the very people that it purports to benefit. As Polikoff observes,

> Even if the constituency for gay rights groups is only gay and lesbian families, and not all those harmed by outdated notions of family in Social Security law, the decision to seek equality under the current law for a minority of married same-sex couples ignores the needs of all the other married same-sex couples who would benefit more from reform of the system for everyone. In this case, equality for some reinforces injustice for many.

(Ibid.: 550 (footnote omitted))

In 2013, the deviousness of political emancipation could be seen in two US Supreme Court decisions. On consecutive days in June of that year, the Court demonstrated how the political emancipation of sexual orientation could indeed allow other modes of exclusion to act after their own fashion. On 26 June, in *United States v Windsor*,[5] it struck down the Defense of Marriage Act (DOMA), a ruling that allowed married same-sex couples in states that allow same-sex marriage to claim federal benefits. Writing for the majority, Justice Anthony Kennedy argued, 'The federal statute is invalid, for no legitimate purpose overcomes the purpose and effect to disparage and to injure those whom the State, by its marriage laws, sought to protect in personhood and dignity.'[6] Kennedy went on to state: 'By seeking to displace this protection and treating those persons as living in marriages less respected than others, the federal statute is in violation of the Fifth Amendment.'[7] In the ruling, the Court thus abolishes heterosexuality as a qualification for marriage, ostensibly emancipating gays and lesbians in the US from the restrictions of homophobia.

However, one day before the Supreme Court's decision on DOMA, the court struck down a key section of the Voting Rights Act.[8] That portion mandated that states with histories of voter suppression receive clearance from the US Justice Department or a federal court before making changes to voting procedures or before redrawing electoral districts, moves that have been used to suppress the voting power of racial minorities. With the two decisions, the Court extended protections for marriage equality, while weakening protections against voter suppression and racial exclusions at the ballot box. Placed together, the Court's repeal of DOMA and its invalidation of the Voting Rights Act suggest that the mainstreaming of homosexuality within the US took place via the marginalization of anti-racist protections. One way to read the Court's decisions is as the outcomes of a historiographical operation in which gay rights enable the state to act in its own unequal manner with respect to racial inequality. Rather than articulating sexuality as an interruption to the state's manoeuvres – as a refusal to take the state as an intermediary – the gay rights movement produced the conditions whereby sexuality could facilitate the state's racial exclusions.

While groups such as Gay Liberation Front and Third World Gay Revolution dispatched sexuality to ally with critiques of western imperialism, the gay rights movement's emancipation of sexuality through the state also facilitates the state's militaristic and imperial agendas. We can think of the Shepard–Byrd Act's merger into a National Defense Authorization Act, for instance, as yet another demonstration of the consequences of sexual orientation's liberation through the liberal state, a liberation that quite literally expands the powers of the US military industrial complex. In this instance, not only does political emancipation work towards the expansion of civil society's investment in private property, as Marx argues in 'On the Jewish question', but political emancipation also fosters the growth of the state's military forces. The National Defense Authorization Act, therefore, illustrates the ways in which militarization is articulated partly through the cultural integration of forms of difference, such as sexual orientation. In *The Prince*, Machiavelli discusses the relationship between the military and cultural formations. He states, for example:

> The main foundations of all states (whether they are new, old or mixed) are good laws and good armies. Since it is impossible to have good laws if good armies are lacking, and if there are good arms there must also be good laws . . .
>
> (1988: 42–3)

As observed in the annotation to the text, '"Laws" here should probably not be understood in a narrow sense: rather [Machiavelli] had in mind "laws" and "customs" (or unwritten laws); in short, the factors making for political and social cohesion and stability' (ibid.: 43 n. 'd'). The state is produced in the overlaps between culture, military and the law, all of which were – in Machiavelli's theorization of the modern state – theorized as technologies of order.

Culture, law and the military come together in the gay rights movement and the National Defense Authorization Act enacting hate crime protections. In particular, the gay rights movement uses the law to integrate homosexuality within the ideological parameters and administrative procedures of the state, in effect using the state to achieve a kind of cultural transformation within US society. That transformation also opens the door for, not only gay participation within the military, but also the expansion of the military. In other words, the rights-based emancipation of sexual orientation allows the state to achieve social cohesion and stability, but a social cohesion and stability that expand the state's military capacities. As a bill that simultaneously invoked anti-racism and gay rights as measures of progress and extended the military budget, the Shepard–Byrd Act expresses the connection between the law, the military industrial complex and the domain of culture. The Act expresses an emergent discursive climate in which the extensions of US empire and the hegemonic affirmation of minority identity become part of the US nation-state's production of an anti-racist and anti-homophobic social order.

By subjugating the histories of revolutionary articulations of race and sexuality, the state emancipates to the detriment of the historical complexities and contradictions that make up racial and sexual formations. Marx engages the state's suppression of social complexity in *The German Ideology*, when he writes:

> Since the state is the form in which the individuals of a ruling class assert their common interests, and in which the whole civil society of an epoch is epitomised, it follows that the State mediates in the formation of all common institutions and that the institutions receive a political form. Hence, the illusion that the law is based on the will, and indeed on the will divorced from its real basis – on free will.
>
> (Marx and Engels 1974: 80)

As Marx suggests, the state mediates by suppressing actual material and historical complexities and contradictions. With the Shepard–Byrd Act and the efforts around marriage equality, the state attempts to mediate queer sexuality and, in doing so, designates it as one of the common institutions in the national body. As the state becomes the mediator of queer sexuality, it divorces queer sexuality from histories of radicalism, particularly ones that challenged the sexual regulations of the state, as well as its technologies of egalitarianism. Hence, the deviousness of the state lies in its 'emancipation' of sexual orientation as a means to devise newer ways to enact its exclusionary agendas.

The past and future repoliticizations of sexuality

We are in a moment in which institutions of power, such as the state, are – with the assistance of the gay rights movement – arrogating histories of minority difference to themselves, arrogating them in order to extend the boundaries of the state's powers. The history of radical anti-racist and queer social movements within the US reveals the contingency rather than the historical necessity of rights-based models, and the dangerous rather than benign nature of that arrogation. Part of why the history of these movements matters is precisely because this is a history in which groups such as Gay Liberation Front and Third World Gay Revolution insisted that sexuality and sexual freedom be part of conversations and projects that worked to promote freedoms *from* state and military violence, economic deprivation and imperialism.

In many ways, ours is a moment ripe for the devious inventions of political emancipation, given that we live in a time in which a state such as the US is modelling ways to absorb insurgent demands of minoritized social groups, while providing the conditions for social exclusions to persist and advance. This is the historical context in which the US gay rights movement emerges, one in which the state moves from being officially white supremacist to being officially liberal anti-racist, as social theorist Jodi Melamed has argued (2011), a historical context in which minority difference is subjected to the distortions of institutional incorporation, as I have argued elsewhere (Ferguson 2012). As a mode of power, the contemporary historiographical operation associated with gay rights seizes the past in order to delimit our options for the present and the future. Touching on this, de Certeau argues that 'history is always ambivalent: the locus that it carves for the past is equally a fashion of making a place for a future' (1988: 85). As the gay rights movement subjugates the histories of radical articulations of queerness and race, it works to convince us that the present and the future – as far as queerness and other forms of minority difference are concerned – belong primarily to the state and its machineries.

Indeed, as Robert Leckey's introduction to this volume suggests, the theme of 'After legal equality' can be seen as a challenge to the deviousness of political emancipation – that is, the designation of the state as the official envoy of minority constituencies. As he states (1),

> Groups seeking equality sometimes take a legal victory as the end of the line. Once judgment is granted or a law is passed, coalitions disband, and life goes on in a new state of equality. For their part, policymakers may assume that a troublesome file is now closed.

We can read this argument as one that walks in line with the analyses that I have attempted to advance in this chapter – the presumption that rights-based actions will bring an Eden of equality to marginalized communities, and the subjugation of all historical knowledge that contradicts that presumption. Leckey goes on to state,

> This collection, and the larger project of which it is part, arises from the sense that law reforms made under the banner of equality invite fresh lines of enquiry. For example, such reforms may worsen the disadvantage of other groups, as where recognizing same-sex couples can indirectly intensify distinctions by race or class.

(Ibid.)

Leckey's argument here coincides with one made Polikoff, in which she contends:

> The gay rights movement should stand for both equality and justice. Fighting for marriage is different from fighting for equality. And fighting for the current legal consequences of marriage when those consequences are unjust, even to the majority of same-sex couples that marry, is different from fighting for justice.
>
> (2009: 545)

As this volume and other efforts suggest, an era of suspicion has re-emerged. Activists, artists and scholars are increasingly pointing to minority difference's mediation by modes of power. We can read the critique of gay rights within this new emergence. We might also read it as an attempt to repoliticize minority difference, in general, and sexuality, in particular. As de Certeau puts it, 'A "repoliticization" of the human sciences is needed: progress may never be measured or attained without a critical theory of the current status of these sciences in society' (1988: 63). In the context of sexual freedom, we might say that a repoliticization of the desire for rights is needed, one that questions whether rights are part of the 'science' of people's full emancipation. What is at stake here is not simply the past, but also our sense of a future in which sexuality and other modes of difference can be deployed to elaborate critical ruptures and affiliations.

Notes

1   The White House, 'Remarks by the President at Reception commemorating the enactment of the Matthew Shepard and James Byrd, Jr. Hate Crimes Act', 28 October 2009. Online. Available at: www.whitehouse.gov/the-press-office/remarks-president-reception-commemorating-enactment-matthew-shepard-and-james-byrd- (accessed 5 July 2013).
2   Ibid.
3   388 US 1 (1967).
4   In the US, for instance, the adoption of affirmative action policies did not end racial discrimination, but, in fact, allowed for racial exclusions under the cover of a legal prohibition against discrimination (see, e.g., Crenshaw et al. 1996).
5   133 SCt 2675 (2013).
6   Ibid., 2696.
7   Ibid.
8   Shelby County v Holder 133 SCt 2612 (2013).

References

Crenshaw, K., Gotanda, N., Peller, G. and Thomas, K. (eds) (1996) Critical Race Theory: The Key Writings that Formed the Movement, New York: New Press.
Davis, A. (1991) 'Tactfulness of the heart: Jean Genet and the Black Panthers', Interactivist Info Exchange, 25 May. Online. Available at: interactivist.autonomedia.org/node/42692 (accessed 5 July 2013).

de Certeau, M. (1988) *The Writing of History*, trans. T. Conley, New York: Columbia University Press.

Ferguson, R.A. (2012) *The Reorder of Things: The University and Its Pedagogies of Minority Difference*, Minneapolis: University of Minnesota.

Joseph, P. (2009) 'Rethinking the Black Power era', *Journal of Southern History*, 75(3): 707–16.

Kissack, T. (1995) 'Freaking fag revolutionaries: New York's Gay Liberation Front, 1966–1971', *Radical History Review*, 62: 105–34.

Machiavelli, N. (1988) *The Prince*, (eds) Q. Skinner and R. Price, Cambridge: Cambridge University Press.

Marx, K. (1978) 'On the Jewish question', in R.C. Tucker (ed.) *The Marx–Engels Reader*, New York: W.W. Norton.

Marx, K. and Engels, F. (1974) *The German Ideology*, trans. D.J. Struik, New York: International Publishers.

Melamed, J. (2011) *Represent and Destroy: Rationalizing Violence in the New Racial Capitalism*, Minneapolis: University of Minnesota Press.

Newton, H. (1970) 'A letter from Huey P. Newton', *Come Out!*: 12.

Ongiri, A.A. (2009) 'Prisoner of love: Affiliation, sexuality, and the Black Panther Party', *Journal of African American History*, 94(1): 69–86.

Polikoff, N. (2009) 'Equality and justice for lesbian and gay families and relationships', *Rutgers Law Review*, 61(3): 529–65.

Reddy, C. (2008) 'Time for rights? Loving, gay marriage, and the limits of legal justice', *Fordham Law Review*, 76(6): 2849–72.

—— (2011) *Freedom with Violence: Race, Sexuality, and the US State*, Durham, NC: Duke University Press.

Somerville, S. (2005) 'Queer loving', *GLQ: A Journal of Lesbian and Gay Studies*, 11(3): 335–70.

Spade, D. (2011) *Normal Life: Administrative Violence, Critical Trans Politics and the Limits of the Law*, Cambridge, MA: South End Press.

Part III

Sex and love

Chapter 10

Tackling inequality in the intimate sphere

Problematizing love and violence in same-sex relationships

Catherine Donovan

The campaigns for same-sex marriage currently being fought across the world rely (increasingly successfully) on two arguments: that love between adults is a universal sentiment, goal and human right; and that marriage, being based on love, should, therefore, be open to any adult couple, regardless of sexuality or gender identity (e.g., Osterlund 2009; Grossi 2012). Love, in these arguments, is constructed both as a universal feeling and state of being and a socially constructed set of behaviours and regulatory mechanisms. Whereas the former is understood in essentialist terms as part of the human condition, the latter is seen to be flexible, changeable and responsive to changes in societies. Thus are governments exhorted to change with the times and make marriage more inclusive (see Osterlund 2009). In this chapter, love is problematized, and by extension marriage, in order to draw attention to a gap that has appeared in the debates about equality for those in same-sex relationships.

Whereas the focus has been on their claiming rights, recognition and inclusion into society on the same terms as their heterosexual peers, there has been less attention to how issues of equality play out within same-sex relationships. There have been two main strands of arguments against same-sex marriage from within lesbian, gay, bisexual, queer and/or trans (LGBQT) communities. Feminists argue that love, as associated with marriage, has institutionalized women's oppression, and queer theorists argue that love and marriage reproduce heteronormativity (Grossi 2012). Both sets of arguments are concerned (in different ways) with how constructions of marriage, love and the institution of heterosexuality have been based on inequalities and hierarchy, not only of gender and sexuality, but also of social class, 'race' and ethnicity, age, faith and disability. In this chapter, interpersonal violence in same-sex relationships is discussed in order to make the point that, unless we also problematize the abuse of power in the intimate sphere of adult relationships, across sexuality and gender identities, legislative reform risks institutionalizing inequalities of power between intimate partners.

Research on domestic violence and abuse (DVA) in same-sex relationships suggests that these experiences are extraordinarily ordinary. However, in this chapter, it is argued that attention must be paid to understanding the different meanings and impacts of interpersonal violence, in order to name the problem more clearly and develop more appropriate responses to it. The chapter is divided into five sections. In the first, there is a brief discussion of the debates about equality and sameness between people, to problematize the focus on equality in the public and private or intimate spheres. This includes a discussion about interpersonal violence in lesbian and gay relationships. The next outlines the research from the UK on which the following three sections draw. In the third section, feminist approaches to interpersonal violence are summarized and discussed, in order to identify some of their problems in understanding DVA in same-sex relationships and to define DVA. The fourth section discusses and critiques minority stress as an alternative explanation for DVA in same-sex relationships. In the fifth, the discussion turns to the role of love in DVA relationships, to make the point that understandings and enactments of love in abusive intimate relationships have been under-researched, even though love figures among the most-often given reasons for victims'/survivors' – regardless of gender or sexuality – remaining in abusive relationships or returning to them. The chapter concludes that it is to equality in the intimate sphere that our attention should be turned, if we are to transform society.

Equality: are we the same or different? Do we want the same or different things?

In many of the equality debates occurring across Western democracies, similar themes emerge: whether those of us who are LGBQT are the same as heterosexual people, and whether we want the same things out of life. Gamson (1994) characterized these debates as between boundary defenders – those who argue with actual or strategic (Plummer 1995) essentialism for equal human rights across sexuality and gender – and boundary strippers – those who argue that equality and categories of sexuality and gender should themselves be problematized for their impact on reproducing heteronormativity. Richardson (2004, 2005) and others have warned against an emerging sexuality and gender fundamentalism, constituting 'good gays', those who apparently conform to heteronormative standards of intimate and family living, and the 'bad gays', those who live outside these standards and transgress social norms of monogamy, family life and the heteronormative social order.

However, there is also evidence from research conducted with those entering civil partnerships and/or same-sex marriages that equality with heterosexuals in legal, economic and consumer rights has had positive outcomes that have not inevitably resulted in conformity to heteronormativity. For example, the work of Fish (2007) and King and Bartlett (2006) suggests that same-sex marriage or civil partnerships might have positive impacts on mental and other health outcomes for partners in these arrangements, similar to marriage's effects for heterosexual partners.

The work of Dickens *et al.* (2009) in the UK and Green (2010) in Canada also suggests that partners to civil partnerships and same-sex marriages, respectively, feel a positive impact in terms of their relationship stability and commitment and of their sense of validity, acceptance and sense of belonging within their wider families and communities. However, these authors also suggest that partners to these legal arrangements do not necessarily reproduce heteronormative relationship dynamics that shape household arrangements or monogamy. On the contrary, many respondents in these studies reported maintaining the importance of negotiation in the organization of their relationships, rather than engaging in any taken-for-granted assumptions about how they might behave based on the traditional marriage model. Thus, many reflected the findings of Weeks *et al.* (2001), who found evidence of an egalitarian ethic that was more possible living in same-sex relationships because of the lack, as particularly the women explained, of gender scripts experienced in prior heterosexual relationships (compare Weston 1991).

Consequently, there is some evidence that legal, economic and consumer rights can be separated from the day-to-day living of intimate lives. The marriage or civil partnership contract, enacted and formally witnessed in the public sphere, does not necessarily lead to heteronormative ways of living in the intimate sphere. However, we might also ask about the methodology of these studies. They are based on self-selected samples that are relatively small and almost never representative, because of the difficulties of achieving a representative sample of those who identify as LGBQT. It is also possible to question who decides to take part in these kinds of study, and whether unhappy or discontented people, or the victims/survivors of interpersonal violence or the abusive partners in these relationships, do so.

There is also the question of the ways in which legislative frameworks such as marriage, which include same-sex relationships on the same basis as heterosexual ones, act as technologies of governmentality, reframing spouses as responsibilized citizens required to care for each other (see Osterlund 2009). In a similar vein, Young (in this volume) shows how Canadian tax laws, now equally applied to those in same-sex relationships, regardless of whether they are married, not only disadvantage couples who have the lowest incomes, but also privilege couples who adopt the nuclear family structure of one partner's being economically dependent on the other.

When the research done on interpersonal violence in same-sex relationships (most of which has focused on lesbian relationships) is considered, the picture of intimacy in the private sphere is different. For example, in her review of the American literature, Turell (2000) found prevalence rates for physical violence in lesbian relationships in the range of 8–69 per cent; for sexual violence in the range of 5–50 per cent; and for emotional violence in the range of 65–90 per cent. For gay men, the range of physical violence found was between 11 and 47 per cent. As discussed in the next section, however, methodological problems caution us to be wary about the prevalence rates that such studies suggest.

Defining DVA and the study

Definitions of interpersonal violence vary across these studies, and there is rarely an attempt to make any distinctions about what kinds of violence and abuse are being reported, so that all violence is counted as the same. This is problematic, because, unless we are able to speak about the motives, impacts, meanings and context of violence and abuse, we are in danger of overlooking salient distinctions. Thus, self-defence, retaliation, mutual abuse and what has been called common couple violence may be assimilated to what Johnson (1995, 2006) has called intimate terrorism, or what Stark (2007) has called coercive control (Hester *et al.* 2010). Another problem inherent in many of these studies is in how they are advertised. Naming intimate partner violence or relationship aggression in the recruitment literature for surveys of self-selected samples can influence both who will engage in the study and what they might speak of.

However, given the apparent normality of interpersonal violence that these studies and studies in ostensibly heterosexual relationships indicate, some have questioned the utility of potentially criminalizing the 'normal behaviour' of intimate partners (Reece 2012). There are several responses to this. They include the reflection that to normalize violence and abuse in intimate relationships might have serious implications for how a society tolerates violence elsewhere, between friends, at school, in the workplace, between parents and children, and so on. In addition, the reality is that using the criminal justice system to respond to interpersonal violence between intimate partners is both extremely difficult (in the UK, the attrition rate is one of the highest of any crime) and highly unlikely.[1] It is also useful to reiterate the argument referred to briefly above, that it is important to identify what kind of violence is being used in what context, in order to make informed decisions about what responses are most appropriate.

This chapter draws on research comparing love and violence in same-sex and heterosexual relationships. We were interested in DVA, as defined currently by the UK government, to include coercive control. Coercive control takes place where one partner acts in various ways (using violence and abuse that may be physical, sexual, emotional, financial, or some combination thereof) in order to exert power and control over his or her partner, such that the latter lives in fear or walks on eggshells in anticipation of the abusive partner's (often unpredictable) behaviour. To address the problem of recruitment outlined above, the research was named as a study of 'what happens when things go wrong' in same-sex relationships, which meant we were able to include a range of different relationship experiences. The study was multi-method, involving a national community survey and interviews.

The survey was answered by 746 people who identified as lesbian, gay male, gay, queer, bisexual and/or trans. The age ranged from 16 years to late 60s, although most people were in their 20s and 30s, and the average age was 35. Nearly two-thirds identified as women (61.3 per cent, 451/736), and more than one-third identified as men (38 per cent, 280/736). Women were most likely to identify as 'lesbian' (69.6 per cent, 314/451), and men mainly identified as 'gay man' (76.4 per cent, 214/280). More women than men defined themselves as bisexual (10.4 per cent, 47/451, compared with 3.9 per cent, 11/280 of men) or as queer (2.9 per cent, 13/451, compared with 1.4 per cent of men, 4/280). The number of trans respondents was very low (n = 5).

The question about ethnicity used mostly the same categorization as the 2001 UK census, and the profile of our sample reflected findings from the general population. Most respondents identified as white (94.8 per cent, 704/743, compared with 92.2 per cent in the census). The proportions identifying as mixed or Chinese were similar to those in the census. However, there were smaller proportions of Asian or black respondents, possibly because the survey, like the census, did not subdivide the categories of Asian or black.

The income level for respondents was slightly higher than for the population generally. The average (mean) income for all the respondents was £22,432.43, with a median, 'midpoint', income of £25,500. Even so, one in five earned less than £10,000, and nearly one-half earned less than £20,000. The income distribution was also gendered. The largest group of men were earning £21,000–30,000, compared with only £11,000–20,000 for the largest group of women. The educational attainment of the survey respondents was generally much higher than that of the UK population. Half of the respondents (50.5 per cent, 375/744) were educated to at least degree level, compared with 27 per cent in England and Wales generally (2011 census), and very few respondents (3.1 per cent, 23/744 or fewer) had no qualifications, compared with 23 per cent in England and Wales (2011 census) (Hester and Donovan 2009; Hester et al. 2010).

The interview sample closely mirrored the profile for the survey, with the exception that we were singularly unsuccessful at recruiting respondents from black and minority ethnic (BME) groups. Only two women out of a sample of sixty-seven respondents identified as 'black' and 'African', respectively. The rest of the interview sample consisted of twenty lesbians (including one who identified as a trans woman), nineteen gay men, fourteen heterosexual women, nine heterosexual men, three bisexual women and three queer women.

The results showed that just over 38 per cent (n = 266/692) of the survey respondents said that they had experienced DVA in a same-sex relationship (this was just over 40 per cent (n = 169/421) of women and just over 35 per cent (n = 94/248) of the men). However, it was also the case that just over

54 per cent reported that, in the previous 12 months, they had experienced at least one instance of emotionally abusive behaviour. Just under 18 per cent had experienced at least one instance of physically abusive behaviour, and just over 23 per cent had experienced at least one instance of sexually abusive behaviour. Men were significantly more likely to report experiences of forced sex, refusal of a request for safer sex and rejection of safe words in S/M sex.

Among the top ten most reported emotionally abusive behaviours experienced were 'having your age used against you' and 'having your education used against you'. In addition, among those respondents who identified as a member of a BME group, 'having your race used against you' was also in their top ten (though the numbers were too small to be statistically significant). These findings do suggest, however, that some LGBQT people might also draw on socially constructed inequalities between groups in society to establish relationships of unequal power and abuse in their same-sex intimate relationships.

Interviews explored a best and a worst relationship experience, asking about how they had met, how their relationships were organized, whether they loved each other, and how they knew that (see Donovan and Hester, 2014, for more discussion of this). Of the women interviewed, nineteen gave accounts of DVA in female same-sex relationships, and thirteen gave accounts of DVA in heterosexual relationships. Just over one-half of the gay men interviewed said that they had experienced DVA in an intimate relationship.

Feminist approaches to DVA

Feminist approaches to DVA argue that the problem is one of heterosexual men for heterosexual women. They argue that, when severity of impact is taken into account, including domestic homicide and repeat victimization, women are among the worst affected victims/survivors of DVA, as well as the most often identified victims/survivors. This argument has been successfully deployed in the UK such that the Coalition government's policy on DVA is encapsulated in the *Call to End Violence Against Women and Girls Action Plan* (Home Office 2011: 6), which states that gender is the most important risk factor when considering interpersonal violence. Evan Stark (2007) argues that the focus on physical violence is a red herring and offers coercive control as a way of describing a pattern of behaviours that cumulatively result in heterosexual men being able to control their female partners. Stark further argues that coercive control is constituted through socially ascribed gendered behaviours and expectations that exist in public and private spheres, and, as such, it is only attributable to heterosexual men in abusive relationships with heterosexual women. However, in our study, we found evidence that coercive control was experienced in same-sex relationships, regardless of gender (Donovan and Hester 2014; see also Ristock 2002).

The question then becomes whether or not the feminist approach is applicable to abuse and violence in same-sex relationships. This approach has problematized the ways in which the institution of heterosexuality is supported, reinforced and reflected in private and public spheres, positioning men as facing the public sphere, as providers, heads of household, disciplinarians and decision-makers, with their roles socially valued, and positioning women as facing the private sphere, as nurturers, carers, waiters and the wooed, with less social value attached to their roles. For example, women's paid work is often seen as secondary to their main role as wife and mother, which is reflected in inequalities in pay between women and men and their tendency to fit paid work around childcare responsibilities and, therefore, be more numerous in part-time work. Such structured dependency can have consequences for those women who are victims/survivors of DVA, as their options to leave can feel constrained by their unequal access to resources.

Others have rejected the feminist approach to intimate partner violence, precisely because it is heterosexist, problematizing as it does masculinity and institutionalized heterosexuality, with its associated structured dependency that positions women unequally (e.g., Island and Letellier 1991). Further critiques have questioned the ways in which such a model reifies binaries of perpetrator/victim and male/female, which, it is argued, do not allow different kinds of DVA story to be either told or recognized by victims/survivors or practitioners (e.g., Ristock 2002). In response to these critiques, it can be argued that not enough is known about the experiences of those in abusive LGBQT relationships to reject wholesale the feminist focus on DVA as the exertion of power and control. Furthermore, although it is clear that DVA is not just a problem of heterosexuality, we may still be able to explore the implications of heteronormativity as it is constituted in practices of love, to shed light on how and why abuse might occur in intimate relationships, regardless of gender and sexuality. This will be explored further below.

One cause for caution with the feminist account of DVA arising in the LGBQT context is that the public story of DVA (Donovan and Hester 2010) might in itself be a barrier impeding those in same-sex relationships from recognizing and identifying experiences as abusive. The public story constructs DVA as a heterosexual problem, a problem of physical violence and a problem of gender: the bigger, stronger man being (physically) violent to the smaller, weaker woman. As a result, abusive experiences in same-sex relationships can be minimized as bad luck or a wrong choice in a partner, a problem that can be redefined as an individual problem requiring privatized solutions. In our survey, over one-third of those who said that they had sought help for their experiences did so with counsellors or therapists. Only 10 per cent reported their experiences to the police, the last of a list of possible sources of help offered. In contrast, in heterosexual relationships, the British Crime Survey[2] shows that nearly one-third of women reported their experiences to the police, who were the second source of help after friends and family (Donovan et al.

2006; Smith *et al.* 2012). In any event, in North America, the critique of the feminist approach to understanding DVA has been the catalyst for another focus for study: that of minority stress, to which we now turn.

Minority stress and its impacts on DVA

Minority stress is defined in various ways, but most often focuses on the negative implications for the behaviours of LGBQT people of living in a heterosexist and homophobic society: 'experiencing psychological and social stresses that arise from one's minority status' (Mendoza 2011: 170). Most studies have suggested and tested the hypothesis that experiences, or fear of experiences, of homophobic bullying and/or hate crime, stigma or discrimination, in combination with a closeted life, might bring about such stress that a partner might enact violence and abuse on their partner. Some variations of definitions have led to different methodologies and different variables being tested, which results in a patchy picture of results. Mendoza did not find evidence of any causal relationships between measures of homophobia, stigma and discrimination and DVA, yet concludes that experiences of homophobia and discrimination (but not stigma) 'contribute to the likelihood of partner abuse in gay male relationships' (2011: 178). For Mendoza, being closeted is a maladaptive behaviour, but, echoing other work, it will be argued here that decisions about not coming out might be taken for very rational reasons of protection, as well as for more positive reasons such as taking opportunities to develop a counterculture, networks and identity that are supportive (e.g., Seidman *et al.* 1999). Balsam and Syzmanski (2005) recognize the social contextual factors that might prevent people from coming out, but they also suggest that the impact of homophobia and heterosexism contributes to the context in which DVA takes place. Again, the results reviewed suggest correlations rather than causation, and yet there is a growing focus on minority stress as providing a unique factor for DVA in same-sex relationships that makes it distinct from DVA in heterosexual relationships.

Although the arguments for minority stress apparently ask for recognition of the different sociocultural context in which those in same-sex relationships might enact intimacy, their focus is psychological and individualistic. The abusive partner is pathologized as enacting maladaptive behaviours that are the result of the psychological damage done by a stigmatizing and discriminatory society. This might be part of the picture of DVA, and yet it is difficult to explain how and why one partner more than the other might be impacted by internalized homophobia, discrimination or stigma, or why one partner more than the other might be more likely to use violence as a result. In our survey, we found that threats to out a partner were identified as a factor in people's experiences of emotional abuse, including threats to out someone who was a parent. This would suggest that, in a society organized around the heterosexual assumption (Weeks *et al.* 2001), it is possible that particular ways of being controlled based on sexuality might act to isolate victims/ survivors from potential sources of support.

In the interviews, further accounts emerged of the ways in which sexuality might be implicated in the control of a partner's behaviours and experiences within a same-sex relationship. There were reports of abuse, from those who had been most recently out and/or in their first same-sex relationship (Donovan *et al.* 2006; Donovan and Hester 2008; see also Ristock 2002), by partners who had more experience of being out and/or of having same-sex relationships. In this way, the intersection of age and experience can act to place those with less experience in a subordinate position (Donovan and Hester 2014). In addition, abusive partners might denigrate LGBT activities, the local scene or other LGBT potential friends, with the effect of preventing their partner from going out into the scene, maintaining LGBT friendships and/or having access to potential LGBT sources of support or role models for how non-abusive relationships might be enacted. Some women talked about having felt unsure and undermined about whether they were 'real' lesbians, because of the ways in which abusive partners behaved.

Another way that sexuality might be used to control a partner was by abusive partners explaining that they did not want to be out and thus expected their partners not to bring LGBT friends to the house or to be too out publicly or to engage in LGBT community activities, all this to protect the abusive partner's desire to remain in the closet. All of these behaviours lead to similar impacts in isolating victims/survivors from potential sources of help or community knowledges (Weeks *et al.* 2001) that might have enabled them to realize their experiences as abusive. By undermining the confidence of victims/survivors, such conduct made them more reliant on their abusive partners. In these instances, using actual or perceived fears about being part of a minoritized community to control somebody's behaviours is only possible in a context that provides evidence that those fears are rational in some way.

The lack of community knowledges, in combination with other impacts of the heterosexual assumption, could also lead to the normalization of abuse. In their accounts of abusive relationships, interview respondents talked of not having known what to expect or how same-sex relationships were supposed to work, or of assuming that what had been experienced was to be expected. For example, Emma, a white, self-identified queer woman who was seventeen in her first same-sex relationship, explained: 'I just thought this is how relationships are'. Edward, who was a white, self-identified gay man and sixteen when in his first same-sex relationship, said: 'I didn't know any differently'. Thus, normalization of abuse might be the result of heterosexist and homophobic constructions of lesbian and gay life, such that it is imagined as, or expected to be, unhappy, abusive and/or violent.

An added factor that exacerbated these experiences was the isolation in which many respondents lived their relationships. This became apparent when comparing the accounts of abusive relationships across sexuality. Although, in our study, questions were not asked about the involvement of respondents' family of origin in their relationships, heterosexual women almost always spontaneously referred to their parents when giving an account of how they had met their abusive partner. This occurred most often in relation to their rationale for getting married, when their parents had expected it or talked them into it, and sometimes in terms of their parents' active collusion with keeping the abusive relationship together. Accounts of those in same-sex relationships almost never referred to their parents. This suggests that those entering their first same-sex relationship might do so in isolation from their families of origin. If this means that individuals in same-sex relationships may escape their parents' pressure to enter or stay in an abusive relationship, it also makes it more difficult for their families to be available to provide support if the relationship goes wrong, or for the victim/survivor to ask for help from family members who have not been told about the relationship.

This suggests that the focus that minority stress places on individualized adaptations to a heterosexist and/or homophobic society is problematic, given the broader social and cultural impacts on LGBQT people of the heterosexual assumption. Controlling behaviours based on sexuality could be prevented if community knowledges were more available for young people, or those entering their first same-sex relationships, to be able to identify their experiences as abusive; if fears about being outed held no power; and if stereotypes and damaging ideas about what it is like to be lesbian or gay or in a same-sex relationship could be successfully challenged, with more positive role models being represented in mainstream media and everyday life.

Heteronormative constructions of love and intimacy

Contemporary arguments by which love is the central definer of marriage reflect a more recent history of marriage that, hitherto, was an economic, legal and political contract, securing the property and power of men (see Grossi 2012; Donovan and Hester 2014). Essentialist ideas about love construct it as a universal human emotion that is inexplicable, magical and uncontrollable. However, the arguments against same-sex marriage focus on love as being best illustrated, not only in heterosexuality, but in a particular model of heterosexuality, as lived through the nuclear family and marriage: lifelong monogamy, fidelity, reproduction and complementary gender roles arising from and through dominant ideas about femininity and masculinity (see Harding, in this volume). Heterosexual women are constructed as nurturers and carers engaging in the emotion work that keeps relationships and families together, while heterosexual men are constructed as initiators, decision-makers and providers. These ideas are pervasive and underpinned by essentialist ideas about what is natural and/or 'God given', so that those in same-sex relationships are not seen as able to authentically love. However, LGBQT people assert that they do love and can love in similar ways to heterosexual people. The overwhelming majority of respondents we interviewed attested to the role of love in their abusive relationships, in terms both of what drew them to their abusive partner and why they stayed (see also Fraser 2008).

Love can be expressed as feelings, values and practices. As hooks (2000) has argued, very often feelings and values are given precedence over practices: declarations of love can be made and elicit strong feelings, in spite of how partners treat each other. Our research suggests that love is implicated in DVA relationships and in similar ways across gender and sexuality. This should not be a surprise. As Hart, a pioneer in placing DVA in lesbian relationships on the public agenda, argued in the mid 1980s, lesbians and, we might add, gay men, bisexual, queer and/or trans people grow up in the same society as heterosexual people. They grow up, in the main, in heterosexual families, and they witness, observe and interact with the ways in which love is constituted through a heterosexual, gendered lens, such that, as she says, 'the same elements of hierarchy of power, ownership, entitlement and control exist in lesbian family relationships' (Hart 1986: 175).

In this chapter, it is argued that there exists a dominant, heteronormative set of understandings, expectations and values that are embedded in relationship practices and practices of love and that influence how love is felt, understood and enacted across sexuality and gender (Donovan and Hester 2014). In simplistic terms, relationships where DVA is experienced, regardless of gender and sexuality, can be articulated through two rules: the relationship is for the abusive partner and on the latter's terms; and the victim/survivor is responsible for the abusive partner and the relationship (Donovan and Hester 2010). These rules can be seen to reflect a heteronormative construction of a love relationship, in which one is 'in charge' and the other is responsible for the emotion work that keeps the relationship together. A range of abusive behaviours can be utilized, typically (but not exclusively) emotional and emotionally coercive sexual abuses by female abusive partners, and typically (but not exclusively) physical and physical sexual abuses by male abusive partners, even after the relationship has ended, the effect of which is to either (re)establish these rules or to punish the victim/survivor for breaking them.

Thus, although gender is implicated, it is so in complex ways. Gender norms can be both predictive of, and overturned by and through, relationship practices (see also Collier, in this volume, in relation to men and fathering), not just across relationships, but also within the same relationship, depending on the circumstances and context. For example, masculinity is traditionally associated with key decision-making and setting the terms in a relationship. However, we found that abusive partners enact these relationship practices, regardless of sexuality or gender. Femininity is associated with caring and nurturing behaviours. However, in the accounts we were given, the victims/survivors enacted these relationship practices, regardless of sexuality or gender

(Donovan and Hester 2011). Expressions of love and need/neediness are also identified with femininity, and yet we found that those who were abusive most often enacted these practices of love in order to elicit care, forgiveness, protection, loyalty and a sense of responsibility for the abusive partner in the victim/survivor.

Victims/survivors were often able to explain why their abusive partners behaved the way they did, referring to unhappy childhoods, problems with substance use, being different from other people, having unhappy workplaces, being terrified of responsibility, and so on. Their abusive partners had disclosed these experiences to excuse their behaviours and elicit forgiveness and care. For example, Kenneth, a white, self-identified gay man who was HIV-positive, talked about how his abusive partner, who was much younger than him and also HIV-positive, relied on Kenneth to keep him going with his medication:

> I wouldn't forgive it, but . . . he'd grown up in an abusive family . . . abusive father, but yeah, he got violent towards me. Never seriously hurt me. But, on more than one occasion – p'raps three or four occasions, kicked and hit. And that was absolutely awful. . . . He died at age twenty-six . . . so he died like two and a half years after we split up. Um, and he was . . . as healthy as I am at the moment when we split up. . . . I'm not saying that I kept him alive but . . . he would constantly say to me . . . how he really admired the way I coped with HIV. Um, looked up to the way I handled taking the drugs and that. He really didn't like it . . . I mean, bit odd for someone who would push anything down his throat, um, but in terms of taking medication he was terrible, and really didn't like it at all. And he did and he admired me for that, and he did say that I kept him alive, that I gave him a reason to wanna keep going.

Being responsible for the relationship and feeling emotionally strong are most often associated with masculinity, and yet, typically, victims/survivors, regardless of gender or sexuality, enacted these practices of love. For example, Amy, a white, self-identified lesbian, explained how she could not leave her abusive partner, because she felt responsible to stay and help her through her decision to seek help for the causes of her alcohol abuse:

> Yeah . . . I thought . . . the nice side of her outweighed the ugly side of her, for want of a better word. Um. Yeah, and I felt like it wouldn't be fair for me to say, 'oh, right, I've seen this behaviour, it's really ugly, I'm going, bye', after a couple of years or something. It wasn't fair at all. So I did feel responsible to try and help her out and try and look after her and try and support her. . . . But also I think I felt a greater responsibility because it was the first time in all of that time that she'd ever disclosed the alcohol use and the events which led to the alcohol use. You know, and a lot of that stuff was around abuse. So it was very difficult.

In Western societies, we increasingly invest in love as a definer of self-fulfilment as represented by being part of a couple (e.g. Evans 2003). Yet we have not yet fully explored and interrogated how love might be enacted in ways that challenge heteronormative ways of living love. Unless we challenge the assumptions, values and expectations that are embedded in relationship practices and practices of love, we risk reinforcing relationship contexts in which DVA can occur. Grossi (2012) explains how, when love emerged to redefine the purpose of marriage in the mid nineteenth century, it was seen as radically subversive, championing the agency of individual women and men against the existing purpose of marriage to secure the agendas of men or families. She goes on to argue that it is this radical feature of love that must be utilized to counter the heteronormativity that might either exclude same-sex relationships from marriage or, by including them in marriage, undermine their potential to radicalize intimacy and family life.

The feminist approach to understanding DVA has focused on patterns of behaviour that result in coercive control. This analysis provides us with tools to recognize and name experiences as DVA, as opposed to other kinds of interpersonal violence. This is important in order to identify what kinds of response will best address the violence and abuse. The feminist approach has also provided an analysis that foregrounds the social and cultural context in which gendered norms of behaviour in private lives can, not only produce contexts, opportunities and vulnerabilities for DVA to occur, but also make recognition difficult because of their normalizing tendencies. It is suggested that gender in heterosexual relationships may act similarly to the heterosexual assumption in same-sex relationships: both may help to make sense of how victims/survivors might be positioned as vulnerable and unable to name their experiences of DVA and might find difficulties in seeking help. Both may also normalize violence and abuse. However, the suggestion is also that an exploration of how love is heteronormatively gendered in more complex ways might help in identifying experiences of DVA across sexuality and gender, providing explanations about how and why victims/survivors remain in abusive relationships or return to them.

Conclusion

In this chapter, the argument has been made that discussions about equality have, in the main, been focused on formal equalities enacted in the public sphere, and that what is needed, in addition, is to problematize inequalities in the form of DVA in the intimate sphere and beware of how what are understood as legal equalities – for example, same-sex marriage – might unintentionally further embed heteronormative inequalities in how intimacy is practised. The case has been made that the current focus on minority stress as an explanatory tool for DVA in same-sex relationships is problematic, because of its focus on individualized, psychopathologized responses to heterosexism and homophobia. Instead, it has been suggested that there are many social and cultural impacts of the heterosexual assumption that influence and shape, not just the behaviours of abusive partners, but also those of victims/survivors and how they understand their experiences. This is particularly the case for those entering their first same-sex relationship. For example, the public story of DVA is implicated in acting as a barrier to those in same-sex relationships recognizing and naming their experiences as DVA, which impacts on their ability to seek help.

The feminist approach that has problematized heterosexuality as the dominant context in which DVA can occur has also, itself, been problematized for its tendency to reify gendered behaviours in embodied women and men. This has led to a discussion about how heteronormative constructions and meanings of love are implicated in experiences of DVA across gender and sexuality. These dominant constructions of love, often reified in (same-sex) marriage, position partners in relationships of inequality and dependency and imbue relationship practices and practices of love with expectations that foster loyalty, privacy, commitment to forever and fidelity, which, when enacted, keep victims/survivors glued into abusive relationships. It has been argued that, although gender is implicated, it is so in more complex ways that position the abusive partner enacting practices of love more associated with femininity (expressions of need/neediness) and victims/survivors enacting relationship practices more often associated with masculinity (feeling emotionally stronger than their abusive partners and responsible for them). The result is confusion about what is being experienced, especially as abusive relationships are not only or always necessarily experienced negatively (see also Fraser 2008).

Looking forward, it is suggested that we should problematize heteronormative constructions of love – and marriage – that are based on expectations of inequalities between partners to a relationship, and give those entering same-sex relationships the skills to have the confidence and self-esteem to recognize, resist and leave abusive relationships. This means that, in debates about same-sex marriage, we should be cautious about the ways in which heteronormative practices of love and relationship practices can be reinforced through marriage laws and enacted and/or expected in same-sex relationships.

Love is understood, in dominant discourses, to conquer all, to withstand everything thrown at it, and to enable partners to stand together through thick and thin and against the world. In some respects, fighting to have same-sex love perceived this way as well has been a valiant goal, when society has said that those in same-sex relationships cannot know what authentic love is because they are not heterosexual. However, in other respects, these constructions of love can also benefit those who are willing to employ abusive behaviours that establish relationship rules in their favour. Discussions about (in)equality need to be taken into the intimate sphere to challenge (hetero)-normalized intimate relationships based on inequalities and abuses of power.

As Harding argues in this volume, in relation to family law, heteronormativity prevails even after equality. She focuses on the ways in which laws are interpreted in heteronormative ways that do not recognize the diversity of family life of lesbians and gay men, and on how judicial interpretations are not able to accurately recognize the law's implications, so strong are the heteronormative assumptions and expectations about family and parental relationships. In this chapter, the point is made that it is the intimate couple that should be encouraged to consciously question the assumptions and expectations that heteronormativity provides about adult intimacy, love and marriage, in order to challenge relationships of inequality, dependency and/ or violence and abuse.

Note

1   According to the British Crime Survey, only 16 per cent of those who say they have experienced violence and/or abuse ever report those experiences to the police (Smith *et al.* 2010). It is even less likely to be reported by those in same-sex and/or trans relationships (Donovan *et al.* 2006).
2   The British Crime Survey has recently been renamed the Crime Survey England and Wales to make clear that there is a Scottish Crime Survey that has been conducted separately for some time.

References

Balsam, K.F. and Szymanski, D.M. (2005) 'Relationship quality and domestic violence in women's same-sex relationships: The role of minority stress', *Psychology of Women Quarterly*, 29: 258–69.

Dickens, S., Mitchell, M. and O'Connor, W. (2009) 'The impact of the Civil Partnership Act on the lives of same-sex couples', *Benefits*, 17(3): 237–48.

Donovan, C. and Hester, M. (2008) ' "Because she was my first girlfriend, I didn't know any different": Making the case for mainstreaming same-sex sex/relationship education', *Sex Education: Sexuality, Society and Learning*, 8(3): 277–87.

—— (2010) 'I hate the word "victim": An exploration of recognition of domestic violence in same sex relationships', *Social Policy and Society*, 9: 279–89.

—— (2011) 'Exploring emotion work in domestically abusive relationships', in J. Ristock (ed.) *Intimate Partner Violence in LGBTQ Lives*, New York: Routledge.

—— (2014) *Domestic Violence and Sexuality: What's Love Got To Do With It?* Bristol, UK: Policy Press.

—— Holmes, J. and McCarry, M. (2006) *Comparing Domestic Abuse in Same Sex and Heterosexual Relationships: Initial Report from a Study Funded by the Economic & Social Research Council*, Sunderland, UK: University of Sunderland/University of Bristol.

Evans, M. (2003) *Love: An Unromantic Discussion*, Cambridge: Polity Press.

Fish, J. (2007) 'Getting equal: The implications of new regulations to prohibit sexual orientation discrimination for health and social care', *Diversity in Health and Social Care*, 4: 221–8.

Fraser, H. (2008) *In the Name of Love: Women's Narratives of Love and Abuse*, Toronto: Women's Press.

Gamson, J. (1994) 'Must identity movements self-destruct? A queer dilemma', *Social Problems*, 42: 390–407.

Green, A. (2010) 'Queer unions: Same-sex spouses, marrying tradition and innovation', *Canadian Journal of Sociology*, 35(3): 399–436.

Grossi, R. (2012) 'The meaning of love in the debate for legal recognition of same-sex marriage in Australia', *International Journal of Law in Context*, 8(4): 487–505.

Hart, B. (1986) 'Lesbian battering: An examination', in K. Lobel (ed.) *Naming the Violence: Speaking Out about Lesbian Battering*, Washington, DC: Seal Press.

Hester, M. and Donovan, C. (2009) 'Researching domestic violence in same-sex relationships – a feminist epistemological approach to survey development', *Journal of Lesbian Studies*, 13: 161–73.

—— and Fahmy, E. (2010) 'Feminist epistemology and the politics of method: Surveying same sex domestic violence', *International Journal of Social Research Methodology*, 13(3): 251–63.

Home Office (2011) *Call to End Violence Against Women and Girls: Action Plan*, London: HM Government.

hooks, b. (2000) *All About Love*, New York: William Morrow.

Island, D. and Letellier, P. (1991) *Men Who Beat the Men Who Love Them: Battered Gay Men and Domestic Violence*, New York: Harrington Park Press.

Johnson, M.P. (1995) 'Patriarchal terrorism and common couple violence: Two forms of violence against women', *Journal of Marriage and the Family*, 57: 283–94.

—— (2006) 'Conflict and control: Gender symmetry and asymmetry in domestic violence', *Violence Against Women*, 12: 1003–18.

King, M. and Bartlett, A. (2006) 'What same sex civil partnerships may mean for health', *Journal of Epidemiological Community Health*, 60(3): 188–91.

Mendoza, J. (2011) 'The impact of minority stress on gay male partner abuse', in J. Ristock (ed.) *Intimate Partner Violence in LGBTQ Lives*, New York: Routledge.

Osterlund, K. (2009) 'Love, freedom and governance: Same-sex marriage in Canada', *Social and Legal Studies*, 18(1): 93–109.

Plummer, K. (1995) *Telling Sexual Stories: Power, Change and Social Worlds*, London: Routledge.

Reece, H. (2012) 'Domestic autonomy takes another beating', *Spiked*. Online. Available at: www.spiked-online.com/site/article/12904 (accessed 29 June 2013).

Richardson, D. (2004) 'Locating sexualities: From here to normality', *Sexualities*, 7(4): 391–411.

—— (2005) 'Desiring sameness? The rise of a neoliberal politics of normalisation', *Antipode*, 37(3): 515–35.

Ristock, J. (2002) *No More Secrets: Violence in Lesbian Relationships*, London and New York: Routledge.

Seidman, S., Meeks, C. and Traschen, F. (1999) 'Beyond the closet? The changing social meaning of homosexuality in the United States', *Sexualities*, 2(1): 9–34.

Smith, K., Flatley, J., Coleman, K., Osborne, S., Kaiza, P. and Roe, S. (2010) *Homicides, Firearm Offences and Intimate Violence 2008/09 (Supplementary Vol. 2, Crime in England and Wales)* 3rd edn, London: Home Office.

—— Osborne, S., Lau, I. and Britton, A. (2012) *Homicides, Firearm Offences and Intimate Violence 2010/11 (Supplementary Vol. 2, Crime in England and Wales)*, London: Home Office.

Stark, E. (2007) *Coercive Control: How Men Entrap Women in Personal Life*, Oxford: Oxford University Press.

Turell, S. (2000) 'Seeking help for same-sex relationship abuses', *Journal of Gay and Lesbian Social Services*, 10: 35–49.

Weeks, J., Heaphy, B. and Donovan, C. (2001) *Same Sex Intimacies: Families of Choice and Other Life Experiments*, London: Psychology Press.

Weston, K. (1991) *Families We Choose: Lesbians, Gays, Kinship*, New York: Columbia University Press.

Chapter 11

(Re)inscribing the heteronormative family

Same-sex relationships and parenting 'after equality'

Rosie Harding

UK artist Edward Monkton[1] has a range of philosophical cartoons, 'the INTERESTING thoughts of EDWARD MONKTON', commonly sold as greetings cards, mugs, coasters and other such products. One of his cartoons is called 'The LAW of STRAIGHTNESS', with a picture of pencils and the caption, 'my pencils are STRAIGHT'; of socks – 'my socks are STRAIGHT'; a pillow – 'my pillow is STRAIGHT'; and some chips – 'my chips are STRAIGHT'. Below this are the words:

EVERYTHING must be STRAIGHT or else the World will EXPLODE*

*Those who do not believe in the Law of Straightness will not BE SAVED

As with any artistic work, there are a number of different possible interpretations of this cartoon, and perhaps the most immediately obvious is that it is referring to tidiness and, particularly, an obsessive-compulsive approach to tidiness. However, this cartoon also raises complex and intertwined questions regarding the nature of the regulation of sexuality in contemporary Western societies. One way to frame these questions is to ask: What does it mean to think about 'the LAW of STRAIGHTNESS'? There are two aspects to this: (1) the LAW and (2) STRAIGHTNESS. In using the term 'the law', we implicitly accept a monist or singular idea of law – that there is something inherently coherent, and therefore privileged, about this singular entity that is described as law. When combining this with a concept of 'straightness', we are led to the concept of heteronormativity: 'the institutions, structures of understanding, and practical orientations that make heterosexuality seem not only coherent – that is, organized as a sexuality – but also privileged' (Berlant and Warner 2000: 312).

In this chapter, I seek to explore the ways that the 'law of straightness' is still manifest in contemporary English family law, even 'after equality' and taking into consideration the recent legal shifts in the ways that lesbian and gay lives are recognized and regulated in English law. I argue that, by exploring the multiple facets of legal regulation of the family, we can gain a greater understanding of both 'law' and 'heteronormativity'. In so doing,

I demonstrate that 'the family' is actually a monist construct that limits, rather than facilitates, human expression. I approach this issue through two distinct questions. First, how does a monist or singular understanding of law, sexuality and family operate to limit the possibilities for true egalitarianism? Second, how can a conceptually plural understanding of law, sexuality and family assist in challenging heteronormativity? I explore these questions through two contemporary contexts, same-sex marriage and the recognition of legal parents where children are born to same-sex couples.

In the first part, I provide a brief overview of how the concepts of legal pluralism and heteronormativity can be used to interrogate contemporary understandings of 'the family' in parliamentary discourse. I then turn to provide a critical discourse analysis (van Dijk 1991) of expressions of heteronormativity in contemporary lesbian and gay family law. Critical discourse analysis seeks to be explicitly emancipatory, paying close attention to the ways that power relations (Foucault 2002) are constructed and operationalized, as well as highlighting practices of resistance (Harding 2011). It aims to explore 'how competing interpretations achieve hegemony and how meanings of language are accepted and applied within practical contexts' (Harvie and Manzi 2011: 82). In the second part, I use critical discourse analysis to examine the parliamentary discourse during passage of the Marriage (Same Sex Couples) Bill 2013. In the third part, I analyse judicial discourse in the decision of *Re G; Re Z*, in which two known sperm donors were granted leave to apply for contact with children born to female same-sex couples in civil partnerships.[2] In the critical discourse analysis that follows, I use quotations to allow the reader to hear the voices of their speakers, and to see words and phrases in their discursive context, revealing the layered meanings of the language used. I conclude by arguing that, in spite of egalitarian reform, contemporary discourse about same-sex relationships and parenting reinscribes heteronormativity on to lesbian and gay family life.

The law of straightness: exploring legal pluralism and heteronormativity

In previous work (Harding 2011), I argued for a nuanced understanding of heteronormativity as an example of a plural legal framework. I suggested that drawing heteronormativity into understandings of legal pluralism has three main benefits: first, it can expose the contingency of law and the ways in which even egalitarian legal change can be understood in terms of protecting current axes of privilege. Second, it can expose the coercive force of heteronormativity. Third, it casts a light on the experiences of other domains of oppression, including sexism, racism and class privilege.

My approach to legal pluralism has most in common with those who advocate a 'new' legal pluralism (e.g., Griffiths 1986; Moore 1986), which focuses on the idea that not all laws or things that are experienced as like law can be traced back to a source in government. I draw this insight together with Tamanaha's (2000: 313) approach to legal pluralism that, 'law is whatever people identify and treat through their social practices as "law"'. I am also attentive to the ways that narrative exposes everyday understandings of law, and that a critical approach to legal pluralism can 'investigate how narrating subjects treat law' (Kleinhans and Macdonald 1997: 46). My approach to heteronormativity seeks to explore the operation of norms about heterosexual ways of living and being that pervade all aspects of life for LGBT individuals. Like Chambers, I argue that heteronormativity is experienced as a regulatory practice, because 'heterosexual desire and identity are not merely assumed, they are expected' (2007: 665). In this chapter, I seek to bring these nuanced concepts of legal pluralism and heteronormativity to bear on understandings of 'family' in English law.

There has been a tremendous shift in legal recognition of lesbian and gay families over the course of the last quarter-century. In 1988, the infamous Section 28 was enacted, which sought to outlaw local authorities from 'promoting homosexuality' in general and, in particular, to refrain from promoting 'the teaching in any maintained school of the acceptability of homosexuality *as a pretended family relationship*'.[3] This provision was just one of a series of legislative interventions at that time that sought to insulate the heteronormativity of the family from the 'threat' of lesbian and gay parenting (Cooper and Herman 1991). Twenty years later, the Human Fertilisation and Embryology Act 2008 enabled two women to be listed on a child's birth certificate as 'mother' and 'parent', provided the agreed parenthood provisions were met.[4] Where a female parent is recognized as the legal parent under that legislation, 'no man is to be treated as the father of the child',[5] 'for any purpose'.[6] This recognition of lesbian parenting in legislation can, on a straightforward reading, be understood as a simple recognition framework, one that reinvents the family as no longer heteronormative.

As ever when it comes to family law, the situation is far more complex than this. Prior to the attainment of legal equality in parental status and marriage rights, the impact of such change had the potential to be either assimilationist or transformative. Not surprisingly, the experience 'after equality' appears similarly bifurcated. As will become apparent in the chapter's following parts, the legacy of Section 28 and the implicit heteronormativity of the family survive in contemporary parliamentary and judicial discourse. For example, in *Re G; Re Z*, the two applicant known donors were repeatedly given the title of 'biological father' by the judge, as he granted each of them leave to apply for contact orders. Here, we see the reinscription of heteronormative understandings of family into a situation where the children in question were legally fatherless. Similarly, an amendment to the Marriage (Same Sex Couples) Bill was proposed (but not passed) that would have inserted a provision into the Education Act 1996, stating that, no school shall be under any duty . . . to promote or endorse an understanding of the nature of marriage and its importance for family life and the bringing up of children, that runs contrary to the designated religious character of the school.

The fear expressed through this proposed amendment was that a teacher who, for reasons of religious conscience, does not agree with same-sex marriage would be disciplined for not representing the legal 'truth' of marriage, and expressing a religiously based view that marriage is for different-sex couples only.

Parliamentary discourse: love makes a family?

The Marriage (Same Sex Couples) Act 2013 extends civil marriage to same-sex couples in England and Wales and, thus, follows on from the 'legal equality' for same-sex couples implemented by the Civil Partnership Act 2004.[7] It will also enable some religious same-sex marriages to be recognized in English law. The first same-sex marriages took place in March 2014. This legislation was introduced by the Conservative–Liberal Democrat coalition and was decided on a free vote. The legislation enjoyed wide support in Parliament, including from the main opposition party (Labour), but proved controversial among a minority of MPs and Lords and sparked a great deal of discussion in Parliament and the British media. The parliamentary discourse explored here is drawn from the Commons Second Reading Debate (5 February 2013). This debate lasted just over six hours and constitutes 109 pages (59,484 words) of single-spaced Hansard text. Debate on the second reading is the first opportunity that MPs have during the progress of a bill to debate its substantive content and, as such, it holds an important place as an expression of whether the bill is likely to succeed or not. This Bill had majority support in the Commons, as demonstrated by the overwhelming majority of MPs who voted in favour of it at Second Reading (400 Ayes, 175 Noes).

There were two competing discourses of the purpose of marriage expressed in these debates, both of which can be tied to heteronormative understandings of the purpose and function of marriage: that marriage is either about 'love' or 'procreation'. It can be seen in analysis of this debate that those who spoke in favour of same-sex marriage primarily constructed the purpose of marriage as 'love'; those who opposed focused on the issue of 'procreation'. In her introduction of the Bill on behalf of the government, Maria Miller, the minister for women and equalities, focused on 'love':

What marriage offers us all is a lifelong partner to share our journey, a loving stable relationship to strengthen us and mutual support throughout our lives. I believe that that should be embraced by more couples. The depth of feeling, love and commitment between same-sex couples is no different from that depth of feeling between opposite-sex couples. The Bill enables society to recognise that commitment in the same way, too, through marriage.[8]

There are two phrases worth closer attention in this description: 'lifelong partnership' and 'loving stable relationship'. Both of these phrases hark back to different aspects of the legal and academic critique of definitions of marriage. Recall, for example, the 'definition' of marriage put forward by Lord Penzance in *Hyde v Hyde and Woodmansee*: marriage is 'the voluntary union for life of one man and one woman to the exclusion of all others'.[9] Although Probert (2007) has persuasively argued that this 'definition' can actually be more usefully considered to be a 'defence' of marriage (in *Hyde*, from the threat of a potentially polygamous marriage under the Mormon faith), it is clear that there are echoes of this approach to marriage in the minister's comments. Indeed, arguably the only change to the *Hyde* definition that is put forward by the minister is the deletion of the requirement for the parties to a marriage to be of different sexes. The themes of 'for life' and the limitation to two parties certainly remain in this construction of same-sex marriage. More interestingly, the inclusion of 'love' into any legal definition of marriage is a departure from previous legal understandings of marriage, though the minister does not see this as a problem. Later in her speech, for example, she went on to say:

Some say that the Bill redefines marriage, but marriage is an institution with a long history of adaptation and change . . . Suggestions that the Bill changes something that has remained unchanged for centuries simply do not recognise the road that marriage has travelled as an institution.[10]

A second proponent of the view that the purpose of marriage is 'love' was Yvette Cooper, MP (Labour). Consider her contribution to the debate:

Couples who love each other should be able to get married, regardless of their gender and sexuality. We should enjoy that and we should celebrate that. We all love a good wedding: we pause when we walk by a church or a registry office and we smile at the couple coming out in a cloud of confetti, because we think it is a great thing that a couple want to get married and want to celebrate that . . . We should celebrate the fact that different couples want to get married – that is exactly what we should support. This is not just about the wedding; we love a wedding, but we also all love the idea of a long, stable marriage. We love the idea of a golden or diamond wedding anniversary, where the couple are still caring for each other, even though they are bickering over the biscuits. We also all clearly like a good party, too.[11]

Here, we see that, not only are (long, stable) marriages conflated with wedding celebrations, but that the celebration of 'love' (particularly through length of marriage – represented through her discussion of golden and diamond wedding anniversaries) is presented as the most important aspect of marriage. In a similar vein to the minister, Cooper also described the changing nature of marriage:

> We cannot hide discrimination simply by calling it a definition. Marriage has changed many times over the centuries – and thank goodness for that. For hundreds of years, women were treated as property in marriage, handed from their fathers to their husbands and denied rights of their own. Until the 1990s, women's bodies were effectively treated as their husbands' property. If a husband raped his wife, it was not even treated as a crime. Civil marriage was introduced over 170 years ago and was pretty radical at the time, but now, every year, 160,000 of us get married in a civil ceremony. Marriage has changed before, and it should change again.[12]

Cooper's points about the positive changes that marriage has undergone are supported by a wealth of feminist critique of marriage as an institution. Many commentators have argued that marriage is an irredeemably patriarchal institution that has been the cause of centuries of oppression for women and, as such, should be wholly and completely dismantled (e.g., Robson 1998; Jeffreys 2004). Importantly, this anti-marriage position used to have far more support than it does now: the institution of marriage is now generally considered less problematic, even for some radical feminists, than it was in the 1970s (Finlay and Clarke 2003). No doubt this is, in part, because of the changes to marriage discussed by both Maria Miller and Yvette Cooper in these debates. For those who still do oppose marriage per se, however, the possibility of same-sex marriage remains anathema. In the words of Sheila Jeffreys (2004: 330): 'marriage exists to form the cement for the heteropatriarchy'.

Such critiques were noticeable by their absence in the parliamentary debate. Indeed, the suggestion from Sir Roger Gale (Conservative) that, 'if the Government are serious about this measure, they should withdraw the Bill, abolish the Civil Partnership Act 2004, abolish civil marriage and create a civil union Bill that applies to all people, irrespective of their sexuality or relationship',[13] was greeted with disdain and described as 'profoundly offensive'.[14]

The first mention of 'procreation' as the main purpose of marriage in these debates also came from Cooper, who set out an early critique of this perspective:

> Some people oppose same-sex marriage because they believe that marriage is by definition about the procreation of children. However, that is not

true of civil marriage, and that has been the case for over a century. Many marriages are childless, and we do not prevent people who are too old or too sick to have children from getting married. We do not do fertility tests at the altar. Yes, in vast numbers of families, marriage is an important starting point for a loving family bringing up children, but gay couples bring up children too.[15]

Like the discourse of 'love', defining marriage by reference to procreation is a departure from current law. Although a (different-sex) marriage is still technically voidable on the basis of non-consummation, there is no requirement for procreation in determining the legality of marriage.[16] Consider this contribution from John Glen, a Conservative backbench MP:

> The assumption of the Bill is that marriage is just about love and commitment. Of course marriage is about love and commitment, but it is also about the complementarity, both biologically and as a mother and father, of a man and a woman who have an inherent probability of procreation and of raising children within that institution.[17]

Here, it is the mere biological capability of a different-sex couple to procreate that is presented as the purpose of marriage. The source of this construction of procreation as the purpose of marriage is not the legal definition of (civil) marriage. Rather, it stems from the reasons for marriage set out in the Book of Common Prayer 1662, which remains a foundation of the established Church of England. There are plural sources of law that underpin marriage in English law. These include: the common law definition of marriage, the rules in the Matrimonial Causes Act 1973, the Canon Law by which the established Church conducts legal marriage (a marriage entered into through the rites of the Church is recognized as a valid legal marriage in English law) and Article 12 of the European Convention on Human Rights. Each of the legal sources seeks to draw on its own implicit understanding of what marriage means and requires, and procreation is a recurrent theme. Historically, however, procreation has not been a legal purpose of civil marriage. Nevertheless, in part because of the established nature of the Church of England, the plural framework of marriage law in England retains procreation as part of the legal discourse around marriage.

A further layer of confusion in this love or procreation debate, of course, can be found in the judgment from Sir Mark Potter P in the only English same-sex marriage case considered by the courts to date. In *Wilkinson v Kitzinger*, he conflated the religious definition of marriage according to the rites of the Church of England with the formalities of civil marriage and suggested that to recognize same-sex marriage would be to 'fail to recognise physical reality'.[18]

Although the physical act of procreation necessarily requires both male and female gametes, clearly this does not prevent same-sex couples from having and raising children. As David Lammy, MP (Labour), put it:

> Let us use today to return to a discussion of what marriage ought to be about. When I married my wife, I understood our marriage to have two important dimensions: the expression of love, fidelity and mutuality over the course of our life together; and a commitment to raise children. Gay men and women can now raise children – this House made that decision – so let us not hear any further discussion about having a family as if gay men and women cannot have that.[19]

The parliamentary discourse about procreation as the foundation of marriage is, therefore, better read as another means of protecting (heteronormative) marriage from the threat of same-sex couples. It is clear from this discourse that, rather than being essentially about either love or procreation, the main purpose of marriage is to support the (heteronormative) family. As I have argued before, 'the heteronormative image of "the family" (with all its concomitant gender/race/class implications) remains dominant and entrenched in the social imagination; a social category which excludes many alternative family forms, not only same sex relationships and families' (Harding 2011: 43).

The heteronormative family is as pervasive in these debates about same-sex marriage as it has been in others. Consider this contribution to the debate from Tim Loughton, MP (Conservative), who sought to remind Parliament that civil partnerships have already achieved 'equality':

> I supported the Civil Registration [sic] Act 2004. It should have been introduced earlier and it gave same-sex couples the same rights under the law and the tax system that I enjoy as a married person. I do not regard a couple's civil partnership as inferior or unequal to my marriage; it is simply different. That Act was an end in itself; it achieved equality . . . The real problem is not a lack of equality under the law but people's perceptions of a lack of equality for those with different sexual persuasions. We must redouble our efforts to root out that lack of equality, but changing the nature and the word of a ceremony will not do it and we completely mislead ourselves if we think that it will.[20]

Critiques of different but equal status within same-sex marriage debates have been somewhat ubiquitous, and so I shall not retread them here (see Peel and Harding 2004; Harding 2007). As I have argued previously, lesbians and gay men almost universally seem to regard civil partnership as 'not enough' (Harding 2006; Harding and Peel 2006). Consequently, it seems that civil partnerships (where they are available to same-sex couples only) will remain most appropriately understood as mere 'stepping stones' (Waaldijk 2001) or 'equality practice' (Eskridge 2002), rather than as a meaningful, egalitarian alternative to marriage (Peel and Harding 2004).

In these parliamentary debates on the Marriage (Same Sex Couples) Bill, the conflicting ideologies that underpin plural legal frameworks were placed in sharp focus. Of course, it is possible to understand same-sex marriage through lenses of either 'love' or 'procreation'. Indeed, in my previous research with lesbians and gay men, both 'love' and considering having children were given as reasons for entering into legally recognized relationships, whether civil partnerships or marriage (Harding 2011). However, reading these debates leaves an uncomfortable sense that the plurality of perspectives on marriage actually all point in the same, heteronormative direction. Simplistically, we could construct the arguments about 'love' as being about equality of recognition of same-sex sexuality, and those about 'procreation' as being concerned with protecting the privileged position in law of the potential biological outcome of heterosex, but to do so would be to elide the real source of tension in the love/procreation fault line: that not only is heterosexuality expected in relation to parenting, it is seen as normative, natural and desirable.

Judicial discourse: empowering lesbian mothers?

The ubiquity of heteronormativity is just as apparent in contemporary judicial discourse on lesbian and gay families. Consider *Re G; Re Z*. The facts of the case are rather complicated. They involve two applications for leave to apply for contact orders made by two men in a civil partnership with each other, S and T, regarding two children, G and Z, for whom they acted as known donors. G was conceived following self-insemination using sperm S donated to D and E, a lesbian couple in a civil partnership. Z was conceived following self-insemination using sperm T donated to X and Y, a second lesbian couple, also in a civil partnership. Both children were conceived following the reforms of the Human Fertilisation and Embryology Act 2008 and, as such, had their mother and (second female) parent listed on their birth certificates. Following the rules under section 45(1), the two men are 'sperm donors' and, as such, are not to be treated in law, for any purpose, as the fathers of the children conceived from their donation (s 48(1)). To complicate matters further, S had previously acted as a known donor to another child, F, born to E prior to the 2008 Act. Given the law at that time, S was that child's legal father, and he was pursuing a second action respecting that child for a range of orders, including matters such as contact, joint residence and parental responsibility. In sum, E is the legal mother of F and G; D is E's civil partner and legal parent of G; S is the legal father of F and has no legal relationship to G; F and G are full-blood siblings; X is legal mother of Z; Y is X's civil partner and legal parent of Z; T has no legal relationship to Z.

The differing situations of one of the lesbian couples, D and E, and their two children, born before and after the legal reforms, respectively F and G, helpfully represent the fundamental legal shift that was enacted by the Human Fertilisation and Embryology Act 2008. F was conceived prior to the passing of the legislation in March 2008 and was born in December 2008. The new parenting provisions apply only to children conceived after 1 April 2009; G was conceived in December 2009 and born in September 2010. Thus, S, the known donor for both F and G, is considered to be the legal father of F, but a legal stranger to G, despite the similar circumstances of their conception.

There were a range of disagreements hinted at between the parties as to the nature of the contact that had happened between the known sperm donors and the children before the applications to the courts. None of the parties had drawn up a written agreement prior to the birth of any of the children about the extent, nature or frequency of contact between the known donors and the children. It suffices for present purposes to note that, although each of the known sperm donors had experienced some contact with the child born of his donation, their demands for frequent contact had become unwanted, inconvenient or otherwise more significant than the children's legal parents had intended or desired.

S requested leave of the court to apply for orders relating to contact, residence and parental responsibility in respect of G. T requested leave to apply for contact with Z. Under section 10 of the Children Act 1989, both men had to seek leave of the court prior to making an application for an order under section 8.[21] Under section 10(9), when determining whether to grant leave, the court must have regard to

> (a) the nature of the proposed application for the section 8 order; (b) the applicant's connection with the child; (c) any risk there might be of that proposed application disrupting the child's life to such an extent that he would be harmed by it.

Before exploring the outcome of this case, it is interesting to note some of the implicit undercurrents in the relationships among the parties. Consider the following excerpts from the judgment. E stated:

> We wanted a known donor to make it possible for the child to find out more about its background. We were not looking for a father, we didn't want involvement, we, that is D and I were to be the parents.[22]

By contrast, S stated:

> Importantly, I would be known to the child and to the rest of the world as its father, although it would not carry my name. I did not mind about the name, it was more important for me to be known to the child as its

father, and to play the role perhaps as a friendly, caring and involved adult. The mothers did not request or want a financial contribution.[23]

It is important to draw out two points of contrast. First, E's reference to 'involvement' contrasts with S's reference to a 'financial contribution'. Each draws on different discursive understandings of the role of a father in a child's life, as a caregiver ('involvement') or as a provider (through financial contributions). Whereas, in the past, the attribution of fatherhood has, to a greater or lesser extent and through a variety of means, prioritized the attribution of financial responsibility for children, contemporary fatherhood discourse seeks to foreground gender neutrality and equality in parenting (Collier and Sheldon 2008). By specifically disclaiming her family's need for a 'father' and by focusing on a lack of 'involvement', E is drawing on both of these discourses. In contrast, S seems to be more concerned with 'involvement' and does not appear to draw the link between financial contribution to the upbringing of the child and parenthood.[24] He appears to consider that one can be a 'father' without either the financial responsibility that rests with legal parents or any day-to-day involvement in childcare.

Interestingly, gendered power dynamics play out in the discussion relating to financial resources. It becomes apparent that S and T have considerably greater financial resources than D and E (and possibly also X and Y). This raises questions about the justice of enabling known donors, with no financial responsibility for their progeny, to essentially force a child's legal parents into a protracted court battle that they cannot afford, particularly in the face of recent cuts to legal aid and increased incentives to use private ordering and mediation for family disputes in England.[25]

Second, consider how the parties use the terminology of 'parenthood'. E describes herself and D as G's 'parents' and S as a 'known donor'; S describes D and E as 'mothers' and himself as a 'father'. This difference in terminology lies at the heart of the conflict in this case. In English law, a child can have only one 'mother'; the gestational mother is always given this status, irrespective of genetic connection. Under the Human Fertilisation and Embryology Act 2008, a child can either have a 'parent' *or* a 'father', not both.[26] The term 'known donor' is, therefore, utilized by E (G's mother) to discursively highlight that G has a 'parent' and no father. S, in seeking to establish a parental connection, elides D (G's 'parent') into E, as one of G's 'mothers'. This may seem like a simple linguistic manoeuvre, but it is not. It invokes the weight of social approval associated with the term 'father', as the embodiment of 'safe familial masculinity' (Thomson 2008: 113), in contrast to the spectre of the 'sperm donor', potentially constructed as engaging in 'a masturbatory act done for "beer money"' (Thomson 2008: 113). By eliding D (G's 'parent') into E (G's 'mother') through the use of the word 'mothers', S is, therefore, attempting to improve his own position in the wider construction of family, by leaving space for a 'father' as the second and contrasting type of legal parent.

More generally, counsel for the two men and Mr Justice Baker in his judgment repeatedly referred to the couples of D and E and of X and Y as 'mothers'. Consider the following excerpt from one of the final paragraphs of the judgment:

> It was always part of the plans in both cases that there should be some contact between the children and their biological fathers. Equally, both S and T should reflect on the fact that the primary family unit for these children is with their mothers and this court will, when considering their substantive applications, look very carefully to ensure that any risk of harm to the children is avoided. These mothers understandably feel very vulnerable by the challenge to their family units. Notwithstanding the great social changes that have facilitated the creation of these new types of family, mothers in the position of D and E, and X and Y, understandably continue to feel vulnerable, and this court will take that vulnerability into account when considering the applications for contact.[27]

Here, even in the context of cautioning the men that the court may not grant the contact orders they request, we see Baker J referring to them as 'biological fathers' and to all four of the women as 'mothers'. By referring to the men as 'biological fathers', Baker J is drawing the discursive power of 'father' on to their side of the dispute. Moreover, by not referring to D or Y, the civil partners of the women who had carried the children, as 'parents', but merging them into a category of 'mothers', he is concurrently erasing their legal status in this judicial discourse. This, perhaps, comes across even more powerfully in the following excerpt:

> The 2008 Act denies the biological father the status of legal parent, but it does not prevent the lesbian couple, in whom legal parenthood is vested, from encouraging or enabling the biological father to become a psychological parent. On the contrary, it empowers the lesbian couple to take that course as the persons in whom parental responsibility is vested.[28]

In this passage, the discursive power of 'mother' has been replaced with 'the lesbian couple', whom Baker J constructs as having a responsibility to encourage or enable 'the biological father to become a psychological parent'. This appears to be the crux of the reasoning in the case. By considering known donors to be 'fathers' of children for whom 'the lesbian couple' have legal parenthood, Baker J is artificially elevating the importance of fathers and concurrently reinserting the (negatively construed) discursive impossibility and invisibility of lesbianism, motherhood and parenthood (Arnup and Boyd

1995). Arguably, rather than emphasizing the difference between legal parents and those who do not have a legal relationship to the children, the use of the prefix 'biological' simply reinforces the donors' entitlement to the sociocultural privileges that stem from being a 'father'.

The practice of using known donors has a long history in lesbian and gay parenting culture. Although knowing one's biological origins is culturally assumed to be a good thing, forcing women to undergo unnecessary stress and financial outlay to defend their families against unwanted interference is unlikely to be in the best interests of any child. It would be a missed opportunity if, rather than emphasizing what is good about constructing families with known donors, cases such as *Re G; Re Z* coerce lesbians who want to have children into using licensed clinics, with anonymous donor sperm, in an attempt to gain a higher level of security from unwanted interference with their families.

The never-ending reinscription of heteronormativity on the family

Through this chapter's critical discourse analysis, I have sought to demonstrate how parliamentary and judicial discourse that has arisen 'after equality' has continued to draw on heteronormative ideals of the family. In many respects, this continued presence of heteronormativity is no great surprise: feminist commentators on the pitfalls of same-sex marriage have consistently argued that seeking inclusion in heteronormative legal institutions will simply lead to further assimilation of lesbian and gay families into those very same heteronormative legal institutions (e.g., Polikoff 1993). Similarly, as Robert Leckey (2013: 16) has recently argued, changes to recognition frameworks for lesbian (and gay) parents create new dangers that might result in constraining 'the diversity of queer kinship'.

I do not seek to argue, either that 'fathers' are not, or should not be, important, or that 'love' or 'procreation' are not, or should not be, considered reasons for marriage. Many people, gay and straight, do marry or enter into civil partnerships for love (although see Donovan's problematization of discourses of love, in this volume) or to gain access to the legal rights and responsibilities that will enable them to most effectively support their children. Importantly though, lesbian and gay equality must have some substantive content, or we risk the continued reinscription of heteronormativity on to lesbian and gay lives. It is not appropriate to simultaneously grant 'equal' legal status to the adult relationships of same-sex couples or to non-biological lesbian parents and then to undermine that very same recognition with a refusal to accommodate lived difference into that 'equality'. Another example would be Monk's 'too gay to foster' case study (in this volume), which highlights the expectations of heteronormative relational performance when same-sex couples seek to become parents. We need to be attentive to the possibilities that are both created and foreclosed by these new 'after equality' legal frameworks.

We know that lesbian and gay relationships and families are different. Rather than falling back on heteronormative proscriptions of what 'marriage' or 'family' means, 'after equality' legal frameworks need implementation in ways that acknowledge these differences. In the process, we must ask questions such as the following: What are the foundational purposes of same-sex marriage? Why do same-sex couples (want to) marry? How are 'known donors' understood within lesbian and gay family contexts? Should formal legal frameworks accommodate 'known donors'? If so, how? Can children have more than two legal parents?[29] What about other people with possible parental claims (e.g., surrogate mothers or birth parents of adopted children)? The answers to these questions will only become apparent in time, following judicial determinations and socio-legal research within the new legal frameworks for lesbian and gay families.

The danger is that contemporary legal frameworks enforce the performance of heteronormative familial lives on lesbian and gay families. If we had a tendency towards conspiracy theories, we might argue this is all part of an underlying governmental aim, made visible through the requirement for same-sex couples to be in civil partnerships in order to access 'legal parent' status for the mother's partner, or to be able to access new fast-track surrogacy procedures. However, unless we challenge the legal reinscription of understandings of the (singular, heteronormative) 'family' on to same-sex relationships and lesbian and gay parents, we run the risk of reinventing the 'known donor' as substantively the same as the biological 'father', constructing same-sex relationships as the same as heterosexual marriage and missing out on the transformative potential of new equality frameworks in family law. If we do, we will lose the value and difference that alternative family forms can offer. It seems that the real work of transforming the 'law of straightness' must begin 'after equality'.

Acknowledgements

With thanks to Elizabeth Peel, Robert Leckey and all of the 'After equality' workshop participants for their constructive comments and criticism.

Notes

1 Edward Monkton is the alter ego of artist Giles Andreae. A range of Edward Monkton cartoons can be viewed on his website. Online. Available at: www.edwardmonkton.com (accessed 30 June 2013).
2 *Re G (A Minor); Re Z (A Minor)* [2013] EWHC 134 (Fam).
3 Local Government Act 1988, s 28 (emphasis added) (repealed by the Local Government Act 2003). See Cooper and Herman (1991) for a nuanced discussion of the governmental conditions that made this legislation possible.

4 Sections 42–6.
5 Ibid., s 45(1).
6 Ibid., s 48(2).
7 Importantly, unlike the case in some other jurisdictions where civil unions or domestic partnerships have been created to be substantially distinct from marriage, the legal consequences of English civil partnership are almost identical to legal marriage. In the Marriage (Same Sex Couples) Act 2013, Parliament has retained the small differences between how formalized same- and different-sex relationships are treated in law (the lack of a consummation requirement and the removal of adultery as a ground of dissolution). See Herring, in this volume; Barker 2006.
8 HC Deb 5 February 2013, Col 125.
9 (1866) LR 1 P&D 130.
10 HC Deb 5 February 2013, Col 126.
11 HC Deb 5 February 2013, Col 134–5.
12 HC Deb 5 February 2013, Col 140.
13 HC Deb 5 February 2013, Col 152.
14 HC Deb 5 February 2013, Col 152 (Chris Bryant).
15 HC Deb 5 February 2013, Col 140.
16 The House of Lords case of *Baxter v Baxter* [1948] AC 274 conclusively held that use of contraception did not negate consummation.
17 HC Deb 5 February 2013, Col 190.
18 [2006] EWHC (Fam) 2022 at paras 118–20.
19 HC Deb 5 February 2013, Col 193.
20 HC Deb 5 February 2013, Col 157–8.
21 Only those who are listed under s 10(4) or s 10(5) may apply as of right for an order under s 8. This includes parents, guardians, persons that the child has lived with for more than three years and persons in whose respect the child is legally considered to be a 'child of the family'.
22 *Re G (A Minor); Re Z (A Minor)* [2013] EWHC 134 (Fam) at para 5.
23 Ibid. at para 6.
24 D, as G's legal parent from the conception prior to the 2008 reforms, has financial responsibility for him. S, as a known donor, has no obligation to provide financial support.
25 Legal Aid, Sentencing and Punishment of Offenders Act 2012; Children and Families Act 2014.
26 See ss 45(1), 48(1).
27 *Re G (A Minor); Re Z (A Minor)* [2013] EWHC 134 (Fam) at para 136.
28 Ibid. at para 118.
29 Clearly they can in British Columbia, Canada (Boyd, in this volume). Questions then include how multiple legal parents experience their different roles, and how those legal possibilities are interpreted and applied.

References

Arnup, K. and Boyd, S. (1995) 'Familial disputes? Sperm donors, lesbian mothers and legal parenthood', in D. Herman and C. Stychin (eds) *Legal Inversions: Lesbians, Gay Men and the Politics of Law*, Philadelphia: Temple University Press, 77–101.
Barker, N.J. (2006) 'Sex and the Civil Partnership Act: The future of (non) conjugality?', *Feminist Legal Studies*, 14(2): 241–59.
Berlant, L. and Warner, M. (2000) 'Sex in public', in L. Berlant (ed.) *Intimacy*, Chicago: University of Chicago Press, 311–30.

Chambers, S.A. (2007) '"An incalculable effect": Subversions of heteronormativity', *Political Studies*, 55: 656–79.

Collier, R. and Sheldon, S. (2008) *Fragmenting Fatherhood: A Socio-Legal Study*, Oxford: Hart.

Cooper, D. and Herman, D. (1991) 'Getting "the family right": Legislating heterosexuality in Britain, 1986–1991', *Canadian Journal of Family Law*, 10: 41–78.

Eskridge, W.N. (2002) *Equality Practice: Civil Unions and the Future of Gay Rights*, New York: Routledge.

Finlay, S.-J. and Clarke, V. (2003) '"A marriage of inconvenience?" Feminist perspectives on marriage', *Feminism and Psychology*, 13(4): 415–20.

Foucault, M. (2002) *Power: Essential Works of Foucault 1954–1984*, Vol. 3, (ed.) J.D. Faubion, trans. R. Hurley, London: Penguin.

Griffiths, J. (1986) 'What is legal pluralism?', *Journal of Legal Pluralism and Unofficial Law*, 24: 1–56.

Harding, R. (2006) '"Dogs are 'registered', people shouldn't be": Legal consciousness and lesbian and gay rights', *Social and Legal Studies*, 15(4): 511–33.

—— (2007) 'Sir Mark Potter and the protection of the traditional family: Why same-sex marriage is (still) a feminist issue', *Feminist Legal Studies*, 15(2): 223–34.

—— (2011) *Regulating Sexuality: Legal Consciousness and Lesbian and Gay Lives*, London: Routledge.

—— and Peel, E. (2006) 'We do? International perspectives on equality, legality and same sex relationships', *Lesbian and Gay Psychology Review*, 7(2): 123–40.

Harvie, P. and Manzi, T. (2011) 'Interpreting multi-agency partnerships: Ideology, discourse, and domestic violence', *Social and Legal Studies*, 20(1): 79–95.

Jeffreys, S. (2004) 'The need to abolish marriage', *Feminism and Psychology*, 14(2): 327–31.

Kleinhans, M.-M. and Macdonald, R.A. (1997) 'What is a *critical* legal pluralism?', *Canadian Journal of Law and Society*, 12(1): 25–46.

Leckey, R. (2013) 'Two mothers in law and fact', *Feminist Legal Studies*, 21(1): 1–19.

Moore, S.F. (1986) 'Legal systems of the world', in L. Lipson and S. Wheeler (eds) *Law and the Social Sciences*, New York: Russell Sage Foundation.

Peel, E. and Harding, R. (2004) 'Divorcing romance, rights and radicalism: Beyond pro and anti in the lesbian and gay marriage debate', *Feminism and Psychology*, 14(4): 588–99.

Polikoff, N.D. (1993) 'We will get what we ask for: Why legalizing gay marriage will not "dismantle the legal structure of gender in every marriage"', *Virginia Law Review*, 79(7): 1535–50.

Probert, R.J. (2007) '*Hyde v Hyde*: defining or defending marriage?', *Child and Family Law Quarterly*, 19: 322–36.

Robson, R. (1998) *Sappho Goes to Law School*, New York: Columbia University Press.

Tamanaha, B.Z. (2000) 'A non-essentialist version of legal pluralism', *Journal of Law and Society*, 27(2): 296–321.

Thomson, M. (2008) *Endowed: Regulating the Male Sexed Body*, New York: Routledge.

van Dijk, T.A. (1991) *Racism and the Press*, London: Routledge.

Waaldijk, K. (2001) 'Small change: How the road to same-sex marriage got paved in the Netherlands', in R. Wintemute and M. Andenaes (eds) *Legal Recognition of Same-Sex Partnerships: A Study of National, European and International Law*, Oxford: Hart, 437–64.

Chapter 12

Sexuality and children post-equality

Daniel Monk

Children have been the focus for gay and lesbian[1] legal and political campaigns in a variety of contexts: parental residence (custody) disputes, access to adoption and fostering services and assisted reproduction, and concerns about homophobic bullying and sex education. These have all given rise to similar claims and conflicts in most Western jurisdictions, but the differences have much to tell us about the politics of national histories, cultures and memories (Stychin 1998; Bradley 2005), and so it is important to note that this chapter draws on stories from England.

Issues related to children are particularly well placed to unmask the cultural and political dimensions to sexual orientation claims as they go beyond, and indicate the limits of, arguments based on 'negative' human rights claims premised on privacy and adult autonomy, for, where children are concerned, whether in the context of the legal regulation of the family, reproduction or education, the focus on the rights of the child has legitimized a particular interventionist engagement by the state. At the same time, the concern with 'the child' has long been recognized as providing a thin mask for, and being intimately connected with, concerns with the future and, indeed, the very survival, of society as a whole (Jenks 2005). Consequently, in many jurisdictions, these disputes have represented the 'final hurdle' in the move towards formal equality. So, although homosexual acts were (partly) decriminalized in England in 1967, that critical legislative moment was not perceived as incompatible with much *later* explicit judicial and legislative prejudice in the context of children, for example, lesbian 'custody' cases (Beresford 2008) and the notorious Section 28 of the Local Government Act 1988, which aimed to protect children from the 'promotion of homosexuality' (Monk 1998).

Of course, in this post-equality era, much has been achieved. The age of consent was equalized in 2000; the right to adopt was formally extended to lesbian and gay couples in 2002; Section 28 was repealed in 2003; same-sex relationships were recognized in 2004; and homophobic bullying in schools was explicitly condemned by all political parties in the 2010 general election.

Reflecting and acknowledging this new terrain, critique has shifted to question the terms of inclusion (Brown 1995; Duggan 2003; Stychin 2006), a turn that has added a new perspective to earlier feminist and gay liberationist concerns about the tensions between formal and substantive equality and the problematic silencing of 'difference'. These frameworks have helped illuminate the continuing problematic role of 'the child' in debates about children and relationship recognition (McCreery 2008), parental status (McCandless and Sheldon 2010), education (Monk 2011a) and parenting conflicts *between* gays and lesbians (Diduck 2007; Leckey 2013).

This chapter aims to demonstrate the discursive and political tenacity and malleability of 'the child', that it 'does a lot of work'. For it is through 'the child' that the prejudices and fears of traditional conservatives linger and assert 'respectability', and, at the same time, liberal rights agendas legitimize a counter assertion of respectability. Moreover, although queer theory provides a key tool for critiquing the latter, it also, in places, demonstrates an investment in the category of 'the child' (Lesnik-Oberstein 2008a), often using it to both assert and valorize 'the outsider'. The focus here is on two distinct, contemporary experiences of gay and lesbian encounters with children. The first is the experience of a gay male couple that encountered resistance to being accepted as suitable foster parents, because of their openly non-monogamous relationship. The second is the relationships gays and lesbians construct with 'godchildren', as expressed through their wills.

The first came to light after I was asked to advise the men, the second through empirical research. These 'methods' – the fact that the experiences take place outside statutory reform agendas and litigation strategies, and indeed beyond the focus of radical queer political discourses – are significant, for, although one aim here is to draw attention to potentially 'hidden stories' of contemporary gay and lesbian connections with children within legal frameworks premised on equality, a further aim is to demonstrate what happens, and what is done to grass-roots stories, in order to make them fit within both liberal rights agendas and queer critiques. Consciously reading them both through and against these discursive grains, the aim here is to create a space for a 'quiet empiricism' (Moran 2009), raising questions more than offering answers.

Too gay to foster?

The fact that gay men and lesbians have cared for and provided homes for children, both those of other people and their 'own' (Lesnik-Oberstein 2008b), is not new. However, what is relatively new is the extent to which they have been able to do so, either as individuals or with a partner, openly and with confidence that their sexuality will not prove to be any form of barrier or hindrance. In England, as elsewhere, progress has been incremental and often in the face of fierce opposition (Hicks 2006a, 2006b; Brown and Crocker 2008). However, formal legal equality has now been achieved: the principle of equality is routinely asserted in case law relating to private law disputes;[2]

the Adoption and Children Act 2002 permits gay and lesbian couples to adopt; and the Equality Act 2006 requires adoption and fostering agencies, including those of a religious foundation,[3] to provide their services in a non-discriminatory fashion. Moreover, against a background of increased demand, the government has funded recruitment campaigns for foster carers that explicitly target gays and lesbians (Brown and Cocker 2008).

It was against this background that I was contacted in 2011 by a gay couple that had recently been rejected as prospective foster carers.[4] They were in a long-term relationship and had entered a civil partnership. Initially, the response from the local social services was extremely welcoming, and they effectively 'ticked all the boxes' in the assessment. That their sexuality per se was not a problem was not a surprise: the local authority was well known for its pioneering support for gays and lesbians and proudly flies a rainbow flag during LGBT History Month. Just at the end of the lengthy assessment exercise, however, one of the men disclosed to a social worker that they were not monogamous, that they had an 'open relationship'. Almost immediately, without any further questioning and with minimal explanation, their suitability as foster carers was effectively transformed from 'ideal' to 'untouchable'. After a protracted appeal process lasting over a year, and with little support, they were finally accepted as suitable foster carers by the local authority for a child of any age. However, almost two years later, they have yet to be matched with a child,[5] and, as a result, the outcome is ambivalent, and the message to men in a similar position is far from clear.

Using law to challenge the local authority is far from straightforward. First, the local authority would arguably have treated an opposite-sex couple in the same way. Consequently, the case is not one of direct discrimination, and indirect discrimination is notoriously difficult to establish. Second, the European Court of Human Rights has made plain that there is no 'right to foster'.[6] Fostering is a service provided for children, and, in England, as elsewhere, the legal framework is governed by the overarching principle that the child's interests are paramount. Similarly, although a landmark European Court of Human Rights decision has recently recognized that a gay couple is capable of forming a 'family life',[7] such a right is not absolute and can be infringed by the state in order to protect the rights of others. In other words, the right of the child trumps any rights of the adults to non-discriminatory treatment. The rights of the child and non-discrimination are not, of course, always in conflict. Indeed, quite the reverse. In Re G in 2009, a rule preventing unmarried couples from adopting was overruled in the interests of the child, and a parallel could be drawn to a 'blanket rule' against a non-monogamous couple.[8]

Gay rights organizations have played a critical role in the use of litigation to protect the interests of gay men and lesbians, but, in this case, the response to the men was at best ambivalent. This can partly be explained by the legal complexity of the case, but not totally. In 2011, the Christian Legal Centre supported an action brought by a married couple who argued that concerns expressed by social workers about their homophobia effectively meant that their chances of being accepted as foster carers were impossible, and they went to court to seek clarification.[9] As with the gay couple in this case, they had not actually been rejected as foster carers. Consequently, as Munby LJ noted, the proceedings were 'most unusual . . . about a principle *in abstracto*'.[10] What distinguishes the cases and explains the pre-emptive proceedings in one rather than the other is activist strategizing.

The Christian applicants presented a perfect test-case opportunity in the recent and ongoing strategic attempt to demonstrate that they are the 'new' victims, and that their rights are 'trumped' by gay rights.[11] In other words, from the perspective of the Christian Legal Centre, they were not simply suitable foster parents but also ideal litigants, whereas, from the perspective of gay rights organizations, the non-monogamous gay couple may or may not have been considered suitable carers, but, for reasons explored below, they were most definitely not suitable litigants. Test cases premised on equality claims utilize arguments based on sameness,[12] particularly in the context of family life. However, although for the Christian Legal Centre religious faith was a 'difference' that it wished to draw attention to and indeed be proud of, in the case of the non-monogamous gay couple, the difference was problematic, to say the least.

People across a spectrum of positions express concern about, or are troubled by the thought of, non-monogamous foster carers. That the case divides opinion reveals the conditionality of gay parenting rights and, in particular, how pragmatic political narratives interconnect with those premised on child welfare; in other words, how the figure of the child serves as a discursive site for performing 'good' gay parenthood. For these reasons, the case also reveals the crudeness of the term 'homophobia' as a label or theoretical frame of reference for capturing differential treatment in an age of formal legal equality.

The initial immediate, almost visceral, response of the local authority – in particular its desire for the couple to simply disappear – undoubtedly reflected the deep cultural and social symbolic investment in the monogamy/non-monogamy binary and the extent to which 'consensual non-monogamies continue to be demonized, pathologized, marginalized and subject to the social regulation of ridicule' (Barker and Langdridge 2010: 756). Not surprisingly, and correctly in law, the responses to non-monogamy were 'translated' into and expressed as concerns premised on the welfare of the child.

One concern was that their open relationship would require the men to lie to the children about their whereabouts. The men's response to this was that adults do not tell children about everything they do or see, that it would be acceptable to say they were 'visiting a friend' and draw a veil over the details, and that doing so would be analogous to telling a child they were going to see a film (which might be 'X rated') and not narrating the details. As Carol Smart has argued, secrets can serve legitimate functions (2007: 108).

The concern about dishonesty is paradoxical, for it was their honesty that distinguished them from both those couples that know how to play the game and those practising *non-consensual* non-monogamy. The main 'child welfare' concern, however, focused on the indirect impact of non-monogamy on the men, both individually and as a couple.

Concern was expressed that it might expose them, as individuals, to physical harm. Although plausible, the same could be said of most sports. However, in this context, the cultural association of promiscuity with risk makes the equation more compelling. To a certain extent this mirrors English criminal law's heteronormative binary, whereby boxing and homo-social 'horseplay' are legal, whereas consensual SM sex is criminal (Bibbings 2000).

More fundamental was the perception that there must be something wrong with their relationship, which would impact on the stability they would be able to offer a child. There are curious echoes here of earlier cases in English family law where, notoriously, a mother would lose custody of her children if she had committed adultery, for, in the words of a judge, 'a bad wife is by definition a bad mother'.[13]

The assumption that a non-monogamous relationship is not in the 'best interests' of a child is less likely to be expressed in such explicitly moralistic language (and certainly not in terms that express an explicit patriarchal, gendered 'double standard'). Today, it is expressed as a therapeutic concern through the language of responsibilization (Reece 2009). In other words, an open relationship nowadays is less likely to be considered 'sinful' or immoral, particularly by professionals committed to 'non-judgmental' and 'non-discriminatory' practice (Brown and Cocker 2010), but instead it is more likely to be viewed as possible evidence of 'unresolved issues', emotional crisis and instability. The point here is not that these concerns are necessarily inappropriate; rather, it is to notice the malleability and inherently value-based underpinnings of judgments premised on 'child welfare' (Reece 1996).

Hicks argues that the fears and prejudices about gay men as dangerous, predatory perverts coalesce with, and are reinforced by, perceptions of gay men as promiscuous, and that they combine to arouse suspicion among social workers about the motives of gay men wishing to foster or adopt (2006a: 102–3). Consequently, 'to express the idea that someone might be a gay parent and also a person with sexual desires is a problem' (Hicks 2006a: 103), and a gay man desiring to foster while at the same time explicitly desiring sex outside the conjugal couple is uniquely problematic. One way in which agencies discursively enable gay men to be deemed suitable as foster carers is a process whereby they are 'reimagined as maternal or, indeed, feminine' (Hicks 2006a: 100). Emphasizing their 'nurturing' qualities distinguishes them from heterosexual men and defuses the threat of their sexuality. This process, which of course has much to say about dominant understandings of 'motherhood' and female sexual desire, was not possible here, for openly seeking sex outside a relationship resolutely placed the couple in the socially constructed category of 'male'.

'Having children' is sometimes perceived or read as a sign of 'growing up' and drawing attention to promiscuity within the gay community as a form of negative stereotyping.[14] Shonkwiler observes how 'asserting maturity through parenthood specifically counteracts the standard narrative of homosexuality as a failure to develop a fully adult sexual identity' and that, '[to] voluntarily subordinate one's hard-won "liberated" political gay identity to the strictures of family nurturance is seen as a new kind of social maturity' (2008: 547, 557). A gay couple that wishes to foster and to have an open relationship is, within this framework of knowledge, inherently and deeply suspect. They fail to demonstrate the maturity required to be a good parent, not only by acknowledging their sexual desires, but also by proudly asserting their desire to act on them. In this way, they are not simply 'too male', but, more significantly, 'too gay'.

This perspective is reinforced in the extensive literature about gay parenting and gay non-monogamy. The growth of both reflects increasing interest in what can broadly be described as intimate citizenship. However, there is almost no overlap or cross-referencing between the two: in academia, parenting and sex appear to occupy self-contained parallel universes.[15] The gay couple here troubles this division and, in wanting a child *and* a 'gay lifestyle', they are deemed 'selfish', that most damning of labels (with deep, Christian foundations) that is used to delegitimize all forms of 'unnatural' desire for children (whether by the single, the 'old' or the disabled) and also, paradoxically, gays who don't want children and who opt for a 'gay lifestyle' over children. As Hicks' research indicates, 'sameness' accounts by gay parents sometimes set up relationship hierarchies in which gay couples with children are more respected than others (2006b: 767). So it was within this double bind of selfishness that this out and proud gay couple found itself.

Research and anecdotal evidence suggest that gay and lesbian applicants for fostering and adoption are aware of the need to edit, to 'present' or perform in a particular way. Cook (2014: 140), for example, quotes a gay man who successfully adopted a child saying, 'We could really have ruined our chances of adopting by shocking some people whose sensibilities and whose experiences and attitudes to sexual emancipation are quite different from mine. We weren't asked,' he said, 'and we didn't offer any frightening information. We were playing the system and felt that we had to in a way.'

By failing to play the game, the couple in this case further exposed themselves to allegations of 'naivety'. This response arguably is a comment on their lack of social and political capital, in other words, their failure to know the (unwritten and hidden) rules. Moreover, it is a response that demonstrates the extent to which particular views of 'suitability' are either pragmatically acknowledged or accepted and internalized.

Lisa Duggan's concept of 'homonormativity' (2003), Gayle Rubin's classic work on inside/outside sexualities (1984) and Wendy Brown's identification of the conditionality of inclusion (1995) all, in different ways, offer critical frameworks that reveal the 'logic' underlying the silencing of the couple and the necessity of rendering invisible the evidence that consensual non-monogamy is 'the taken-for-granted mode of relating in much gay culture' (Barker and Langdridge 2010: 788). Making families, having children and parenting are complex and hugely varied lived experiences. However, at a discursive political and symbolic level, these activities, and crucially the expression of desire to participate in them, are explicitly utilized to demonstrate the normality of gay men and lesbians. As McCreery notes (2008), arguments for gay marriage are often premised on children's rights arguments. This case reveals the 'fearful pragmatism' of such claims, for, in this case, the couple's honesty could be read as evidence of, rather than a lack of, both stability and commitment. (Indeed, the reason why the couple disclosed their open relationship was to *emphasize* the stability of their relationship.)

At the same time, it is possible and important to note how 'queer' critiques have the potential to silence other readings of the story, and in particular the narrative of the men themselves. From their perspective, the issue was explicitly about and expressed through a discourse of 'gay rights'. Moreover, the meaning they attached to non-monogamy within their relationship cohered with and reinforced Klesse's findings that, for many gay men, open relationships are in significant respects highly conventional, being exclusively based around an 'emotionally exclusive' dyadic couple (2007). In other words, although a commitment to 'coupledom' is perfectly compatible with a celebration of 'gay marriage', it is distinct from, if not at odds with, more transgressive or queer celebrations of non-monogamy.

One social worker expressed the view that the men could not have an open relationship because they were in a civil partnership. This is a particularly ironic view, bearing in mind that none of the numerous references to sex in the law relating to marriage, most notably adultery, applies to civil partnerships (Barker 2006; Stychin 2006). But it could be argued that, *through* their engagement with law, here through opting for legal recognition of their relationship and simultaneously being open about non-monogamy, they bring to the fore difference. In effect, the story could be used to support certain progressive gay marriage arguments that suggest that, by participating in mainstream civic institutions (in this context, relationship recognition and local government fostering), they help to bring about changes in those institutions, rather than the institutions' simply imposing norms on them. In particular, to the extent that they have required a local authority to engage with their experiences, it could be argued that they have challenged assumptions about parenting within family law that prioritize a focus on adult sex lives over day-to-day childcare (a shift called for by Herring, in this volume). It is too early, and arguably optimistic, to tell the story as a success, especially as wide, discretionary decision-making power in this field lacks the certainty offered by test cases or legislative victories. And it is important to emphasize that the aim here is not to suggest that these alternative readings are in any way more valid than the queer readings. It is simply to acknowledge that engagement with the law by the men has begun a process, a conversation that forces people to think about difference.

Queer 'godparents'?

In this second case study, I draw on a small empirical research project that explored gay and lesbian will-writing practices in England.[16] Although not suggesting that gay and lesbian experiences are in any way either monolithic or unique, the premise for exploring 'difference' in this context was based on the combined impact of the following four factors. First, formal legal equality is relatively recent, and, consequently, the evidence that heterosexuals often do not make wills because of assumptions about the legal protection provided by inheritance law for their immediate family or kin (Brooker 2007) is far less likely to apply. Second, gays and lesbians are, to date at least, less likely to have children – a key motive for writing wills – and distinct legal implications exist when they do. Third, the impact of HIV/AIDS – confronting mortality collectively and community-based will-writing services – created a particular shared experience and memory of inheritance conflicts (Monk 2011b). Fourth, testamentary freedom, where upheld, has provided and continues to provide gays and lesbians with a legal space for 'coming out', to actively constitute their significant relations, rendering non-heterosexual relations visible and giving wills a political significance (Monk 2011b, 2013).

The research took the form of semi-structured interviews with ten solicitors with collective experience of writing wills for gay men and lesbians (although not exclusively) over a period of twenty-five years. Here, I focus on just one aspect of the data: the 'godparent' role, formal or otherwise. Albeit for different reasons, these stories, like those of non-monogamous foster parents, are hidden from law and, indeed, from academic research. Indeed, if foster, adoptive and non-biological parenting is still sometimes placed slightly lower in the parental hierarchy than 'natural' or genetic parenting (Hicks 2006a), then the 'godparenting' role (religious or otherwise) is not even on the map.

Recent research in the UK about will-writing practices found that godchildren figured hardly at all (Humphrey *et al.* 2010; Douglas *et al.* 2011). In my research, this finding was mirrored in the experiences of those lawyers who had relatively few gay or lesbian clients. For example, in answer to the question, 'What about godchildren? Children of friends?':

Virtually never. I'm still in touch with my godmother but I don't think she's recognized me in her will. No, the godparent relationship sadly is over.

(Lawyer 1)

However, in answer to the same question, the lawyers who had a large number of gay and lesbian clients had a very different response. For example:

Yes, godchildren in particular and of course that applies to gay clients as well as straight clients [pause] but particularly with gay clients . . . I often wonder if married couples appoint gay friends to be godparents, knowing that they're not going to have their own children and perhaps it's a good idea from a monetary aspect and certainly I do feel that my gay clients perhaps think more of their godchildren than straight clients . . . certainly with gay people, godchildren do feature.

(Lawyer 5)

They too benefit, that's definitely a feature with gays . . . It's not uncommon I would say but it's certainly, children of friends to benefit without question. Godchildren? Often the same, one and the same aren't they?

(Lawyer 8)

Absolutely. A lot of gay people are godparents now . . . there is that much more so than previously, they will leave something to children or acknowledge children, they are there, they think about them, they have these relationships now and they can be acknowledged publically I suppose.

(Lawyer 9)

As Lawyer 8 emphasized, even where the expression 'godchild' was used, it was clear that this had little, if anything, to do with religion. That is a reflection of the secularity of mainstream British culture and, in addition, of the, perhaps telling, absence of any alternative non-religious label or descriptor for this type of adult–child relationship.

As Lawyer 9 above suggests, it may be that, for gays and lesbians, these relationships are more common now than previously. Compared with the testimonies of the lawyers quoted above – who are all currently in practice – the reference to godchildren was less pronounced by those lawyers who wrote wills only during the late 1980s and early 1990s (predominantly for gay men with HIV/AIDS). The popularity of gay men as godfathers is, it would seem, more than an anecdotal journalistic myth (Turner 2003; Waters 2009), and Lawyer 5's reference to the motives of the parents might, tentatively, also explain why it seems more likely to be men than women who are chosen.

It is possible to read the place made for godchildren/children of friends in gay and lesbian wills in a queer celebratory fashion that emphasizes 'difference'. This reading challenges the applicability to gays and lesbians of the finding by Douglas *et al*. that,

> in so far as it has been suggested that people may be seen as having a 'personal community' – 'a specific subset of people's informal social relationships . . . [which] represent people's significant personal relationships and include bonds which give both structure and meaning to their lives', these do not seem to impinge on their views when it comes to determining inheritance.
>
> (2011: 246–7 (footnote omitted))

One result of this is that, despite 'equal rights' found in family law more widely, the exclusion of non-traditional family forms from the intestacy rules means that, for gays and lesbians, testamentary freedom and will-writing, with all the attendant risks and expenses (Monk 2011b), remain as critical as ever. It should be made plain from the outset that the argument here is not that these relationships should be recognized in law (even if such a task were feasible). Rather, it is that the focus on obtaining legal recognition of relationships (of whatever forms) obscures and creates silences about the significance – emotionally – of such forms of 'connectedness' (Smart 2007: 189).

A further queer celebratory reading would be to view these relationships through the lens of Eve Sedgwick's understanding of the avuncular. Crucially, she argues that avuncular relationships do not simply expand the notion of the family, but destabilize and trouble children's understanding and experience of family, that 'the move from "kinship" to "family" is "avuncular suppressive"' (1994: 62). Suggesting that we 'forget the name of the Father. Think about your uncles and your aunts', she comments: 'It is the very badness of their fit with . . . streamlined modern models of "family" – that makes them such good places to look for . . . resistance to the sleek "same"/"different" scientism of modern gender and sexual preference' (Sedgwick 1994: 60).

From this perspective, it is precisely because gay and lesbian godparents *don't* have their own children, because they fail to conform to the new model of 'respectable' gay parenting noted in the context of good foster parents, that they are *good godparents*. As Sedgwick notes, because their 'intimate access to children needn't depend on their own pairing or procreation, it's very common, of course, for some of them to have the office of representing nonconforming or non-productive sexualities to children' (1994: 63).

Like the non-monogamous foster parents, the desires of the queer godparents (particularly those without their own children) fail to conform to the assimilated model of gay and lesbian parenting, for the 'natural' desire for a child is replaced with a desire for a relationship with other people's children.

In this way, these godparents communicate a queer message to children that there is more in life than partnership and parenting. Moreover, making the avuncular relationships visible in wills adds materiality to queer stories of kinship that, too often, in celebrating alternative kinship, fail to examine this dimension. However, this dimension provides a particularly productive space for thinking about relationality (Heaphy *et al.* 2013: 106). As Shonkwiler notes, 'Family is not just whom you "choose"; it is also who you spend your money on . . . money becomes a way to construct the category of family in recognizably social terms' (2008: 552).

Alongside these celebratory readings of 'difference' and the avuncular (which, in some respects, mirror the queer celebratory literature about non-monogamy), I want to add more cautious and ambivalent interpretations. Such an approach serves, not only to demonstrate the limitations of the above readings, but also to highlight the fact that they are precisely that, readings, and that, in analysing empirical data, as with theoretical work, it is all too easy to emphasize the responses that one wants to hear. This is particularly the case in the context of work on queer kinship, as Heaphy cautions: 'narratives about lesbian and gay reflexivity sometimes confuse analysis with prescription, and actualities with potentialities' (2008: abstract). The data here provide an interesting complication that arose when the distinction between godchildren/children of friends and nieces and nephews was addressed. Here, the biological/non-biological distinction so 'problematic' for critical and queer commentators was clearly in evidence.

One of the participants initially suggested that his gay and lesbian clients did not distinguish the two categories and commented that a typical perspective was: 'Absolutely, equally, equally, it's our close friend . . . not biologically related but, yes you can be very close to these children' (Lawyer 9). However, this was later complicated:

> If somebody is going to leave a bequest or make provision for nieces or nephews and they have godchildren, quite often if they are giving pecuniary legacies, then it is the same, there's no distinction. If it's a division of residue estate it's often the case that it would be the family that would take a bigger share.
>
> (Lawyer 9)

Similarly, another also suggested that the two are treated equally, in terms of lifetime gifts, but later noted:

> My clients sometimes think in terms of need and sometimes they just, there is that nexus, well, some of this money might have been family money and blood is thicker than water, so and although I love my friends, my money will go back to my family, possibly more if it's family money, rather than they've actually earned it all themselves.
>
> (Lawyer 5)

Alongside this evidence of a more traditional familial approach to inheritance, all the lawyers stressed that, for gays and lesbians in particular, their treatment by their family and, especially, the degree of acceptance of their sexuality were critical factors that trumped any notion of biological family obligation. As one noted:

> Wanting to exclude family, family difficulties definitely have often been a factor, namely my siblings, my parents, my children, whoever don't recognize my relationship and I don't want them to get anything so it's more of a, rather than wanting to positively provide for somebody, they positively do not want to provide for the people who disapprove of them, so that's quite a common one.
>
> (Lawyer 8)

Moreover, one noted a shift here: 'A lot of older gay people I've made wills for don't refer to family, it's more likely to be younger people that still have relationships with their family' (Lawyer 9).

What these observations suggest is that gays and lesbians, in constructing their 'inheritance family', rather than operating outside the traditional family form or rejecting family, negotiate and play with different understandings of family. The observation above that younger gays and lesbians are more likely to refer to their birth families in their wills is not surprising, certainly in the UK, where attitudes to sexuality have changed dramatically, but it provides an important reminder that the loss of families of birth was, for many, not simply a positive act of celebrating the alternative offered by 'families of choice'. Indeed, it coheres with research that points to the ongoing significance of the nuclear family (Humphrey *et al.* 2010; Douglas *et al.* 2011) and with Heaphy *et al.*'s (2013) recent work on the 'ordinariness' of the personal lives of younger gays and lesbians.

Taking godparent–godchild relationships seriously provides a grounded resource or space for demonstrating ways in which some gay and lesbian kinship practices may indeed be different from mainstream norms, and, at the same time, for showing how, in the desire to create and acknowledge relationships with children and people from younger generations, gay men and lesbians engage with, rather than operate outside, these norms. In other words, this research draws on, but at the same time troubles and complicates, queer critiques. In emphasizing the differences, terms such as 'personal life', 'intimate citizenship' and 'queer kinship' have been introduced, as an explicit challenge to the concept of 'family'. Although these terms can be used alongside family, an implicit and problematic binary is too often imposed. In this vein, Gillies notes the risks associated with decentring 'family'. In a provocative argument that has been strongly criticized (Wilkinson and Bell 2012), she argues that progressives should reclaim 'family' as a flexible, enduring and necessary sociological framework alongside 'personal lives'; that '[f]amily, as a pliable but historically located framework is best able to demonstrate how continuity is interlaced with change' (Gillies 2011: 10.2). From this perspective, gay and lesbian 'godparents' may be very queer *and* intimately connected to family, rather than against it.

Conclusion

Observing the use made of child welfare arguments in the context of gay marriage debates, McCreery (2008: 202) argues:

> For same-sex marriage to have a transformative impact on society, its proponents must reject the pragmatic impulse to reify a normative vision of family. *This means accepting couples who choose to remain childless; acknowledging that individuals have a right to complicated sexual histories, desires, and activities.*

This critique highlights how both non-monogamous foster couples and childless 'godparents' represent, at least at the discursive level of political representation, challenges to a particular form of mainstream equality politics. In both cases, the engagement with 'the child' is scripted, not simply differently, but in ways that draw on and perform a type of difference that emerges and 'makes sense' within queer discourses. Both stories can be located outside legal norms: in the former, outside dominant assessments of child welfare; in the latter, beyond the conjugal and blood-orientated rules of intestacy. In both cases, rights claims, although possible in theory, not only are questionable on practical and principled grounds, but are again incompatible with formal legal equality claims.

At the same time, both stories reveal an investment in parenting and in inheritance (the future) and, in so doing, sit awkwardly within some queer scholarship. Halberstam describes 'queer time' as 'the potentiality of a life unscripted by the conventions of family, inheritance and child rearing', and she refers to wills as a key tool of 'middle class logic' (2005: 2, 5). In Edelman's polemic, 'the queer' is positioned against 'the child' as the embodiment of an antisocial and future-negating heroic (2004). As expressions of desire for a child and for validating and acknowledging relationships with children, the stories here could, plausibly, be read as 'assimilationist' by a queer politics that too often desires clarity in the form of 'simplistic violent hierarchies of politics as either progressive or reactionary' (Moran 2009: 312). Put crudely, neither is assertively 'outside' enough, in both cases, precisely because of their engagement with 'the child'. The point here is not that queer critiques are wrong; on the contrary, they present insightful, distinctive and searing critical tools for analysis. Rather, by being located ideologically and politically in a crudely fixed oppositional dialogue with mainstream liberal rights agendas, queer critiques risk a lack of attention to empirical complexities and messiness. Telling these particular and distinct stories, then, is part of a broader project that suggests that, 'more attention should be paid to connections and intimacies, no matter how strange or unexpected: of progressive and reactionary formations and trajectories intimately entwined rather than necessarily violently separated and opposed' (Moran 2009: 312).

In a post-equality age, 'the child' will remain as potent as ever, both for liberal rights agendas and for queer critics fearful of assimilation. Paradoxically, telling stories that emphasize incoherence is one way of making sense of this new terrain.

Notes

1 Not discounting the insights of queer theory, 'gay and lesbian' is used here both to foreground gender and because these are the expressions used in the narratives and stories recounted here.
2 See *Re G (Children)(Residence: Same-Sex Partner)* [2006] UKHL 43, [2006] 1 WLR 2305; Beresford (2008).
3 See *Catholic Care (Diocese of Leeds) v Charity Commission of England and Wales* [2012] UKUT 395, [2013] 1 WLR 2105.
4 I want here to acknowledge and thank the two men for sharing their experiences with me and Helen Reece, who visited the couple with me and later supported them during the appeal process.
5 This stage of the process is less researched but critical in the context of gay and lesbian adoption, as they are perceived as more accepting of 'difficult to place' children; see *MA v London Borough of Camden* [2012] EWCA Civ 1340.
6 *EB v France* (2008) 47 EHRR 21.
7 *Schalk and Kopf v Austria* [2010] ECHR 995, 53 EHRR 20.
8 *Re G (Adoption: Unmarried Couple)* [2008] UKHL 38, [2009] 1 AC 173. See Reece (2010).
9 *R (Eunice Johns and Owen Johns) v Derby City Council and Equality and Human Rights Commission* [2011] EWHC 375 (Admin). The court rejected the request and emphasized that enquiring into 'the attitudes of potential foster carers to sexuality' was 'relevant when considering an application for approval' (at para 109).
10 Ibid., para 20.
11 See also *Eweida and Others v UK* [2013] ECHR 37, 57 EHRR 8.
12 An important exception is immigration law; see Lord Rodgers' judgment in *HJ (Iran) and HT (Cameroon) v Secretary of State for the Home Department* [2010] UKSC 31, [2011] 1 AC 596.
13 *Re L* [1962] 1 WLR 886, 889–90.
14 It mirrors debates about blood transfusions, where HIV is effectively de-gayed in order to legitimize an 'equal right' to give blood. In both cases, the association of gay men with promiscuity is highly problematic.
15 The exception is Brown and Cocker, who refer to it, tellingly, in the context of 'earlier relationships' (2010: 27).
16 'Writing wills/dealing with intestacy: Gay and lesbian perspectives'. This research was funded by a Socio-Legal Studies Association Small Research Award. It forms part of a broader project examining the politics of inheritance and sexuality, drawing on literary, archival and doctrinal sources.

References

Barker, M. and Langdridge, D. (2010) 'Whatever happened to non-monogamies? Critical reflections on recent research and theory', *Sexualities*, 13(6): 748–72.

Barker, N. (2006) 'Sex and the Civil Partnership Act: The future of (non) conjugality?', *Feminist Legal Studies*, 14: 241–59.

Beresford, S. (2008) 'Get over your (legal) "self": A brief history of lesbians, motherhood and law', *Journal of Social Welfare and Family Law*, 30(2): 95–106.

Bibbings, L. (2000) 'Boys will be boys: Masculinity and offences against the person', in D. Nicolson and L. Bibbings (eds) *Feminist Perspectives on Criminal Law*, London: Cavendish.

Bradley, D. (2005) 'A note on comparative family law: Problems, perspectives, issues and politics', *Oxford University Comparative Law Forum*, 4.

Brooker, S. (2007) *Finding a Will: A Report on Will-Writing Behaviour in England and Wales*, London: National Consumer Council.

Brown, H.C. and Cocker, C. (2008) 'Lesbian and gay fostering and adoption: Out of the closet into the mainstream?', *Adoption and Fostering*, 32(4): 19–30.

—— (2010) 'Sex, sexuality and relationships: Developing confidence and discernment when assessing lesbian and gay prospective adopters', *Adoption and Fostering*, 34(1): 20–32.

Brown, W. (1995) *States of Injury: Power and Freedom in Late Modernity*, Princeton, NJ: Princeton University Press.

Cook, M. (2014) *Queer Domesticities: Homosexuality and Home Life in Twentieth Century London*, Basingstoke: Palgrave.

Diduck, A. (2007) '"If only we can find the appropriate terms to use the issue will be solved": Law, identity and parenthood', *Child and Family Law Quarterly*, 19(4): 1–23.

Douglas, G., Woodward, H., Humphrey, A., Mills, L. and Morrell, G. (2011) 'Enduring love? Attitudes to family and inheritance law in England and Wales', *Journal of Law and Society*, 38(2): 245–71.

Duggan, L. (2003) *The Twilight of Equality? Neoliberalism, Cultural Politics, and the Attack on Democracy*, Boston: Beacon Press.

Edelman, L. (2004) *No Future: Queer Theory and the Death Drive*, Durham, NC: Duke University Press.

Gillies, V. (2011) 'From function to competence: Engaging with the new politics of family', *Sociological Research Online*, 16(4): 11.

Halberstam, J. (2005) *In a Queer Time and Place*, New York: NYU Press.

Heaphy, B. (2008) 'The sociology of lesbian and gay reflexivity or reflexive sociology?', *Sociological Research Online*, 13(1): 9.

Heaphy, B., Smart, C. and Einarsdottir, A. (2013) *Same-Sex Marriages: New Generations, New Relationships*, Basingstoke, UK: Palgrave Macmillan.

Hicks, S. (2006a) 'Maternal men – perverts and deviants? Making sense of gay men as foster carers and adopters', *Journal of GLBT Family Studies*, 2(1): 93–114.

—— (2006b) 'Genealogy's desire: Practices of kinship amongst lesbian and gay foster carers and adopters', *British Journal of Social Work*, 36(5): 761–76.

Humphrey, A., Mill, L., Morrell, G., Douglas, G. and Woodward, H. (2010) *Inheritance and the Family: Attitudes to Will-Making and Intestacy*, London: National Centre for Social Research.

Jenks, C. (2005) *Childhood*, 2nd edn, London: Routledge.

Klesse, C. (2007) *The Spectre of Promiscuity*, Aldershot, UK: Ashgate.

Leckey, R. (2013) 'Two mothers in law and fact', *Feminist Legal Studies*, 21(1): 1–19.

Lesnik-Oberstein, K. (2008a) 'Childhood, queer theory and feminism', *Feminist Theory*, 11(3): 309–21.

—— (2008b) *On Having an Own Child: Reproductive Technologies and the Cultural Construction of Childhood*, London: Karnac Books.

McCandless, J. and Sheldon, S. (2010) 'The Human Fertilisation and Embryology Act (2008) and the tenacity of the sexual family form', *Modern Law Review*, 73(2): 175–207.

McCreery, P. (2008) 'Save our children/Let us marry: Gay activists appropriate the rhetoric of child protectionism', *Radical History Review*, 100: 186–207.

Monk, D. (1998) 'Beyond Section 28: Law, governance and sex education', in L. Moran, D. Monk and S. Beresford (eds) *Legal Queeries: Lesbian, Gay, and Transgender Legal Studies*, London: Cassell.

—— (2011a) 'Challenging homophobic bullying in schools: The politics of progress', *International Journal of Law in Context*, 7(2): 181–207.

—— (2011b) 'Sexuality and succession law: Beyond formal equality', *Feminist Legal Studies*, 19(3): 231–50.

—— (2013) 'EM Forster's will: An overlooked posthumous publication', *Legal Studies*, 33(4): 572–97.

Moran, L. (2009) 'What kind of field is "law, gender & sexuality"? Present concerns and possible futures', *Feminist Legal Studies*, 17(3): 309–13.

Reece, H. (1996) 'The paramountcy principle: Consensus or construct?', *Current Legal Problems*, 49(1): 267–304.

—— (2009) 'Parental responsibility as therapy', *Family Law*, 39: 1167.

—— (2010) '"Bright line rules may be appropriate in some cases, but not where the object is to promote the welfare of the child": Barring in the best interests of the child?', *Child and Family Law Quarterly*, 22(4): 422–48.

Rubin, G. (1984) 'Thinking sex: Notes for a radical theory of the politics of sexuality', in C. Vance (ed.) *Pleasure and Danger*, Boston: Routledge & Kegan Paul.

Sedgwick, E.K. (1994) *Tendencies*, London: Routledge.

Shonkwiler, A. (2008) 'The selfish-enough father: Gay adoption and the late-capitalist family', *GLQ: A Journal of Lesbian and Gay Studies*, 14(4): 537–67.

Smart, C. (2007) *Personal Life*, Cambridge: Polity.

Stychin, C. (1998) *A Nation by Rights*, Philadelphia: Temple.

—— (2006) 'Family friendly? Rights, responsibilities and relationship recognition', in A. Diduck and K. O'Donovan (eds) *Feminist Perspectives on Family Law*, London: Routledge-Cavendish.

Turner, J. (2003) 'Gay godfathers are chic so why do gay fathers still freak us out?', *The Times*, 13 September.

Waters, D. (2009) 'Gay godfathers rule', *The Guardian*, 4 April.

Wilkinson, E. and Bell, D. (2012) 'Ties that blind: On not seeing (or looking) beyond "the family"', *Families, Relationships and Societies*, 1(3): 423–9.

Index

For Product Safety Concerns and Information please contact our EU
representative GPSR@taylorandfrancis.com
Taylor & Francis Verlag GmbH, Kaufingerstraße 24, 80331 München, Germany

9 781138 644762